Public Theology and Civil Society: Constructive Formation

Paul S. Chung

Public Theology and Civil Society: Constructive Formation

First Edition: 2022

ISBN: 9781524316662
ISBN eBook: 9781524316815

© of the text:
   Paul S. Chung

© Layout, design and production of this edition: 2022 EBL

All rights reserved. No part of this publication may be reproduced, distributed, or transmitted in any form or by any means, including photocopying, recording, or other electronic or mechanical methods, without the prior written permission of the Publisher.

*Celebrating my grandson,
Yohan Junghoon Morrow (June 18, 2020)*

Table of contents

Introduction 11
Chapter 1 Moral Duty 31
Chapter 2 Utilitarianism 70
Chapter 3 Social Contract 108
Chapter 4 General Will 157
Chapter 5 Cosmopolitan Principle 200
Chapter 6 Christian Realism 248
Chapter 7 Religious Socialism 292
Epilogue 341
Bibliography 350
Index 361

Acknowledgement

Public theology focuses on social, cultural, and institutional spheres as their distinguished regimes located in civil society stratified in a hierarchical manner. It acknowledges that the latter is imbued with the neocolonial reality between the metropolis and periphery. In this combined regime, public theology shares in the modernist issues of liberty, justice, democracy, and recognition, while taking into account the postcolonial condition.

My concern is to develop public theology as a way of helping the faith community understand what is really happening in society and culture, as well as throughout the globe. Actualizing the meaning of the Gospel, public theology serves for the church to be faithful to responsibility, shalom, and solidarity with those on the margin.

I appreciate Prof. Craig Nessan for his friendship that has blossomed during my faculty time at Wartburg Theological Seminary and continues in my life as a parish pastor.

I extend my thanks to my friend Peter Watters, who is a promising scholar. He has done a fine job in editing and improving the book project in terms of linguistic skill and significant comments. Finally, I extend my gratitude to Prof.

Kirsi Stjerna, who endorses my study of public theology and civil society in terms of project of incomplete modernity in a postcolonial context.

Easter 2021
Paul S. Chung
Hercules, CA

Introduction

This book is an attempt to articulate public theology in constructive formation by critically involving the philosophical tradition of political modernity, civil society, colonialism, and racial justice. It seeks to configure public theology and civil society in taking on the significance of the incomplete project of modernity in dealing with Christian realism and religious socialism.

In a nutshell, public theology (*theologia publica*) is concerned with the public affairs or institutions of society (*res publica*) to promote the common good in society. Civil society etymologically originates in a political community (Aristotle) or Greek polis (city-state) in which free citizens live as political subjects on equal footing by participating in the formation of public opinion and in the decision-making of public and political affairs under the rule of law.

Civil society in the sense of *res publica* (a republic), seen in the modern political democratic context, is made up of non-governmental organizations and institutions. It underlays freedom of speech and an independent public opinion while safeguarding the interests and will of the citizen; the sphere of civil associations is defended against the domination of political society (the state) and the privileged strata of economic society (bourgeois dominion).

According to Jürgen Habermas, the term public sphere (*Öffentlichkeit*) was formed and took on its social function during the eighteenth century in Germany. It was specifically a part of civil society, which was established as the economic realm of commodity and its system of exchange and social labor governed by its own laws.[1]

Despite the plethora of definitions, I appropriate a concept of civil society along with a democratic notion of the citizen regarding popular sovereignty in the political community under a general will (Rousseau). It is significant to safeguard the concept of civil society and citizen against bourgeois society, in which an egoistic private life seeks one's own affairs as the bourgeoisie in the commercial society; it utilizes other people as a means for own purpose.

However, being a part of the community, a citizen is interested in contributing public affairs to the common good and justice, while a bourgeoisie is primarily concerned with his/her private economic affairs.

In the political community, according to Marx, the citizen is valued as a communal being, while in civil society he/she "is active as a private individual, treats other men as means, degrades himself to a means, and becomes the plaything of alien powers."[2]

Given Marx's definition, it is worth considering how influential Hegel's definition of the political State over religion and civil society (as a bourgeois society) remains in Marx's distinction of civil society and State. However, Marx's limitation can be seen in his identification of bourgeois as a member of civil society, while undermining the citizen as an individual with political rights.

For the task of public theology and civil society, it is important to develop a theological position in dealing with the public arena concerning theories of justice, democracy, and liberty. I weigh in the significance of the legacy of incomplete modernity

---

[1] Habermas, *The Structural Transformation of the Public Sphere*, 2.
[2] "On the Jewish Question," in *Karl Marx Selected Writings*, 46.

to express its own distinguished regime in interrogation with the western tradition of liberal democracy and its cosmopolitan project; it is on the threshold to global sovereignty and world society in the aftermath of colonialism. The western tradition of enlightenment and modernity entails a major contribution to liberty, human rights, democracy, and scientific progress. But it has caused detrimental consequences of under-modernity in terms of slavery, colonialism, and laissez-faire capitalism on a worldwide scale. This postcolonial problem features public theology in constructive formation, which is undertaken in a sociological, hermeneutical framework.

Public Theology in a Diverse Spectrum

Public theology is conceptualized in a diverse framework. Jürgen Moltmann takes on public relevance within the confines of political theology in which he focuses on the significance of modernity by requiring an explicit public theology. His project of "God for a secular society" strives for public theology, which is involved in the public affairs of society and state. It seeks to develop public theology in examining God in the project of the modern world, in which he critically examines Thomas Hobbes' political theory of Leviathan and develops a critical political theology. Furthermore, for Moltmann, public theology is embedded with a postcolonial reality, because Western modernity entails its colonial tradition.

Moltmann juxtaposes Luther's Reformation theses on the entrance of the castle church in Wittenberg (1517) with Hernando Cortes' colonial conquering of the city of the Aztecs in 1521. When the Enlightenment was embodied in Lessing and Kant and culminated in their writings, numberless

African slaves were being sold to America through triangular international trade.[3]

Public theology is distinguished from political theology in the sense that the former is primarily involved in the philosophical tradition of political modernity while drawing attention to its negative colonial side and racial justice. Thus, I locate the regime of public theology in the complex reality between modernity and the religious socialist tradition according to Reinhold Niebuhr, Paul Tillich, and Karl Barth (Dietrich Bonhoeffer included in this prophetic direction).

These great theologians remain classic examples of prophetic public theology by appraising the western tradition of political democracy and promoting prophetic justice and emancipation. Thus, I involve unveiling economic injustice and possessive individualism within the formal and libertarian frame while undertaking a meticulous and critical interpretation of the religious socialist principle.

A project of public theology in this construction is involved in taking issue with a dialectic of enlightenment and progress, which entails the gloomy side of colonialism. Without critical analysis of modernity and colonialism, there would be no serious project for considering public theology and civil society in a genuine sense.

On the other hand, public theology offers a general framework in an interdisciplinary, or social scientific manner in order to facilitate the responsibility of the church for the common good and advocacy for those on the margins in undertaking social ethical guidance in the problems of civil society in democratic, pluralistic affairs.

A neo-Orthodox model (Max Stackhouse) is grounded in the social gospel tradition and Reinhold Niebuhr, in which

---

[3] Moltmann, *God for a Secular Society*, 1. 12.

Stackhouse discusses the significance between theology and economic justice. It tends to bring the sociology of Max Weber into effect in expressing Christian economic responsibility and justice. It combines social sciences with natural scientific findings in dealing with ecumenical relations, global problems, interreligious dialogue, and multicultural diversity in face of a postcolonial challenge.[4]

A critical theoretical inquiry (David Tracy) takes into account Habermas' theory of communicative rationality in analyzing the structural change of the public sphere. Tracy delineates three publics in terms of church, academy, and culture. His public theology is of a constructive character which is conceived in the church and reflected on critically in the academy; it is also meshed with the wider culture.[5]

Tracy elaborates public theology in the method of correlation between Christian theology and philosophical reflection, in which Christian symbols are interpreted in terms of a creative synthesis between critical social theory and philosophical hermeneutics.

In the discussion of public use of reason, Habermas presents a post-metaphysical mode of thought for a complementary learning process between religion and secular reason concerning the importance of the political role of religion. In well-established constitutional states, churches and religious communities contribute to enhancing democracy and human rights in defense of the inclusion of those in minority or marginal groups (Martin Luther King Jr. and the U. S. Civil Rights Movement); in the European context, such political contributions can be seen in the social or religious socialist movement.[6]

---

[4] Stackhouse, *Public Theology and Political Economy*, 1-15.
[5] Tracy, *The Analogical Imagination*, 3.
[6] Habermas, *Between Naturalism and Religion*, 124.

To enhance public use of reason, religious citizens must take an epistemic stance toward other religions and liberal political culture, without sacrificing their own identity and claim to truth. Articles of faith should not come into conflict with secular scientific knowledge, egalitarian individual right, and universalistic morality. This epistemic stance calls for the arduous work of hermeneutical self-reflection and the translation of religious discourse, which must be undertaken from the standpoint of religious traditions.[7]

Accordingly, public theology makes the arguments in society, culture, academy, and the church relevant and intelligent to all rational people through a mutually critical correlation and conversation with contemporary cultural situations and non-theological disciplines. According to Tracy, public theology is best comprehended as a fundamental, systematic, hermeneutical, practical, and ethical theology in which the language of analogical imagination and negative dialectics are envisioned in the ever-widening and continual process for semantic retrieval. The present horizon of the reader is to be vexed, provoked, and challenged by the subject matter, or lifeworld of the text which generates a surplus of meaning through a fusion of horizons.[8]

Public theology has both a philosophical and sociological character, through the correlation of dealing with the translation and communication of theological symbols to secular citizens in the public use of reason, as well as to people of other faith communities. It entails a constructive formation as one of the essential features in an interdisciplinary manner.

---

[7] Ibid., 137.
[8] Tracy, *The Analogical Imagination*, 105. 434-35.

Social Stratification and Civil Society

Public theology finds it significant to cope with diverse public spheres in terms of social stratification and civil society. According to Thomas McCarthy, Habermas' theory of structural transformation of the public sphere facilitates the comprehension of the extent to which the historical structures of the liberal public sphere become central to the historical development of democratic theory through the process of rationalizing public authority. This has occurred through the institutionalized influence of informed discussion and reasoned agreement.[9]

Accordingly, Habermas analyzes the bourgeois public sphere. He finds it significant to investigate the category of the public sphere within the broader field, combining aspects of sociology with economics, or constitutional law with political science, or fusing social intellectual history in a social scientific framework. Habermas distinguishes several types of political public spheres, or literary public spheres in the world of letters or representative publicness, which displays inherent spiritual power or dignity before an audience.[10]

Given Habermas' attempt, I strive to incorporate his critical theory into a theory of social stratification by categorizing diverse or multiple fields in civil society. A theory of social stratification (especially Max Weber and Pierre Bourdieu) facilitates a project of public theology in explicating the extent to which many diverse fields or spaces (politics, economics, education, mass media, culture, religion) are interrelated with one another for symbolic and economic goods. In this generative way of analyzing the buried structures of various social worlds or multiple realities, it is important to draw attention to the mechanisms of production, reproduction, and transformation in the social fields.

---

[9] Habermas, *The Structural Transformation of the Public Sphere*, xii.
[10] Ibid., Xv.

The objectivity of the first order, the facticity of social fact is constituted by the division of labor in production, distribution of material resources, and different forms of capital. In the objectivity of the second order there is a system of classification and rationalization that functions as a symbolic structure in shaping and conditioning practical activities of agents such as to conduct, thoughts, judgment, or disposition (social habitus) among others.[11]

To the degree that civil society is disenchanted from the magical power of the world, it has entered into the system of rationalization, specialization, and relations of power in social facts and relations of meaning in a symbolic template, which would occur between groups and classes. This social structure is embedded with class struggle for symbolic goods and capital in diverse forms through status and a class struggle (political power, education, culture, social relationship, and religious authority). A reality of the life-world (meaning, morality, culture, and religion) is embedded with the power relations of social structure, which reifies or colonizes the reality of the life-world.

In a similar way, Gramsci makes a distinction between political society and civil society, while reformulating Machiavelli's concept of power in the mixture of consent and coercion. For Gramsci, "the supremacy of a social group manifests itself in two ways, as 'domination' and as 'intellectual and moral leadership. ' ...A social group can, and indeed must, already exercise 'leadership' before winning governmental power;... it subsequently becomes dominant when it exercises power, but even if it holds it firmly in its grasp, it must continue to 'lead' as well."[12]

Machiavelli's theory of political sovereignty is appreciated in Rousseau's theory of civil society and republic democracy.

---

[11] Bourdieu and Wacquant, *An Invitation to Reflexive Sociology*, 7.
[12] Gramsci, *Selections from the Prison Notebook*, 57-8.

Furthermore, Gramsci's theory of hegemony finds its influence in the postcolonial study of global sovereignty and critique of Eurocentric discourse.

Thomas McCarthy provides a critical-theoretical insight into characterizing postcolonial theory in a genealogical sense, especially in dealing with racism and imperialism. He offers a contribution to the critical history of the present in taking issue with neocolonialism and neo-racism, which continue their significance in the present.

Public theology and civil society involve postcolonial reality underlying the relation between metropolis and periphery in the aftermath of colonialism. The term "postcolonial" is used as an umbrella concept in scrutinizing the system of dominant discourse and its power structure in academic literature as well as in colonial relations between the metropolis and the periphery.

What strikes me as a truism is to construct public theology in terms of civic, cultural spheres of social stratification, which are bound to the neocolonial condition. It examines the extent to which postcolonial or neocolonial problematics would unveil the domination and exploitation of the metropolis against the periphery.

Accordingly, I adopt a prophetic form of public theology in scrutinizing the postcolonial condition and its critical method in society, stratified in the hierarchical spectrum, especially in dealing with slavery, racism, and colonialism in the detrimental legacy of European modernity.

Eurocentric Position and Marx in Controversy

In the study of public theology and the incomplete project of modernity, one cannot sidestep Marx's position, which triggers a bitter critique of the problems of modernity and its capitalist order. He becomes the interlocutor with the theological principle of religious socialism, whereas controversial in a postcolonial context.

A postcolonial epistemology is a critical method of discourse in problematizing a western mode of representation, hegemony, and modernity in its developmental scale, by unveiling its Eurocentric assumptions and knowledge system in the relation between the metropolis and the periphery.

The proponents of the Empire such as Michael Hardt and Antonio Negri appropriate Gramsci and Foucault to sophisticate a notion of imperial sovereignty. But they take issue with the Eurocentric assumptions in Marx's position and share in Edward Said's critique of Marx's Orientalism; the "Oriental society" is fabricated in essentializing the Oriental character as static, timeless, and unchanging.[13]

As Said writes, "my contention is that without examining Orientalism as a discourse one cannot possibly understand the enormously systematic discipline by which European culture was able to image—and even produce—the Orient politically, sociologically, militarily, ideologically, scientifically, and imaginatively during the post-Enlightenment period."[14]

In the genealogy of colonial sovereignty, Marx is accused of being a Eurocentric thinker in his position of the British rule in India. Marx's insufficient knowledge of Indian history, culture, and society becomes a target of critique and controversy.

According to Marx, England has the task to fulfill a double mission in India; destruction of the solid foundation of Oriental despotism in the idyllic village communities, as well as regenerating the Asiatic society through the laying of the material foundations. Marx is criticized for building on Eurocentric

---

[13] Hardt and Negri, *Empire*, 125.
[14] "Introduction to Orientalism," in *The Edward Said Reader*, 69-70.

assumptions, in which history outside Europe is conceived only as moving along the path which has already been traveled by Europe itself.[15]

On the contrary, Thomas McCarthy compares Marx's position with James Mill, who was engaged in the East India Company (1819); the latter justified the utmost abuse of European power as an improvement over the exercise of Oriental despotism in its most temperate form. His son, John Stuart Mill (working as Chief Examiner in the East India Company) argues in the introductory chapter of *On Liberty* that "despotism is a legitimate mode of government in dealing with barbarians, provided the end be their improvement and the means justified by actually effecting that end."[16]

Given this, it is necessary to analyze Marx's view of British rule in India (written for the *New York Daily Tribune* in 1853) in which Marx denounces the self-interest of the British rule in the disguise of a civilizing mission as the profound hypocrisy of capitalism in contradiction to J. S. Mill. At least, Marx implies an aspect of rethinking and renewing the less developed society from and for the margins, in which the capitalist mode of production along with progress dethroned "hideous pagan idol, who would not drink the nectar but from the skulls of the slain."[17]

In the midst of the debate, it would be superficial to blame Marx merely as a Eurocentric thinker in justifying capitalist civilization, but an in-depth reading is required in buttressing his critique of Spain's colonialism in the context of primitive accumulation (mercantilist capitalism) in reference to British rule in India. A Christian character of capital accumulation is

---

[15] Hardt and Negri, *Empire*, 118-20.
[16] Mill, *On Liberty*, 10.
[17] Cited in McCarthy, *Race, Empire, and the Idea of Human Development*, 178.

denounced as profound hypocrisy, while his limited knowledge of Indian history, society, or culture may not simply be taken as a fabricator of Orientalist discourse.

Marx's critical view of primitive accumulation is indebted to Adam Smith, who was a staunch opponent to mercantilist slave trade and colonialism. A looking-backward face of Smith, his laissez-faire capitalism is critically analyzed in connection with his moral theory and critique of colonialism in his looking-forward face. In fact, a critical evaluation of the legacy of incomplete modernity cannot be neatly categorized in terms of the inverted logic of Orientalism imbued with a binary opposition.

As Dipesh Chakrabarty writes, "the phenomenon of 'political modernity'…is impossible to *think* of anywhere in the world without invoking certain categories and concepts, the genealogies of which…all bear the burden of European thought and history. One simply can't think of political modernity without these and other related concepts…This heritage is now global."[18]

Western global hegemony in the modern period, together with its political theory, philosophical concepts, and social sciences, has become indispensable in shaping scholarship and its hegemony in our present; it is also required to analyze the system of domination and undertake a critique of Western imperialism. What is substantial is to rethink and renew them "from and for the margins"[19] in social stratification in the metropolis as well as in non-West nations.

In genealogical inquiry of capitalism and power relations, it is indispensable for public theology to learn from Christian political realism as well as from the prophetic tradition of religious socialism (Paul Tillich and Karl Barth).

---

[18] Chakrabarty, *Provincializing Europe*, 4.
[19] Ibid., 16.

Christian Realism and Religious Socialism

For public theology. I begin with a biblical definition of prophetic theology, whose essential character lies in its future orientation, a vision of God's Future, while at the same time, entailing a sharp critique of the status quo in society, culture, and the state. As Walter Brueggemann maintains, "it is the task of the prophet to bring to expression the new realities against the more visible ones of the old order."[20]

Having said this, Reinhold Niebuhr is taken to be a classic example of prophetic public theology, who was deeply engaged in the Western tradition of political democracy and its moral theory, as well as in critical conversation with Marxist theory. He develops the notion of Christian responsibility in creatively interpreting the dialectic between original righteousness and original sin while interacting with the relationship between the city of God and the city of the world through the lens of Augustinian political realism.

Niebuhr's Christian realism provides social ethics with a theological frame of reference in which he seeks to cut loose from the idealistic and utopian illusion among religious liberals and secular intellectuals. It develops an independent Christian ethic in which religion makes a distinctive contribution to morality, comprehending the dimension of depth in life.[21]

Niebuhr calls attention to Berdyaev's view of the myth, according to which myth has validity as a reality, far greater than concept. It has little to do with the illusions of primitive mentality. "Behind the myths are concealed the greatest realities, the original phenomena of the spiritual life…A myth is always concrete and expresses life better than abstract thought can

---

[20] Brueggemann, *The Prophetic Imagination*, 14.
[21] Niebuhr, *An Interpretation of Christian Ethics*, 2-3.

do...A myth presents to us the supernatural in the natural—it brings two worlds together symbolically."[22]

The mythical approach becomes decisive in construing an independent Christian ethic in terms of the ethic of Jesus, which exhibits itself as an impossible possibility through the ideal of sacrificial love and an absolute ideal of nonresistance. The ethic of Jesus serves as an ideal standard only through approximation, and Niebuhr interprets it in terms of discriminate critique. The law of love is a yardstick in choosing greater goods as well as lesser evils.[23]

Niebuhr contrasts a prophetic religion of Jesus with a demonic form of religious nationalism, which demands unconditional devotion to national self-deification.[24] He analyzes love and justice in terms of moral dispositions according to the paradoxical vision of original righteousness and original sin.

Niebuhr provides theological anthropology for undergirding Christian social ethics in terms of love and justice. Love as forgiveness transcends justice (rational ideal of an equal distribution), because it expresses the highest aspirations of human freedom. His realist ethic is expressed in the following manner: "Only a religion full of romantic illusions could seek to persuade the Negro to gain justice from the white man merely by forgiving him. ...Short of the transmutation of the world into the Kingdom of God, men will always confront enemies."[25]

Niebuhr's major concern can be seen in his confrontation with several fronts such as orthodox Christianity, liberal Christianity, and Marxist socialism. Orthodox Christianity has its weakness in its premature identification of the transcendent will of God with canonical, legalist codes. Liberal Christianity inclines to invest

---

[22] Ibid., 8. Footnote 1.
[23] McCann, *Christian Realism and Liberation Theology*, 85.
[24] Niebuhr, *The Nature and Destiny of Man* 1, 214.
[25] Niebuhr, *An Interpretation of Christian Ethics*, 140-41.

and impose the relative moral standards of a commercial culture carelessly and prematurely upon the ethic of Jesus.[26]

Liberal Christianity is instilled with the whole of modern secular liberal culture and commercial value. The kingdom of God is translated into an ideal moral society, identifying middle-class perspectives with eternal values.

On the other hand, radical Christianity attached to Marxism inclines to ascribe the attitudes and values of the workers with the absolute truth. In the case of Marxism, the proletariat becomes the active agent of the revolution, but its utopianism leads to disillusionment.[27]

Against such assumptions, Niebuhr regards the ethic of Jesus as the perfect fruit of prophetic religion in which the moral ideal of love and vicarious suffering make their realization remote and unrealistic in history. The ethic of Jesus in its command of love (even including our enemies) is impossible for human capacity, but it is possible insofar as we are free to aspire to it.

Gospel ethic with the symbol of the kingdom of God characterizes Niebuhr's social ethics in an Augustinian fashion: "The Kingdom of God is always at hand in the sense that the impossibilities are really possible, and lead to new actualities in given moments of history, nevertheless every actuality of history reveals itself, after the event, as only an approximation of the ideal; and the Kingdom of God is therefore not here. It is in fact always coming but never here."[28]

Christian political realism is considerably involved in the moral, political theory of democracy and liberal modernity, and provides some important insights into bridging the problem of public theology with the legacy and project of the incomplete modernity.

---

[26] Ibid., 5.
[27] Ibid., 10-11.
[28] Ibid., 36.

Christian political realism in its critical, constructive appraisal of Marxist theory can be furthered in connection with the political theology of Karl Barth and Dietrich Bonhoeffer, and finally, Paul Tillich's theological philosophical sophistication of the religious socialist principle.

Tillich's critical constructive reading of the religious socialist principle deserves special attention because his earlier position is associated with the political tradition of critical theology at the Frankfurt School (Max Horkheimer). His prophetic public theology can be seen in his systematic theology involved in morality, culture, and religion along with the political dimension.[29]

These public spheres are judged by a biblical symbol of the Kingdom of God, which is transcendent and eschatological. "The Kingdom of God has not yet come…God is not yet all in all, whatever this 'not yet' may mean…: religion itself, namely a religious culture beside a secular culture, a temple beside a town hall, a Lord's Supper beside a daily super, prayer beside work, meditation beside research, caritas beside *eros*."[30]

I compare Tillich's religious socialism with Barth's political theology in its critique of the pathologies of lordless powers in the public sphere. This prophetic experiment recasts public theology in its project of incomplete modernity in terms of responsibility, solidarity, and emancipation.

Christian realism and religious socialism aside, I go further to construct public theology in a social scientific frame of reference in taking on late capitalism and its legitimacy. Emile Durkheim's sociology of division of labor and public morals becomes decisive in cutting across the limitations of Marx's negative position of the social division of labor. Weber's analysis of bureaucracy

---

[29] Tillich, *Systematic Theology* 3, 92.
[30] Ibid., 311.

and his critique of socialism helps to clarify political ethics and parliamentary-participatory democracy in comparison with Tillich and Barth.

A prophetic approach to public theology requires a sociological analysis of the division of labor and moral solidarity, in which Durkheim is valued as the one in steering between Scylla of laissez-faire capitalism (imbued with social Darwinism) and Charybdis of Marxist utopianism.

Argument, Scope, and Direction

Political liberalism in the specific form of Rousseau and Kant shows "a nonreligious, post-metaphysical justification of the normative foundations of constitutional democracy." Situated in the tradition of rational natural law, the theory of political liberalism averts assumptions of classical and religious natural law in the cosmological or soteriological context.[31]

Concurring with this position, I am concerned with an idea of people's consent, which is a central concept of popular sovereignty in Rousseau's social contract theory and its participatory democracy. This position culminates philosophically in Kant's cosmopolitan principle in postcolonial profile. It is also found in a social democratic version of the social contract and its consent through its original position of equality and justice in John Rawls' theory of justice.

In an analysis of the political discourse of modern democracy, I set out to develop a sociological, hermeneutical reading of the tradition of political liberalism and democracy in diverse contexts, which seeks to cut through the limitations of European modernity and its hegemony. This perspective shapes the

---

[31] Habermas, *Between Naturalism and Religion*, 102.

correlation between public theology and civil society, which underlays an incomplete project of modernity and its postcolonial thrust.

Given this, when considering public theology, it is important to involve a comparative study of religion and culture in a democratic, pluralist society toward peace among religions and politics of cultural justice and recognition. The subject matter is organized and thematized in terms of liberty, social justice, and recognition of the Other in the context of modern democracy and civil society. Public theology is configured in this spectrum, in which comparative study of religion is to be undertaken to advance the incomplete project of modernity.

Chapter 1 begins with Kant's moral philosophy and includes a theological appraisal of his achievement. Kant can be featured as an inspiration for public theology and the kingdom of God. I undertake conceptual clarity in discussing his moral philosophy in response to Hegel's critique. Kant remains an important figure for public theology in the views of Albrecht Ritschl and Karl Barth.

Chapter 2 deals with utilitarianism, and I further examine the utilitarian position (Jeremy Bentham and J. S. Mill) and compare their problems with social contract theory, as elaborated in John Rawls' theory of justice. The latter indicates a new and creative synthesis of Locke, Rousseau, and Kant in a social-democratic direction. Of remarkable significance is that I seek to safeguard Adam Smith from utilitarian–libertarian principles while examining his contribution to the moral theory and critique of colonialism.

In chapters 3 and 4, I focus on the political tradition of social contract theory and general will, scrutinizing problematics, contributions, critiques, and limitations of Hobbes, Locke, and Rousseau in reference to a new development of John Rawls. I find in this political tradition of social contract theory (Rousseau, Kant, and Rawls) that the political moral theory of justice, equality, and democracy finds consonant with public theology in its endeavor to strive for justice as fairness, common good, and solidarity in civil society.

In chapter 5, I undertake a study of Kant's cosmopolitan principle which shows a parallel to Smith in their respective critique of colonialism. It is imperative to delve into the Kantian cosmopolitan project, critically revising its limitation of a world republic in its political constitution of international law. The cosmopolitan condition cannot be properly understood apart from Kant's critique of colonialism. The postcolonial reality is intertwined with the liberal democratic critique of colonialism and its cosmopolitan principle of sovereignty.

Chapter 6 delves into Reinhold Niebuhr's Christian political realism, which is based on his creative reading of Augustine. He can be appreciated as one of the best examples representing public theology in the Neo-Orthodox model. He is considerably involved in examining the tradition of liberal democracy as well as Marxist theory and develops the position of Christian political realism. His moral analysis of freedom and responsibility marks an important contribution through his new interpretation of original sin.

In Chapter 7, I take on the significance of Reinhold Niebuhr's Christian political realism in connection with the prophetic tradition of religious socialism in Paul Tillich and Karl Barth. Tillich's socialist principle is compared with Barth's public theology of reconciliation and resistance. A critical rejoinder is undertaken in examining Dietrich Bonhoeffer in terms of Gustavo Gutierrez's theology of under-modernity. To mediate public theology with moral solidarity, I engage in a sociological theory of the division of labor, rationalization, and moral solidarity according to Emile Durkheim and Max Weber. Social scientific theory facilitates public theology in prophetic reasoning of reconciliation and the kingdom of God in cutting across the Marxist reductionist version of the division of labor in the phase of late capitalism.

The epilogue is a reflection on the discussion of public theology and modern theory of civil society and democracy by looking at their relevance for postcolonial reality. A public epistemology in sociological inquiry and hermeneutical seriousness takes on problematic ways of thinking in terms of appreciation of ethical tradition, critical distance (problematization via the immanent critique), and a new synthesis of ethical meaning and practice.

Public theology in constructive formation could be a viable project involving philosophical moral theory and social scientific inquiry, insofar as it is engaged in diverse public spheres embedded within the reality of social, culture stratification in a democratic, pluralist society.

Chapter 1
Moral Duty

What should we do? This question belongs to the basic content of ethical methodology. This question has to do with the tradition of Immanuel Kant's moral philosophy, which is based on duty ethics or rules ethics.

This chapter explores Kant's moral philosophy and radical evil in its religious framework and includes a theological appraisal of him. His kingdom of ends is extended over the social-political realm, in which he develops political reform in a context-sensitive manner in terms of political prudence. In the analysis of morality and politics, I take issue with Hegel's critique of Kant and his theory of religion and morality. Kant can be appreciated as the pioneer for the dialogue between theology and philosophy.

Deontology and Public Use of Reason

The word "deontology" comes from the Greek word *deon* which means duty or that which is obligatory. Moral duties are transcultural and universally binding. Kant's deontology is seen in the public use of reason in his discussion of Enlightenment. The only reason is the supreme principle of morality, which provides a solid foundation for the universality of morality. Reason directs the will. As autonomous and rational beings, we have the ability to use our reason to discern what is right and wrong. It does not need to rely on outside authorities. In dealing with the problem of Enlightenment, Kant defines it as humans exist from the self-incurred minority, which is incapable of using one's intelligence.[1]

Kant maintains that the public use of human reason must be free at all times from restrictions, in dealing with erroneous points in religious and ecclesiastical matters.[2] What is crucial in the Enlightenment is a human release from the self-incurred minority, primarily in matters of religion.

A human being has come of age, which characterizes the Enlightenment person, because it represents human emergence from a self-inflicted state of minority and tutelage, requiring courage to make use of reason. "Have the courage to make use of your own intelligence" (*sapere aude!*) is the slogan of the enlightenment, which emphasizes "an escape from self-caused immaturity."[3]

Kant has almost unconditional faith in reason as representative of the spirit of the eighteenth century. He sets out to "institute a court of appeal which should protect the just rights of reason, but dismiss all groundless claims, …but according to the eternal and unalterable laws of reason."[4]

As Kant writes of the French Revolution with sympathy, "such a phenomenon in human history will never again be forgotten, because it has revealed a disposition and capacity for betterment in human nature."[5] He notices in this upheaval a sign of the kingdom of heaven at hand in the world. Public use of reason requires freedom, which is the basis of morality and goodwill. Human freedom of choice is implicit in the moral law, and it is the sole determining ground of evil.

---

[1] "What is Enlightenment?" in *Basic Writings of Kant*, 135.
[2] Ibid., 137-8.
[3] Ibid., 135; 140.
[4] "Critique of Pure Reason," Ibid., 5.
[5] Cited in Barth, "Kant," in *Protestant Theology in the Nineteenth Century*, 257.

Practical Reason, Evil, and the Idea of God

Kant incorporates the metaphysics of his time (the ideas of God, freedom, and immortality of the soul) into his critique of practical reason. In his critique of pure reason, he is concerned with an object a priori that transcends all experience by accompanying and directing all empirical knowledge. Empirical knowledge is constituted by intuition, which is supplied by sensibility as well as the understanding (source of concepts), both of which are peculiar to human reason. Their object is given as phenomena to us under space and time rather than things in themselves.

We comprehend the existence and attributes of what exists by virtue of the categories a priori (or forms of the understanding); they conceptualize the empirical object in intuition (or sense experience) as an objective reality for the self, making the synthesis of the self and objects possible. Operative with the sense experience, understanding is empirical as well as a priori because it creates concepts for the objects of sense experience.

"Experience," Kant holds, "requires understanding," and one must presuppose "the rules of the understanding as existing within [oneself] a priori," "to which all objects of experience must necessarily conform, and with which they must agree."[6]

In a concrete unity or combination between intuition and concepts which originate in the understanding, genuine empirical knowledge becomes possible concerning what exists; it corresponds to the transcendental act of apperception (or representation) underlying the synthetic a priori, which is *"the highest principle of all employment of the Understanding."*[7] What is striking in Kantian teaching is that an intuition without concepts would be blind, while concepts without intuition are empty.[8]

---

6 "Critique of Pure Reason," in *Basic Writings of Kant*, 13.
7 Ibid., 74.
8 Cited in Barth, "Kant," in *Protestant Theology*, 260.

Kant maintains that pure reason contains a practical motive in itself because there are practical laws. "Pure reason is practical of itself alone and gives (to man) a universal law which we call the *Moral Law*."[9]

God, freedom, and immortality are not to be comprehended as an existent reality, nor objects of our theoretical knowledge. Rather such metaphysical subject matter belongs to primary, practical reason. Kant has "to remove [theoretical] *knowledge* in order to make room for *belief*."[10]

The ideas such as God, freedom, and immortality are indispensable in empirical knowledge, and their regulative use is to be perceived in actual fact, in other words, practice rather than a theory or theoretical knowledge. Their truth is contained in the truth of the will for good, which is subject to the categorical imperative of duty. Reason postulates or pre-supposes the unconditioned in all things by themselves for everything conditioned. The transcendent concept of the unconditioned is demanded by practical reason, the moral use of which does not require the assistance of theoretical reason. The true knowledge of God, freedom, and immortality is knowledge by practical reason, which is accomplished in the moral deed in accordance with duty. All knowledge that transcends every experience has its practical truth as conceived in the form of pre-supposition or postulates, which are accomplished in the moral act.[11]

Kant conceptualizes the notion of a will as good, and it "exists already in the sound natural understanding, requiring rather to be cleared up than to be taught."[12] Goodwill is recognized as unconditional, given, and intrinsic to human beings. The

---

[9] "Critique of Practical Reason," in *Basic Writings of Kant*, 239.
[10] "Critique of Pure Reason," Preface in the Second Edition, Ibid., 19.
[11] Barth, "Kant," in *Protestant Theology*, 262-3.
[12] "Fundamental Principles of the Metaphysics of Morals," in *Basic Writings of Kant*, 155.

condition of goodwill is analyzed through the categorical imperative of duty. A person of goodwill has good intentions and is motivated to act for the sake of duty. People of goodwill are lawgivers unto themselves, imposing the moral law upon themselves.

They would arrive at the same conclusions regarding what is right and wrong. Deontic ethics attentions principally to right conduct. Acting out of duty, goodwill involves the intention to do what is right regardless of our feeling or any reward; in the latter, an action is done out of sympathy in helping others. Such an action may be praiseworthy but has no moral worth. The highest good lies in the moral perfection of the individual.

Human freedom is implicit in the moral law, and it is the ground in determining the reality of evil. Evil is seen as moral deviation. It has little to do with a natural impulse from the original constitution of human nature or transmission of original sin. Evil has been brought by a human being upon him/herself by choice that is contrary to the moral law. But it is radical because it is rooted in humanity itself and ineradicable. It is a propensity rather than a predisposition. By propensity, Kant comprehends the subjective ground of the possibility of a natural inclination (habitual craving, concupiscence). But the will can be appraised as good or evil in terms of its maxims.

The propensity to evil can be seen in the deviation of the maxims from the moral law. It is a natural propensity in human beings toward evil, in reference to three distinct degrees: frailty, impurity, and corruption of the human heart. Kant relates the frailty to Paul's word: "What I would, that I do not!" I adopt the good (the law) into my maxim, but this good, an irresistible incentive is subjectively weaker.[13] By the corruption of the human heart Kant means "the propensity of the will to maxims which

---

13 "Religion within the Limits of Reason Alone," Ibid., 379.

neglect the incentives springing from the moral law in favor of others which are not moral."[14]

Human nature possesses both animal inclinations as well as the capacity to grasp the moral law through reason. Reason is "a point of no return" for ethics which are based on freedom and moral law because evil is rather acknowledged as a "thorn in the flesh."[15]

This position leads Kant to the biblical statement. For instance, as the Scripture says, none is good (the model of good) but God only (whom you do not see) is good. Reason frames a priori simply from the idea of moral perfection (God the lawgiver), connecting with the notion of free will. The duty is free from all experience, and set in the idea of a reason, which determines the will by a priori principles. [16]

Given this, Kant grounds religion within the limits of reason alone, which refers to practical morality; it is concerned with knowledge of our duties as a divine commandment. Faith sees human morality as the essential component of worshiping God. Like Augustine, Kant maintains that a notion of God dwells within our reason from the beginning, thus a knowledge of God is a recollection of God-notion. God within our reason has to be the authentic interpreter of all revelation. The idea of God (religion) has its seat within human moral reason alone. The doctrinal teaching of revelation is not redundant but honored as the shell, which helps to set the religion of moral reason publicly in motion. [17]

A metaphysic of morals is based on the pure conception of the duty, a priori free from everything empirical. The conception of

---

[14] Ibid., 380.
[15] Lehmann, *Ethics in a Christian Context*, 183.
[16] "Fundamental Principles of the Metaphysics of Morals," in *Basic Writings of Kant*, 166-7.
[17] Barth, "Kant," in *Protestant Theology*, 271; 268-9.

the moral law is a priori grounded in reason and exercises on the human heart in terms of reason alone, thus practical.[18] But there is a reality of radical evil as original or latent sin in Pauline sense. We are created good, but inclined naturally to moral corruption. What strikes in Kant's definition of radical evil is the empirical observation of human action contrary to moral law.

But Kant's position has little to do with Augustine's inherited sin by sexual propagation, because "birth need not be the cause of it."[19] The source of evil consists in an expression of freedom because it "can lie only in a rule made by the will for the use of its freedom."[20] It refers to the predisposition to animality in human beings along with humanity (self-love) and personality (respect for the moral law) in him/her; the former implies mechanical self-love for self-preservation, propagation of species in sexual impulse, and the social impulse in interaction with other people. These are called "vices of the coarseness of nature."[21] The idea of moral law is the essence of personality itself, which alone is rooted in practical reason dictating moral laws unconditionally.[22]

Kant's anthropological position is of a theological character. The concept of God is seen in a practical concept of the highest good, which is the object of our will, thus a priori through pure reason. Kant regards the Christian conception of the kingdom of God as that of the highest good, transforming the idea of God as a postulate of pure practical reason. Although the postulation of God is of a practical necessity for morality, a postulate of the pure practical reason, God may be the ground of morality, because no

---

[18] "Fundamental Principles of the Metaphysics of Morals," in *Basic Writings of Kant*, 168.
[19] "Religion Within the Limits of Reason Alone," Ibid., 372.
[20] Ibid., 371.
[21] Ibid., 375.
[22] Ibid., 378.

morality is without belief in God. "But seek first his kingdom and his righteousness, and all these things shall be yours" (Matt 6:33).

This postulate tends to conceptualize God as an immanent thought in human beings, because "God is the morally practical self—legislating Reason"[23] with us. The question of the existence of God is seen in a way that the Idea of God stands to the moral imperative as the highest Principle in morally self-determining Reason.

Duty and Virtue

Kant does not neglect the importance of virtue. Virtues such as compassion, wisdom, generosity, and happiness make it easier for us to do the duty in accordance with goodwill, and they are important to cultivate. We nurture goodwill by forming friendships and exhibiting respect for others.

Although his moral philosophy focuses on duty, a virtuous character is embodied in goodwill. In his *Groundwork of the Metaphysics of Morals,* Kant begins with the importance of goodwill rather than the duty: "It is impossible to conceive anything at all in the world, or even out of it, which can be taken as good without qualification, except a goodwill."[24] A virtuous disposition helps us in our struggle against unruly impulses and obstacles standing in the way of doing our duty. The goodwill "is already present in a sound understanding and requires not so much to be taught as merely to be clarified."[25]

---

[23] Lehmann, *Ethics in a Christian Context*, 188. Lehmann notices in Kant's *Opus Posthumum* a shift from the idea of God as a postulate of the practical reason into an idea of God as immanent.

[24] Kant, *The Moral Law: Groundwork of the Metaphysic of Morals*, 1.

[25] Ibid., 62.

Kant does not eliminate the importance of virtue in light of goodwill. Virtues such as moderation in the affections and passions, self-control, and calm deliberation are constitutive components in shaping the intrinsic worth of the person. Without the principles of goodwill, they do not deserve to be called good without qualification. Goodwill is good simply by virtue of the volition, in other words, it is good in itself. Reason has an influence on the will, producing not merely good as a means to something else. Rather it is good in itself, thus reason was absolutely necessary for that.[26] "This must be the supreme good and the condition of every other, even of the desire of happiness."[27]

Thus, according to Lehmann, "the goodwill, moreover, although its moral worth is determined by its direct and intrinsic exhibition of duty as the highest Good (*summum bonum*) may also, when conjoined with happiness, be regarded as the complete Good (*supremum bonum*)."[28]

In the tradition of Aristotle, we become moral and happier through the repeated performance and practice of good actions. The nonrational nature of emotion is an important component of moral goodness, as guided under the control of reason. Living well and doing well are identified with being happy. Virtues involve living according to reason, and it is essential in achieving the good life, happiness, and inner harmony. Virtue comes about as a result of habit, a settled disposition of the mind in observing the mean state against that of excess or that of a defect. The reality of evil would be found in the extreme through its domestication, thus only with a parenthetical concern.[29]

---

[26] "Fundamental Principles of the Metaphysics of Morals," in *Basic Writings of Kant*, 152.
[27] Ibid., 154.
[28] Lehmann, *Ethics in a Christian Context*, 180.
[29] Ibid., 170.

This ethical perspective may find a place in Kant's position of the relation between duty and virtue. Kant's moral view incorporates significance of the virtue into the deontic framework. Nonetheless, it is Hegel that takes issue with Kant's moral view of the world, arguing that Kant left ethical life to be derivative.

Hegel and Ethical Life

In the *Philosophy of Right*, Hegel distinguishes morality from ethical life. The "ought-to-be" is in the moral sphere, while it becomes an "is" only in ethical life (consisting of family, civil society, and the state).[30] (§ 108) The right of moral includes three aspects in dialectically related manner: purpose (responsibility and means), intention (happiness), and the good (freedom realized) (§ 114).

Hegel argues that Kant defines the pure unconditioned self-determination of the will as the root of duty. The latter has the firm foundation and point of departure in terms of its infinite autonomy, exclusively adhered to a moral position; however, Kant's philosophy of morality makes no transition from morality to the sphere of ethics. Thus, he reduces the morality to "an empty formalism" in the absence of contradiction only for "the preaching of duty for duty's sake" (§ 135).

In *Phenomenology of the Mind*, Hegel characterizes Kant's philosophy of morality in terms of the moral view of the world, in which the universality is epitomized in the soul of the acting individual; the latter regards itself to be the self-regulating source of all universal condition of action through ethical consciousness of duty. Therefore, Hegel argues that Kant defines morality

---

[30] Hegel's *Philosophy of Right*, 1942.

as "the relation of actions to the autonomy of the will, i. e. to possible universal legislation through maxims of the will."[31]

Although "duty constitutes the sole essential purpose and object of self-consciousness,"[32] Hegel argues that duty remains one of the essential features of ethical life. The moral view of the world consists in the dialectical relation or mediation between the implicit aspect of morality (sensibility) and its explicit aspect (moral duty) through antithetic and conflicting moments and presuppositions. Thus, Hegel appeals to the tradition of the Greek ethical theory, because "the moral consciousness cannot renounce happiness and drop this element out of its absolute purpose."[33] Sensibility is a moment of this dialectical process in producing unity with the moral consciousness, a moment of actuality; in other words, "sensibility should be in conformity with morality" through dialectical process and mediation.[34]

Given this, Hegel requires or postulates a harmony between morality and nature (or happiness) to exist necessarily for arriving at its actuality. Nature is sensibility taking the form of volition in the shape of impulses and inclinations, and it is opposed to pure will. However, nature lies within consciousness. Pure consciousness takes the relation of sensibility to it for the harmonious, absolute unity of two entities as an essential fact. The opposition between sensibility and pure consciousness should be resolved qua consciousness, which is "always making progress in morality."[35]

However, progress in morality does not mean a moral striving toward perfection for the sake of duty, but it sets out to maintain

---

[31] Hegel, *The Phenomenology of Mind*, 351.
[32] Ibid., 353.
[33] Ibid., 354.
[34] Ibid., 355.
[35] Ibid., 356.

the means mediated in the dialectical movement in which morality and happiness are brought to harmony.

The moral consciousness exists for itself, finding the nature opposing it. This leads to the postulate of the harmony between consciousness and sensibility. Inclinations and impulses are not to be suppressed, but merely to be in conformity or harmony with reason, because self-realizing consciousness is a moral action, taking on the form of an impulse as the realized harmony of impulse and morality.[36]

In critically dealing with the moral view of the world, Hegel argues that the postulated existence that arises by the means containing harmony is implied in the very notion of morality itself; it stands for the unity or actuality, which means happiness. Human existence in general demands and postulates both duty and happiness.

According to Hegel, a moral attitude is assumed in varied and manifold character. As regards the plurality of duties, the many duties qua many are determinate and are not anything sacred for the moral consciousness. Manifold types of moral attitude and duties must be acknowledged as having a substantial existence and value.[37]

This implies Hegel's ethics of recognition, in which the plurality of duties in manifold consciousness is in contrast to a Kantian moral view of the world, which is grounded in pure duty qua pure duty as sacred and substantial. An ethic of recognition postulates that there is another consciousness that renders many different duties sacred; manifold existence opposes and conflicts with the simple nature of duty in the self-identical moral consciousness. But it reaches the unity of the universal and the particular through the dialectical mediation and the

---

[36] Ibid., 364.
[37] Ibid., 356.

harmony between morality and happiness. This immanent unity "becomes now a master and ruler of the world, who brings about the harmony of morality and happiness, at the same time sanctifies duties in their multiplicity."[38]

Within the recognition in mind, a specific duty in the Kantian sense has also validity in its intersubjective relation with other consciousness. If Hegel focuses on the duty as sacred in the dialectical mediation, happiness is taken to be something contingent; it is expected as the result of grace. Duty is still held to be the essential truth since God (the absolute Being) is the object of thought which is something postulated beyond the actual. However, morality is affected and conditioned by sensibility, such that it is not completed. The idle state of incomplete morality exists in the Other, the holy moral legislator.[39]

In the grace of God, the morally imperfect knowledge and will are held to be perfect, and happiness is given as an act of free grace. God distributes happiness according to the merit which is ascribed to the imperfect consciousness. God completes the meaning of the moral attitude in which pure duty and actual reality are affirmed in a single unity through cancellation and transcending (in the sense of sublation).[40]

At this point, Hegel postulates God as the being of necessity for grace and happiness in the dialectical method. The grace of God is necessary only to human happiness, such that God is not connected with the morality qua divine righteousness and commandment. God's free act of grace in connection with righteousness is tailored into Hegel's dialectical method, which is made into the essential nature of God. His dialectic of necessity is based on the identification between God's self-movement in *actus*

---

[38] Ibid., 358.
[39] Ibid., 366.
[40] Ibid., 359.

purus and human self-confidence of thinking (self-theosis) and discards God's incomprehensible sovereignty. It can be argued that Hegel is not capable of acknowledging the actual dialectic of God's grace and righteousness, which is founded upon the freedom of God in love.[41]

In Hegel's dialectic of necessity, there is no longer contradiction with morality in the sense of reconciliation as the higher unity of thesis and antithesis. *Tout comprendre c'est tout pardoner!*[42]

In fact, Hegel is not so enthusiastic about moral progress toward completion but remains realistically the middle state in the sense of reconciliation between morality and natural inclinations. Moral law becomes natural law.[43] However, this reconciling striving has little to do with setting up categorical imperatives in a critique of what exists for justice and the common good.

Kant and Ethical Theory

Hegel's dialectical response to Kant's moral view of the world entails a substantial critique of Kant's moral philosophy. For Kant, human freedom is the fountain of morality, and he argues that all the actions performed with a view to the purpose of well-being or happiness would be prescribed by instinct. Although moderation, self-control, and calm deliberation are good in many respects, goodwill is good in itself which is considered to be higher than the attainment of virtues through inclination and with the greatest endeavor. As Kant writes, "Like a jewel, it

---

[41] Barth, "Hegel," in *Protestant Theology*, 406.
[42] Hegel, *The Phenomenology of Mind*, 388.
[43] Ibid., 363.

would still shine by its own right, as a thing which has its whole value in itself."[44]

Kant reverses the teleological eudemonism by the critical, deontological analysis of pure practical reason under the name of the highest good. He substitutes the ethical principle of the mean and happiness with the categorical imperative of duty. The goodwill as the starting point can be expressed: "I ought, therefore, I can."[45]

His major concern is to establish the basis of obligation (for instance, "Thou shalt not lie") in "*a priori* simply in the conceptions of pure reason," or "*a priori* principles without any empirical motives;"[46] it is not involved in the nature of humans or in the circumstances in the world. If an action should be morally good, it confirms to the moral law, as well as it must be done for the sake of the law.[47]

As we have seen, the cultivation of virtue is acknowledged in terms of goodwill. Kant writes: "The greatest love I can have for another is to love him as myself... Our duties toward ourselves constitute the supreme condition and the principle of all morality...He who transgresses against himself loses his manliness and becomes incapable of doing his duty toward his fellow."[48]

Goodwill alone motivates us to do our duty and virtue. We have a moral duty to help others even when we do not feel sympathy for them. The cultivation of goodwill acknowledges that we have a duty to treat people as beings of infinite value. The duty of self-improvement, which includes the aspect of

---

[44] "Fundamental Principles of the Metaphysics of Morals," in *Basic Writings of Kant*, 152.
[45] Lehmann, *Ethics in a Christian Context*, 179.
[46] "Fundamental Principles of the Metaphysics of Morals," in *Basic Writings of Kant*, 147-8.
[47] Ibid., 148.
[48] Kant, "Duties to Oneself," in *Lectures on Ethics*, 118.

cultivating virtue, is one of our most important duties; this is regarded as the final guarantor of happiness.

Cultivating goodwill and a sense of duty is an important corrective to a sentimental approach to morality. Self-esteem is a meaningless concept without being grounded in the cultivation of goodwill. The moral life is one of a continual struggle between moral duty (reason) and self-interest or pleasure, which can at times take priority over goodwill. Our primary moral duty is self-respect and the cultivation of proper self-esteem that is grounded in the worth of humanity. It should come from the comparison of goodwill with moral law rather than from comparison with others.[49]

According to Habermas, the role of rational autonomy in a Kantian sense is not to be devalued in Hegel's ethical thought, which subordinates the individual will to communal ethical life (*Sittlichkeit*) rooted in cultural custom and tradition. In the historical transition from traditional to modern society, religious or metaphysical worldviews remain in recess, such that the autonomous individual becomes central in the moral universe. In his discourse ethical framework, Habermas recasts autonomy and practical reason in the Kantian sense for communicative interaction (speech act) and consensus. His position finds it substantial to take on the significance of the categorical imperative in an intersubjective context in terms of Hegel's theory of recognition.[50]

However, in Habermas' critical analysis of Kant, he tends to sidestep Kant's consideration of Stoic ideas and historical reality. If Hegel finds sensibility as an essential component in dialectical mediation with moral duty for harmony, Kant's ought/is distinction incorporates the aspect of natural inclination into

---

[49] Ibid., 127.
[50] Habermas, *Justification and Application*, 1.

a historical, cosmopolitan frame of reference, in which the cosmopolitan or world law becomes a condition of universal hospitality.[51]

This implies Kant's ethics of hospitality in response to Hegel's ethic of recognition. It cuts across limitations of Hegel's critique of Kant as empty formalism. I will say more about Kant's ethics of hospitality later in more detail (in chapter 5).

Moral Imperative: Categorical and Hypothetical

An a priori aspect of morality is the metaphysical foundation of morality. Moral duties are absolute, always morally binding regardless of the circumstances. Moral obligations are categorical, and a categorical imperative is a formal principle: we ought to do something regardless of the consequences. It "declares an action to be objectively necessary in itself without reference to any purpose." It "is valid as an Apodictic (practical) principle."[52]

The universal conformity of human action to the law, in general, is to serve the will as a principle. "*Act only on that maxim whereby thou canst at the same time will that it should become a universal law.*"[53] A maxim is the subjective principle of volition or action set by according to the conditions of the subject (its inclination), while the objective principle under the rule of reason is the practical law valid for everybody. It is obligatory for a will, thus called command of reason, in other words, imperative.[54] As a formal principle, the categorical imperative provides a framework for deriving moral maxims or laws.

---

[51] "To Eternal Peace," in *Basic Wirings of Kant*, 448.
[52] "Fundamental Principles of the Metaphysics of Morals," Ibid., 172.
[53] Ibid., 160.
[54] Ibid., 171; 178.

On the basis of the formal principle of universalizability, it refers to agent-centered ethics in which the moral action is undertaken in conformity to principles, maxims, and rules, in which the practical imperative treats humanity as an end itself.

According to the Scripture, we are commanded to love our neighbor, even our enemy. Love, as an affection seated in the propensity of sense, cannot be commanded. But practical love, which is seated in the will and in the principle of action, can be commanded.[55]

However, a prima facie duty is morally binding unless it (the duty not to lie) conflicts with a more pressing moral duty (preventing someone's death). The latter overrides the duty not to lie. This refers to a hypothetical imperative, which acknowledges such lying to a murderer as a way of saving a life. On the other hand, to lie to other rational beings is to offer them a profound insult (against the duty of nonmaleficence or no harm principle). Lying should not be a universal law.

The hypothetical imperative "expresses the practical necessity of an action as means to the advancement of happiness"; it is assertorial.[56] For instance, skill in the choice of means for one's greatest well-being may be called prudence in the narrow sense; it is hypothetical because it is recommended only as means to another purpose.[57] An action as means to something else may be called, and it comes under the hypothetical command of the law.

The hypothetical dimension can be seen in terms of goodwill, which guides virtue of the means, although the moral law is an end itself, and moral duty requires the submission to moral law under the categorical command of the law.[58]

---

[55] Ibid., 158.
[56] Ibid., 173.
[57] Ibid., 173-4.
[58] Lehmann, *Ethics in a Christian Context*, 178.

Kant remains restricted in clarifying the goodwill in regard to virtue since the latter is required more in the specific and particular context. Moral duty without the wisdom of virtue would have a devastating consequence. This refers to the problem of Kant, who focuses on reason as the foundation of morality.

Fundamentally, rational beings have free will and autonomy is essential for dignity, having intrinsic moral worth. The principle of autonomy of the will, which is grounded in the idea of the will of every rational being, gives universal law, thus universal lawgiving can be unconditioned.

The society of all rational beings constitutes the kingdom of ends, which is summed up in the second formulation of the categorical imperative (also known as the practical imperative). "*So, act as to treat humanity, whether in thine own person or in that of any other, in every case as an end in itself, never as means only.*"[59]

Kant's moral philosophy may find its significance in Marx's critique of religion in his moral impulse. As he writes, "to be radical is to grasp the matter by the root. But for man, the root is man himself…The criticism of religion ends with the doctrine that man is the highest being for man, that is, with the categorical imperative to overthrow all circumstances in which man is humiliated, enslaved, abandoned, and despised…"[60]

Marx's position may concur with Kant's universal practical law constituting an objective principle of the will because human beings exist as an end in itself.

---

[59] Ibid., 186.
[60] "Towards a *Critique of Hegel's Philosophy of Right*: Introduction," in *Karl Marx Selected Writings*, 69.

The idea of Freedom, Kingdom of Ends, and the Church

Our actions in the world of sense are mere appearances of causality and are determined by a natural law of desires and inclinations (heteronomy of nature). They rest on happiness. However, we belong to the intelligible world and conceive the causality of the will on the condition of the idea of freedom, which is connected with the conception of autonomy.[61]

Autonomy is connected with the universal principle of morality, which is ideally the foundation of all actions of rational beings. When we think of ourselves as free, we transfer ourselves into the WORLD of understanding and recognize the autonomy of the will with its consequence, morality.[62]

According to John Rawls, Kant's notion of autonomy along with the categorical imperative becomes central, because a person acts autonomously as a free and equal rational being; the moral law governs human conduct in an ethical commonwealth. Moral principles are conceived of as legislation for a kingdom of ends, as acceptable to all as well as the public.

Given this, Rawls describes his concept of the original position in an attempt to interpret the Kantian notion of justice as fairness.[63] The concept of the original position in a purely hypothetical sense becomes crucial in Rawls' definition of justice as fairness in an original agreement in a veil of ignorance based on equality.[64]

Kant maintains that the autonomy of the will is the supreme principle of morality, in a categorical imperative in connection

---

[61] Lehmann, *Ethics in a Christian Context*, 211.
[62] "Fundamental Principles of the Metaphysics of Morals," in *Basic Writings of Kant*, 210.
[63] Rawls, *A Theory of Justice*, 220.
[64] Ibid., 102.

to heteronomy in a hypothetical imperative.⁶⁵ The principle of appropriateness belongs to the latter. The concept of freedom is the key that explains the autonomy of the will, and it can only be shown a priori. Rational beings, which have a will, have the idea of freedom, and they cannot act save under the idea of freedom, in which all moral laws are connected with freedom. Practical reason or the will of a rational being regards itself as free under the idea of freedom.⁶⁶

Freedom is the condition of the moral law, while the latter is the ground of knowledge of freedom in which freedom itself is known. The things in themselves are behind the appearance, but they affect us in the world of understanding.

Reason is the pure spontaneity that is elevated above understanding, which does not contain intuitions like sense. Intuitions arise when we are affected by things, and understanding brings the intuitions of sense under rules, uniting them in one consciousness, without which we could not think at all. A will takes no account of anything under the head of desires and inclinations, "disregarding all desires and sensible inclinations."⁶⁷

The idea of freedom makes us a member of the intelligible world, and in consequence, our actions would always conform to the autonomy of the will. Still, as a member of the world of sense, our actions ought to conform categorically, thus the categorical "ought" implies a synthetic a priori proposition, which contains the supreme condition according to Reason.⁶⁸ "Freedom is only an Idea of Reason."⁶⁹

---

65 "Fundamental Principles of the Metaphysics of Morals," in *Basic Writings of Kant*, 210; 198.
66 Ibid., 205.
67 Ibid.
68 Ibid., 211-2.
69 Ibid., 213.

It is a mere Idea, offering no object to experience, and pure reason acts through mere ideas. Reason becomes practical by moral interest, and it takes a direct interest as the regulative principle in guiding moral law and action. The law exercises the subjective effect on the will, and its objective principle is furnished by Reason alone. If the universal validity of its maxims is alone sufficient to determine the will, "such an interest alone is pure."[70]

Reason is pure spontaneity in the case of Ideas (Ideal Conception), which transcends everything given by sensibility. It exhibits its most important function in distinguishing the world of sense from that of understanding, prescribing the limits of the understanding itself. Pure reason in the intelligible world gives the law categorically. Practical Reason finds itself in the world of understanding outside the appearance, and it conceives of itself as practical and operates freely.[71]

As Barth characterizes, there is one kind of reason in Kant's teaching of practical reason, which is theoretical as well as practical. "Pure reason…is practical reason. Knowledge by pure reason too, the true knowledge of God, freedom, and immortality, is knowledge by practical reason, as it is implicitly accomplished in the deed performed in accordance with duty, and knowledge by practical reason is knowledge by pure reason."[72]

Morality interests us because it is valid for us as human beings. Kant's epistemology is seen in the principle: *"what belongs to mere appearance is necessarily subordinated by reason to the nature of the thing in itself."*[73]

The universal validity of all its maxims as laws, which is a form of pure practical reason, can of itself offer a spring; a cause

---

[70] Ibid., 217, footnote, 18.
[71] Ibid., 216.
[72] Barth, "Kant," in *Protestant Theology*, 262.
[73] "Critique of Practical Reason," in *Basic Writings of Kant*, 218.

determines the will. But to explain how pure reason can be practical is beyond human reason.[74]

With this idea in mind, Kant conceptualizes an ideal kingdom of ends in which the relation of human beings is seen as ends and means. God is the originator or moral world-ruler, who creates a moral people of God, while human beings are members and free citizens of God's kingdom by creating its organizations and institutions. The idea of a people of God is to be realized only in the form of a church. The true visible church exhibits the moral kingdom of God on earth, which requires universality, purity, freedom, and unchangeableness.

The church has to be considered essentially a universal union into one single Church; only morality or purity should be the principle of ecclesiastical union; its characteristic is under the principle of freedom as well as a republic in the relation of the church to political power. The inalterable constitution of the church is the work of God alone, while its administration is alterable in different times and places. The church is defined as a mere representative of a city of God, which is likened to a household under a common divine moral Father.[75]

To the extent that Kant agrees with an innate propensity to transgression ("in Adam, all have sinned"), "sin is represented as resulting from an already innate wickedness in our nature."[76]

However, evil springs only from morally evil rather than from mere limitation in human nature itself, such that human beings are held responsible for the corruption. There is "no conceivable ground from which moral evil in us could originally have come."[77] Despite the first beginning of all evil only through

---

[74] Ibid., 219.
[75] "Religion within the Limits of Reason Alone," Ibid., 412-3.
[76] Ibid., 393.
[77] Ibid.

seduction, human's original predisposition to good is "still capable of an improvement in contrast to a seducing *spirit*."[78]

This perspective leads Kant to characterize Jesus Christ as "the archetype of the moral disposition in all its purity." This archetype as God's very being has come down to us from heaven as "the Word (the Fiat!) through which all other things are, and without which nothing is in existence that is made."[79]

Kant's Christology is embedded with his Trinitarian thinking in which the loving one (Father), representation in the ideal of humanity begotten (the Son), and divine wisdom (the Holy Spirit).[80] In the assumption of human flesh, or in the state of humiliation of Jesus Christ, Kant holds, "a *humanity*... is, in itself, not evil."[81] The Son of God must be our archetype to which human beings strive to elevate themselves through faithful imitation, despite human limitations. Such moral perfection, which becomes the ideal pleasing to God, is possible to an earthly being subject to wants and inclination.

At this point, what strikes in Kant is "*a practical faith in this Son of God*" in order to become acceptable or pleasing to God.[82] An idea of morally well-pleasing to God is present in human reason, thus the archetype is to be sought in human reason; this implies a sign of faith in Jesus Christ in dealing with religion within the limits of reason alone.

---

[78] Ibid., 394.
[79] Ibid., 398-9.
[80] Barth, "Kant," in *Protestant Theology*, 274.
[81] Ibid., 399.
[82] Ibid., 400.

Hegel: Religion and Moral

G. W. F. Hegel (1770-1831) in his early time was engaged in Kant and supported a Kantian religion of morality against the positivity of Christianity, which was embedded with the authority and "enlightened" despotism under Frederick II of Prussia. Hegel develops philosophical theology or philosophy of religion in renewing the doctrine of God and religion, cutting across limitations of Kantian doctrine of God-postulate.

Thus, Hegel reacts against the Kantian distinction between understanding and reason. Hegel involves comprehending the principle of identity and opposition through its isolated reflection about its antagonism. The unity underlying the antagonism is to be grasped and realized for restoring the totality via reconciliation in terms of reason (dialectical thinking) over against understanding (isolating reflection). Spirit (*Geist*) is termed as designating reason as history while viewing the world history as realized in reason in accordance to the rational progress of human consciousness in history and society.[83]

For Hegel "God is the beginning of all things and the end of all things; [everything] starts from God and returns to God. God is the one and only object of philosophy...Thus philosophy *is* theology...is of itself the service of God."[84]

The vocation of philosophy is to know God by defending the rationality of Christian religion or rational content of religion. A biblical idea of God's reconciliation affirms that religion does not surpass all reason, such that philosophy exhibits the rational content of religion by turning the representational language of religion (symbolic and metaphorical) into a conceptual, scientific language. Christianity as the revealed religion has not fully realized the final stage of the self-knowing cosmic *Geist*, in which

---

[83] Marcuse, *Reason and Revolution*, 10; 45.
[84] Hegel, *Lectures on the Philosophy of Religion*, 1: 84.

God is non-identical with the man Jesus, but God is identical/non-identical with all individuals.[85]

Religious language of representation implies a mode of awareness operative within images and symbols in contrast to the full clarity of conceptual thought. Thus, Christianity still lives partly in unhappy consciousness with its unclear language of representation, which is located and expressed between the past of Christ and his final coming.[86]

Represented religion is to be formulated in absolute knowledge with full clarity of speculative thought. For the system of speculative philosophy, Hegel utilizes a doctrine of the Trinity; the being of God discloses itself to be spirit (*Geist*) in its self-revelation to the world by underlying all reality; the Christian doctrine of Trinity becomes central in Hegel's understanding of God as the absolute intersubjectivity, which is differentiated from the Kantian ethical postulate of God as moral preceptor or executor. Gnosis replaces faith because the world exists as an emanation of *Geist*; philosophy ideally transcends faith and grace. Hegel can become a classic example of seeing the evolution of religion in human history, and his onto-theology apprehends God in accordance with human beings or consciousness in its own development and progress.[87]

"God is attainable in pure speculative knowledge alone, only *is* in that knowledge...for He is spirit; and this speculative knowledge is the knowledge furnished by revealed religion."[88]

---

[85] Taylor, *Hegel*, 210.
[86] Ibid., 211. A notion of unhappy consciousness is found in the relation between the individual believer and the priest, who is in direct communication with God. Through obedience to the priest, the individual believer 'disclaims all power of independent self-existence. Hegel, *The Phenomenology of Mind*, 129.
[87] Hegel: *Theologian of the Spirit*, ed. Hodgson, 7.
[88] Hegel, *The Phenomenology of Mind*, 446.

What is striking in Hegel's philosophy of reconciliation is seen in his conception of the death of God in history, which inspires Christian political theology toward a Trinitarian *theologia crucis* in terms of love and liberation. Hegel helps to understand the cross as the history of God through the idea of reconciliation. It is the Spirit as love that abolishes the Other or self-differentiating of God.[89]

Hegel sees the notion of the death of God and its reconciliation in the form of an imaginative term because the divine death belongs to the bitter feeling of the unhappy consciousness. The religious or believing consciousness remains at the level of imaginative or pictorial thinking, which has not the certainty of self-consciousness. The complete reconciliation beyond it has yet to await transfiguration through the absolute knowledge, which is separated from the religious consciousness.[90]

If "the self accomplishes the life of Absolute Spirit," it refers to the last embodiment of spirit, in other words, the absolute knowledge, in which spirit knows itself 'in the form of knowledge of itself.'"[91] In fact, the religious consciousness counters the process of self-consciousness in the sense of beautiful soul, which Hegel defines as "its own knowledge of itself in its pure transparent unity." "It knows this pure knowledge of pure inwardness to be spirit... the self-intuition of God Himself."[92]

Hegel shares self-intuition of God with Aristotle who conceptualizes happiness in the activity of *theoria*, thus perfect happiness implies the disinterested contemplation of truth; Intellect is something divine within us, which is primordial, approximating to the life of the deity; the activity of God is connected with the activity of contemplation.[93]

---

[89] Moltmann, *The Crucified God*, 254.
[90] Hegel, *The Phenomenology of Mind*, 460;462.
[91] Ibid., 469.
[92] Ibid., 467.
[93] Aristotle, *Nicomachean Ethics*, X. VIII. 8.

It is true that Hegel integrates into his dialectical framework Aristotle's logic of movement and unification in the relation between potentiality and actuality, in which each and every potentiality is inherent in the ontological movement and realized in its existence.

If Kant secures the practical reason (in distinction from understanding) as a universal type of moral rationality in the religious sense, Hegel is concerned with the dialectical unity between knowledge and Geist through the historical course of time.

Hegel's onto-theology is expressed in a dialectical framework based on the movement of the Spirit, in which God is the being of necessity in the self-manifestation of the Spirit to the world. His Spirit-centrism would be expressed as a Quaternity (a four in one), because he conceptualizes evil as "the self-concentration of the natural existence of the spirit," while "good... appears as an (objectively) existing self-consciousness."[94]

God is caught to the iron cage of onto-dialectical logic, movement, and progress within the appearance of Quaternity, in which the different, the disadvantaged, the particular are subordinated to the universal of the spirit including good and evil. This implies Hegel's pessimism in renouncing the fight against radical evil.

However, if Hegel's dialectical method is based on the logic of contradiction or opposition given the state of affairs, I argue that dialectical thinking requires a critical complement from the problematic way of thinking, which suspends what is taken for granted and returns to examine what is marginalized, excluded, and subjugated through the power of the universal discourse. Reconciliation is critically seen along with problematization given the universalizing unity of reason.

---

[94] Ibid., 454.

Unlike Hegel, however, reconciliation does not replace eschatology, but the latter takes issue with the status quo of the universally reconciled stage since there is a reality of radical evil in the reconciled world, impersonal forces.

If reason rules the world, world history proceeds rationally from the necessary course of the World Spirit. What is Hegel's God to do with the reality of sinful conditions in history and society? Hegel does not appeal to religion, but the state, the politically organized community in the sense of the Greek polis in restoring the ethical life for public good against Kantian moral radical autonomy.

Theological Appraisal: Kant and Kingdom of Ends

Unlike Hegel's conception of Christianity as the absolute religion, Kant is not merely blind to faith in human progress only based on a human moral basis, but he requires supernatural influence from above to below in re-creating humanity. An evil principle is inhered together with the good, as seen analogously in the Augustinian notion of a *privatio boni*. Kant describes frailty or self-interest or malevolence as the original sin, concurring with St. Paul: "In Adam we have sinned" (Rom 5:12).

This perspective requires rebirth or regeneration undergoing a complete change of heart in terms of a new creation. It is on the threshold to a theological interpretation of Kant. According to Barth, Kant's appeal to the grace of God is embedded with his idea of the kingdom of God, in which God forgives and justifies human beings through the divine Comforter (paraclete). Nonetheless, biblical subjects such as grace, atonement, or election remain parerga of his philosophical religion of reason, which does not refute the possibility of such ideas. Kant remains a great example of inspiring the mutual quality of the relationship between theology and philosophy.[95]

On the contrary, Albrecht Ritschl (1822-89) calls attention to Kant's moral theory and employs the idea of the kingdom of ends in a new way through his theology of justification and reconciliation by qualifying Christian existence in this regard. Thus, the Christian religion is defined as a way of living, which refers to a style of life expressed in ethical vocation. A religious–ethical style of life is a central concept in understanding the whole of Christianity in its historical development.

Ritschl's idea of reconciliation is differentiated from Hegel's reconciliation in the dialectical frame of reference underlying the unity in sublation (*Aufhebung*) between thesis and antithesis. Rather, his reconciliation refers to the kingdom of God in the biblical sense, in which he takes into account Kant's philosophy of the kingdom of ends on earth.

As Barth writes, "Completed reconciliation consists in God's confronting the believer as his Father and justifying him in his child-like feeling of utter trust, giving him spiritual dominion over the world and engaging him in the work in the kingdom of God."[96]

Along with a modern Kantian understanding of human ethical problems and the kingdom of God, Ritschl's ethical theology is mainly based on the doctrine of justification and stands in the Lutheran community. His creative interpretation of Luther in terms of justification and reconciliation and the Christian notion of freedom is not fully assimilated into Kantian practical reason and its optimism of Enlightenment.

Despite his critique of rigid ecclesiastic orthodoxy, Kant seeks to guard the content of faith and incorporate central tenets of

---

[95] Barth, "Kant," in *Protestant Theology*, 288; 297.
[96] Ibid.

the Bible and its morality into rational faith, that is, within the bounds of reason alone.

Kantian rational faith does not discard divine revelation in Jesus Christ as futile and superfluous. But morality is based on the free, rational human being, who is bound by reason to unconditional laws.

Religion, which is grounded on practical reason, does not require any organizational structures anchored in dogmas and ritual observances; rather it focuses on the disposition of the heart to observe moral duties as God's commands. Christian faith is not confused with rational religion of morality, but it constitutes the shell for the rational content of religion, in which God in us is moral law.[97]

Accordingly, reason becomes the standard by which to interpret the Bible and ecclesiastical faith, while functioning as the principal of scriptural exegesis for the sake of moral improvement. As Kant writes, "Scriptural texts which seem to enjoin a merely passive surrender to an external power that produces holiness in us must, then, be interpreted differently. It has to be made clear from them that *we ourselves must work* a developing that moral disposition..."[98]

The grace of justification–in that God has done in Christ for our sake—is replaced by the grace of sanctification in that we ought to do for the moral worth of life. The moral law refers to the biblical notion of a kingdom of God, which is translated into the concept of the highest good in reference to rational postulates of God and immortality of the soul.

The idea of the kingdom of God embraces the religious and the ethical, and it refers to the *summum bonum* as the highest

---

[97] Habermas, *Between Naturalism and Religion*, 214.
[98] Kant, "The Conflict of the Faculties," in *Kant, Religion and Rational Theology*, 268.

human good and final aim for an ethical common task, which is activated in terms of the love of one's neighbor; the supreme good from which all others are derived.

The kingdom of God is divinely ordained in Christ as the highest good of the community, and it forms the ethical idea for members of the community to attain it through moral actualization in the world. Moral vocation is exercised in relation to the world; marriage, family, civic and social life, the nation.

Kant's kingdom of ends is strongly echoed in his moral interpretation of the kingdom of God in which ethical vocation is to fulfill the universal moral law and fellowship of humankind. A biblical concept of the kingdom of God is charged with eschatological meaning, but its central meaning is established on earth in the sense of chiliasm which anticipates the world—disclosing and transforming power of religious semantics. Morality and eschatology belong together.

This model is elaborated in Ritschl's theological deontology, in which the integrative model of justification with reconciliation engenders an ethical practical lifestyle in effecting the social, political cultural realm in light of the kingdom of God.

However, Ritschl identified a Kantian understanding of the kingdom of ends and cultural values to be in harmony with his Prussian time. The universal end of the kingdom is not in conflict with the developed social, cultural structures, but it is performed through the moral fellowship of the family, the national fellowship of the state, and even the combination of nations in world-empire.[99]

In fact, Kant makes room for faith, looking for a rational equivalent to the cognitive and moral attitude of faith. Rather than religious faith, rational faith "is trust in the attainment of an

---

[99] Ritschl, *The Christian Doctrine of Justification and Reconciliation*, 309-12.

aim the promotion of which is a duty but the possibility of the realization of which it is not possible for us to have insight into."¹⁰⁰

However, the Kantian concept tends to be vulnerable to any socio-political ideology, since rational faith relies on the rationality of society or state. A state most certainly arose not out of a Kantian kingdom of ends, but instead violence which used bodies as a means to an end.

Indeed, Kant's interest is not in faith or promise as the content contained in the moral law, but in its moral form of the faith and promise for us to put into practice. It implies "a flattering imitation" of the Christian concept of faith in a Kantian sense, in which moral faith comes from the shell of religious faith.[101]

In so doing, what is striking in Kant's moral philosophy is to realize the promised kingdom of God on earth as the highest good by transposing the transcendental, eschatological idea of the kingdom of God into an inner-worldly utopia.

Without sufficient distinction of the eschatological hope, however, Ritschl would cause an impression of "a Christ of culture," because the complete reconciliation with culture has been achieved through the idea of the kingdom of God. Jesus Christ is ascribed to Kant's idea of the kingdom of ends without reservation. As Ritschl writes, "the Christian idea of the Kingdom of God denotes the association of mankind—an association both extensively and intensively the most comprehensive possible—through the reciprocal moral action of its members..."[102]

This perspective tends to block a path to the eschatological dimension from God's future while subordinating the

---

[100] Kant, *Critique of the Power of Judgment*, 336.
[101] Habermas, *Between Naturalism and Religion*, 222-3.
[102] Ibid., 284. Cited in Niebuhr, *Christ and Culture*, 98.

anamnestic solidarity of the Gospel in the form of *theologia crucis* under the reconciliation with culture.

Barth acknowledges that Ritschl's significance can be seen in his return to the theoretical and practical philosophy of the Enlightenment in its Kantian form. But he is charged with accommodating Protestant theology to the bourgeoisie ideals at the time of Bismarck. Ritschl's ideal of life is "the very epitome of the national-liberal German bourgeois of the age of Bismarck."[103]

Nonetheless, Ritschl's significance can be seen more in his Christocentric theology in rejection of natural religion and his ethical interpretation of eschatology through reconciliation. It is not surprising that Ritschl finds his significance in the circle of religious socialism (Leonhard Ragaz) in Switzerland as well as the social gospel movement in America (Walter Rauschenbusch).

Conclusion: Public Theology and Political Ethics

Kant in his "flattering imitation" of Christian faith leads to considering the institution of the faith community as a people of God under ethical laws. Practical reason is compelled to establish the rational concept of the ethical community in the complex world. In Kant's reflection of the assumption of human flesh, the Word (the Fiat) is the archetype, the exemplar of the ideal of moral perfection. Our common duty is to elevate humankind to complete moral perfection. The idea of a humanity pleasing to God is already present in our reason, residing in our morally legislative reason, which ought to conform to this archetype.[104]

---

[103] Barth, *Protestant Theology*, 642.
[104] Kant, "Religion Within the Limits of Reason Alone," 399-400.

This contrasts with the Protestant grounding of ethics on faith and grace in which there is an emphasis on God's free grace of forgiveness and Jesus as the revealer and mediator of divine agape. The moral virtues or ethical activity in the kingdom of God is not separated from redemption through Jesus and his lordship in the faith community and the world.

Justification as forgiveness of sin is apprehended in faith and the great guarantee and realization of reconciliation, the ideal of life, which is apprehended as an event in the church. Jesus is the archetypal image of humanity, uniting humanity with the kingdom of God. Jesus realizes his own goal as identical with God's own goal, which is also identical with our own goal. Revealing the love of God, Jesus is God. We obtain justification and admission to the kingdom of God only through Jesus in his church, thus we have God in Jesus.[105]

This perspective is differentiated from Kant, who conceptualizes Jesus only as the archetype and God only as moral ruler of the world.[106] Seeking the archetype in our reason, Kant elaborated an idea of an ethical commonwealth in which people are united under laws of virtues alone.[107]

This refers to the church as invisible. It serves as the archetype of what is established by people, the visible church, which refers to the actual union of people in harmony with that idea.[108] The visible church exhibits the moral kingdom of God on earth.

However, what is central in the church is revelation and faith in the God of Jesus Christ underlying justification and reconciliation. The idea of the kingdom of God is historically grounded in the person of Jesus, and it is ethically apprehended.

---

[105] Barth, *Protestant Theology*, 647.
[106] Kant, "Religion Within the Limits of Reason Alone," in *Basic Writings of Kant*, 410.
[107] Ibid., 406.
[108] Ibid., 411.

This is the controlling principle for public theology to engage with civil society through the prophetic reasoning of reconciliation and *theologia crucis*. God's event of reconciliation in the death of Jesus Christ is the theological epistemology by which to cut across the limitation of binary opposition in dialectical logic while leading to recognition of the Other for the common good and solidarity. Theological reasoning of reconciliation does not avert a reality of impersonal forces in our midst, calling for ethical discipleship in fighting evil.

In fact, Kant opens up the space of a moral dimension to civil society in distinction from the political society. Kant writes: "It has, however, a special and unique principle of union, virtue, and hence a form and constitution which fundamentally distinguish it from the political commonwealth."[109]

A political society (juridico-civil) represents people who stand each other socially under public juridical laws, while a civil society (ethico-civil) represents that they are united under non-coercive laws, in other words, laws of virtue alone. The citizen of the political commonwealth remains completely free to enter into an ethical association or group and follow the constitution if an ethical commonwealth rests on public laws and possesses a constitution based on these laws.[110]

This distinction between political society and civil society remains crucial for public theology to deal with civil society through the significance of public morals, defending the civil society against the power of political society.

In his reflection of the relation between morals and politics, Kant elaborates political ethics in terms of a moral politician, which represents a realm of virtue; the ethical state is within the political society. Politics is defined as an applied doctrine

---

[109] Ibid., 406.
[110] Ibid., 407.

of right and law, without which politics becomes the art of prudence to use the mechanism of nature for the governing people. The concept of right and law would be an empty phrase in the political prudence driven by the mechanism of nature.[111]

"Be ye, therefore, wise as serpents."—this is the dictum of politics, yet morals have limiting conditions: as innocent as doves. In the one statement, no conflict of politics would occur with morals, in such co-existence. The totality of civil society can be created on the basis of the collective unity of the united general will. Such civil society brings forth a common will or a common good of justice or perpetual peace.[112]

Kant's concept of the kingdom of ends entails social, political dimensions in the construction of a moral politician in contrast to a political moralist. The former employs the principles of political prudence in correlation with morals and seeks remedy or reform of the deficient in the constitution in accordance with a model in the idea of reason. It appreciates the necessity of change in approaching the final end of the constitution, which is best in accordance with right and law. Thus, this moral politician requires political prudence because a better constitution cannot be undertaken with impetuosity. Kant includes a possibility of revolution in this regard, even though acts of violence would be subject to the penalties of a seditionist.

Kant takes political prudence as the duty to effect reforms in keeping with the ideals of public laws and rights; he even utilizes revolutions as a call of nature to bring about by thorough reforms and a legal institution based upon the principles of freedom. However, the revolutions should not be abused "for the purpose of camouflaging an even greater suppression."[113]

---

[111] Kant, "To Eternal Peace," Ibid., 460.
[112] Ibid., 459.
[113] Ibid., 461-2. Footnote 10.

The task of a moral politician contradicts a political moralist who would fabricate a system of morals, restricting its purpose that brings politics in accordance with morals.[114] Kant is not a rigorist per se in the political field, because he undertakes a critique of despotic moralists in violating the political prudence, as well as moralizing politicians making progress impossible.[115]

Kant concurs with St. Paul: "We wrestle not against flesh and blood (the natural inclinations) but against principalities and powers—against evil spirits."[116]

He favors the duplicity of politics in relation to morals. Politics is readily agreed with morals as ethics in the first sense, sacrificing the rights of people to their superiors. But the politics should bend its knee to morals as a theory of right and law or jurisprudence in the second sense. To thwart the cunning device of secretive politics, Kant writes a political maxim: "All maxims which *require* publicity in order not to miss their purpose agree with right, law, and politics."[117]

Kant's philosophy of religion reinforces its public use of reason, distinguishing the significance of civil society in its ethical commonwealth from political society, which must be ever reformed by the responsibility of moral politicians with political prudence. This stance forms a point of no return for public theology which pursues prophetic reasoning of reconciliation and *theologia crucis* for the kingdom of God against the reality of impersonal forces. Public theology finds a significance in interlocution with Kant's philosophy of religion.

In Habermas' account, "Reason cannot have its religious cake and eat it too. Nevertheless, the constructive intention of

---

[114] Ibid., 465.
[115] Ibid., 462.
[116] Ibid., 397.
[117] Ibid., 475.

Kant's philosophy of religion still merits our attention if we want to know what we can learn from the articulatory power of the major world religions for the practical use of reason under conditions of post-metaphysical thinking."[118]

---

[118] Habermas, *Between Naturalism and Religion*, 227.

Chapter 2
Utilitarianism

Jeremy Bentham (1748-1832) was the representative of classic utilitarianism, and one of his followers was James Mill, a Scottish philosopher and economist. His son, John Stuart Mill (1806-1873) would become the leading advocate of utilitarian moral theory. If God as the creator desires the happiness of creatures as the purpose of creation, utility is of more profoundly religious character than any other. The utilitarian philosopher believes in divine perfect goodness and wisdom.[1] Utilitarian philosophy is critically involved in Kant while elaborating his ethical content in its distinguished value and different orientation.

First, I am interested in examining the utilitarian philosophy in its achievements and shortcomings concerning Jeremy Bentham and J. S. Mill. Mill's philosophy of liberty comes into critical focus on its laissez-faire capitalism, colonialism, and social Darwinism. Second, I safeguard Adam Smith as a moral philosopher in distinction from the utilitarian stance allied with laissez-faire capitalism. Third, Smith's critique of mercantilist colonialism can be seen in its relevance to biopolitical power and even influence on Marx's theory of primitive accumulation in dealing with European colonialism. His theory of division of labor is critically exposed in this regard. A critical analysis of the division of labor and rationalization remains crucial in

---

[1] Mill, "Utilitarianism," in *Classics of Moral and Political Theory*, 1006.

projecting public theology in its moral frame of reference, which is undertaken through structural change.

1. Liberty and No Harm Principle

According to J. S. Mill, our only duties are to maximize happiness (duty of beneficence) and to minimize pain (duty of nonmaleficence) for the greatest number. The question–what ought we to do? —is answered in the way of creating the best possible consequences in terms of utility, which is the ultimate source of moral duty. Utilitarianism has a particular goal as the great net happiness for all, and moral actions should be determined by its consequence.

J. S. Mill takes issue with Kant who lays out a universal principle as the origin and the ground of moral obligation; "So act, that the rule on which thou actest would admit of being adopted as a law by all rational beings."[2] However, Kant fails, according to J. S. Mill, to draw attention to that "there would be any contradiction, any logical (not to say physical) impossibility, in the adoption by all rational beings of the most outrageously immoral rules of conduct."[3]

However, Mill's argument tends to dismiss that Kant's universalization of individual maxim of action and one's action on it does not mean a way of speculating about consequence. Kant insists that an individual maxim ought to accord with the categorical imperative; it refers to the universalizing test or criterion in treating humanity as an end in itself.[4]

Of central importance in utilitarian ethics is the principle of utility underlying Jeremy Bentham's formulation: the

---
[2] Cited in Ibid., 996.
[3] Ibid.
[4] Sandel, *Justice*, 121.

greatest happiness principle concerning the *summum bonum*. The desire for happiness is universal, and humans recognize happiness as the greatest goal. In seeking the happiness of society or the whole community, the right thing to do is a matter of calculating consequences in terms of costs and benefits.

Private utility comes to terms with public utility, to the degree that the good of the world is made up of the good of individuals. "They all enjoin to abstain from whatever is manifestly pernicious to society."[5] Duty as an objective reality is based on belief in God which operates in proportion to the subjective religious feeling; "a person sees in moral obligation a transcendental fact, an objective reality belonging to the province of 'Things in themselves'..."[6]

Mill's concern is that laws and social arrangements should place the happiness of every individual in harmony with the interest of the whole. The cultivation of individuality is one of the essentials of well-being, but only restricted in the case of a nuisance to other people. Emphasis on individual liberty thwarts the authority of any collective to intervene in individual life, though it may be done for self-protection in preventing harm to others.

The primary means of ensuring happiness is to respect the dignity and personal autonomy of others. Conscience, liberty of tastes and pursuit, or human dignity (with no harm principle) is more than a calculator of the common good. Thus, Mill argues against a notion of identifying the government with the people in such a way that would entail coercion. This political power of the government is illegitimate when exerted in accordance with public opinion. "The best government has no more title to it than the worst...mankind would be no more justified in

---

[5] Mill, "Utilitarianism," in *Classics of Moral and Political Theory*, 1005.
[6] Ibid., 1009.

silencing that one person [the contrary person], than he, if he had the power, would be justified in silencing mankind."[7]

J. S. Mill advocates a concept of justice that focuses on one's personal liberty, his/her property, and legally constituted rights. Justice as impartiality becomes instrumental to some other duty or virtues such as human generosity, preference, or beneficence. The utility principle becomes the ultimate appeal in dealing with all ethical issues, and the "no harm" principle is the foundation of freedom. He secures the liberty of the press against the tyrannical system of government.[8] Despite the liberty of the press, punishment is incurred when a critique of corn-dealers or private property as robbery is undertaken orally before an excited assembly of the mob or in the form of a placard.[9]

J. S. Mill reverses Kant's dictum—"So act, that thy rule of conduct might be adopted as a law by all rational beings"—into a rule in which "all rational beings might adopt *with benefit to their collective interest.*"[10]

However, he remains silent as to what constitutes a benefit to the collective interest or what is the collective interest. Mill undermines that society in effect is more than the sum of individual members, guiding and controlling the individual life. Society would provide the individual with a safety net, to the degree that its social formation is rationalized along with moral solidarity in accordance with a social institution, judicial system, or social welfare.

If the utility is the truth according to Mill, individualism prevails over the control of society, leading to the noninterventionism of the government in individual affairs.

---

[7] Mill, "On Liberty," Ibid., 944.
[8] Ibid., 943.
[9] Ibid., 963.
[10] "Utilitarianism," Ibid., 1021.

There is a tendency in Mill to an unfortunate notion of laissez-faire capitalism in the sense of free-market capitalism (separating economics from the state).

Classical Utilitarian Theory and Its Problem

Bentham promoted the classic notion of utilitarianism as a tool of social reform in critical response to the flagrant injustices of his time plagued by the industrial revolution. His time is beset by upheavals of revolution in America and France.

He accepts David Hume's ethics (1711-1776) in which the circumstance of utility is a source of praise and approbation or a foundation of morals. It should appeal to the moral decision in all ethical subjects. The utility "is a foundation of the chief part of morals, which has a reference to mankind and our fellow-creatures."[11] Reason is not the source of conscience or moral good or evil, but it is "the slave of the passions,"[12] since morals excite passions, in terms of producing as well as preventing these. Morality is not discovered only by a deduction of reason, because its rules are not conclusions of human reason.[13]

It is a sentiment that moves us to act virtuously. Sympathy is the great virtue, which runs counter to the lack of sympathy, such as cruelty or resentment, the greatest vice. Moral sentiments have little to do with ethical subjectivism, but they imply a form of knowledge rooted in our constitution and temper. If reason motivates and instructs us to do good, moral sentiments give a preference for the user to act. Both reason and sentiment work

---

[11] Hume, *An Enquiry Concerning the Principles of Morals*, 231.
[12] Hume, "Selections from the Treatise of Human Nature," in *Classics of Moral and Political Theory*, 753.
[13] Ibid., 756.

together in conjunction, though "moral distinctions... are not offspring of reason."[14]

The function of reason is to affirm the social and generous impulses against the more egoistic ones in the form of self-love, such as avarice, ambition, and all of the vulgar improper passions. The sentiment refers to a feeling for the happiness of humankind, standing in favor of those useful and beneficial.

Because "morality is not an object of reason,"[15] Hume's ethical theory of sentiments calls into question the anthropocentric view of a moral community. Rather it encompasses all sentient beings. Every animal has the sense and appetite, being susceptible to all the same virtues and vices as the human species.[16] The pain or pleasure distinguishes moral good and evil.

Hume's theory of morality finds significance in Adam Smith's theory of moral sentiments underlying moral thought and practice. Although the idea of utility remains crucial in Smith accorded with Hume, he does not take it up in the utilitarian sense of social reform.[17]

Adam Smith (1723-1790) did not use the term laissez-faire capitalism, but his most famous phrase "the invisible hand" appears in *The Theory of Moral Sentiments (1759)*, which has been highly praised by Edmund Burke and David Hume; that term had been appropriated to buttress laissez-faire capitalism without intervention from the state. "[The rich] divide with the poor the produce of all their improvements. They are led by an invisible hand to make nearly the same distribution of the

---

[14] Ibid.
[15] Ibid., 761.
[16] Ibid.
[17] Smith, *Theory of Moral Sentiments*. Part IV: "Of the Effect of Utility upon the Sentiment of Approbation;" Chapter I, "Of the beauty which the appearance of utility bestows upon all the production of art, and of the extensive influence of this species of beauty" IV. I. 1-11: 179-87.

necessaries of life, which would have been made, had the earth been divided into equal portions among all its inhabitants, and thus without intending it, without knowing it, advance the interest of the society, and afford means to the multiplication of the species."[18]

Smith's notion of mutual sympathy of sentiment underlying human morality comes to terms with self-interest under the condition of perfect liberty and perfect competition. Competition becomes a chief driving force rather than social utility. In *The Wealth of Nations*, his notion of division of labor and self-interest is directed by the invisible hand to promote an end, which is no part of individual intention: "By pursuing his own interest he frequently promotes that of the society more effectually than when he really intends to promote it."[19]

Nonetheless, Smith might be tolerant of government intervention seeking to reduce poverty. "No society can surely be flourishing and happy, of which the far greater part of the members is poor and miserable. It is but equity, besides, that they who feed, clothe and lodge the whole body of the people, should have such a share of the produce of their own labor as to be themselves tolerably well fed, clothed, and lodged."[20]

Following in the footsteps of Hume, yet sharing in Smith, Bentham defends animal rights and establishes the highest principle of morality as maximizing utility or happiness over against pain; utility implies whatever produces pleasure or happiness by preventing pain or suffering, including animals. The feelings of pain and pleasure become sovereign masters for our moral life, in which the idea of natural rights is scorned

---

[18] Smith, *Theory of Moral Sentiments*, IV. 1. 10.
[19] Smith, *The Wealth of Nations*, 572.
[20] Ibid., 110-1.

as "nonsense upon stilts."²¹ The principle of utility replaces all references to divine command or abstract moral rules because morality is concerned with fashioning the world to be happy.

According to Bentham, God should be seen as a benevolent creator. As he writes, "the dictates of religion would coincide, in all cases, with those of utility, were the Being, who is the object of religion, universally supposed to be as benevolent as he is supposed to be wise and powerful..."²² Might a benevolent God forbid killing a person who suffers, dying in bed? Bentham is reported to have requested euthanasia in his final days, though such request was not accepted.²³

Bentham, trained in the law, comprehends the purpose of the law as promotion of the welfare of all citizens in which individual freedom should be restricted. Against the egoistic tendency of self-preference, he utilizes government to distribute rewards and punishments, counteracting the egoistic tendency of the individual in undermining the general welfare.²⁴

However, J. S. Mill makes the distinction between higher and lower pleasure. "It is better to be a human being dissatisfied than a pig satisfied; better to be Socrates dissatisfied than a fool satisfied."²⁵ It is absurd for Mill to reduce everything to the calculus of pleasure and pain. A moral ideal of human dignity and its principle of liberty is required without dependence on utility itself.

In the context of Christian ethics, Gustafson appreciates the position of classic utilitarian writers in their appeal to experience in the justification of ethics. He finds significance in Bentham's

---

[21] Sandel, *Justice*, 34.
[22] Cited in James Rachels and Stuart Rachels, *The Elements of Moral Philosophy*, 100.
[23] Ibid., 101.
[24] Niebuhr, *The Nature and Destiny of Man*, I: 107.
[25] "Utilitarianism," in *Classics of Moral and Political Theory*, 999.

statement from *An Introduction to the Principles of Morals and Legislation*: "Nature has placed mankind under the governance of two sovereign masters, *pain* and *pleasure*. It is for them alone to point out what we ought to do, as well as to determine what we shall do.... They govern us in all we do, in all we say, in all we think: every effort we can make to throw off our subjection will serve but to demonstrate and confirm it."[26]

Bentham maintains that the utility produces benefit or pleasure.[27] Morality is based on costs and benefits; thus, he reckons social consequence in the full sense through calculating cost and benefits, even in monetary terms. If morality depends only on calculating consequences, a theory of utility reduces certain human rights and moral duties for respecting humanity merely to calculating consequences. "Pleasures... are the *ends* which the legislator has in view...Pleasures and pains are the *instruments* he has to work with."[28]

In the utilitarian assumption, society is simply reduced to the sum of the individual, and social problems are naively seen in terms of the principle of utility in maximizing pleasure and minimizing pain. The community as a fictitious body is constituted by its members.

This perspective sidesteps what causes social problems embedded with social relations and power structures. According to Marx, the theory of utility is based on social facts, and its economic content turns into "a mere apologia for the existing state of affairs."[29] Bentham completely subordinates all existing relations to the relation of utility and elevates utility unconditionally to the sole content of all other relations.

---

[26] Cited in Gustafson, *Ethics from a Theocentric Perspective* II: 102.

[27] Bentham, "An Introduction to the Principles of Morals and Legislation," in *Ethics for Life*, 272.

[28] Ibid., 273.

[29] Marx, "Utilitarianism," in *Karl Marx Selected Writings*, 189.

In his theory of utility, Marx argues, "the bourgeois no longer appears as a special class, but as the class whose conditions of existence are those of the whole society."[30] The theory of utility and its moral reflection are undertaken within a narrow compass because a critique of the social and economic relations is expounded only in a restricted manner and depends on the position of the exploiter. In fact, the utilitarian theory is "prejudiced in favor of the conditions of the bourgeoisie."[31]

Bentham and Panopticon

Despite the limitations, however, Bentham applies his utilitarian calculus to the reform of the criminal justice system, opposing the concept of retributive justice. His alternative plan for a prison system was the Panopticon which was sanctioned by an act of the British Parliament in 1791. But it was not built. His utilitarian theory concerned with equality and impartiality has been influential in improving the current criminal justice system.

In Bentham's Preface to Panopticon, inspection–house, we read about several benefits brought by it: "*Morals reformed—health preserved—industry invigorated—instruction diffused—public burthens lightened*—Economy seated, as it were, upon a rock—the Gordian knot of the Poor-Laws not cut, but united—all by a simple idea in architecture!"[32]

According to the panoptic mechanism, a supervisor is placed in a central tower, while a mad person, a patient, a condemned person, a worker, or a schoolboy is shut up in each cell. The inmate is watched at and spied and is not to know whether he/

---

[30] Ibid., 188.
[31] Ibid.
[32] Cited in Foucault, *Discipline and Punish*, 207.

she is being inspected at any moment; "one sees" in the central tower "everything without ever being seen."[33]

This utilitarian technology is further seen in Bentham's scheme for renewing pauper management in which he propped a self-financing workhouse for the poor; if the beggar on the streets generates the pain of sympathy or disgust, it reduces the utility of the general public. They should be removed from the streets and confined in a workhouse.[34]

To promote the general welfare or happiness, the poor must be deprived of their human rights and freedom. Bentham remains restrained in providing proper concern about human dignity and individual rights, such that power relations and their problem in society remain intact.

It is Michel Foucault that takes issue with Bentham's design of the Panopticon as a classic example of surveillance and control in which power operates in a disciplinary technology. It functions as a laboratory of power engendering homogeneous effects of power in its ability to penetrate into human behavior. As Foucault argues, "knowledge follows the advances of power, discovering new objects of knowledge over all the surfaces on which power is exercised."[35]

The Panopticon represents a schema of power, which is polyvalent in its application as "integrated into any function (education, medical treatment, production, punishment);" it implies a general model of defining and adjusting power relations in the everyday life, making the spread of power effective, "which can be implemented in hospitals, workshops, schools, prisons."[36]

---

[33] Ibid., 202.
[34] Sandel, *Justice*, 35-6.
[35] Foucault, *Discipline and Punish*, 204.
[36] Ibid., 205; 206.

Foucault interprets the Panopticon in the sense that the political power exercises upon the human body through calculation, docility, economic utility, and surveillance. This disciplinary power has its goal to treat the human body as a docile body, which is to be reproductive. The discipline in meticulous control of the body imposes upon a relation of docility-utility, and it became a general formula of domination in the course of the seventeenth and eighteenth century.[37]

The social body comes to terms with power relations, such that a procedure of subordination of bodies must increase the utility of power underlying a perfect disciplinary institution. A utilitarian type of reason serves as technological rationality for consolidating the political power in control of the human body and surveillance of the entirety of human life in society.

Utilitarian Principle and Religious Character

If Bentham has the sole goal of morality to maximize the total utility of the community, it tends to scapegoat an innocent person or group. However, J. S. Mill finds it objectionable. Mill recasts the utilitarian principle with an emphasis on individual rights. Mill's principle of non-maleficence or no harm principle protects someone else's legitimate rights and supports no censorship for a more tolerant society. It is more important than the duty to maximize the happiness of the community.

J. S. Mill's no harm principle affirms that the individual is sovereign over his/her own body and mind. The sovereignty of the individual is justified as a warrant to end the suffering of the person. What is crucial in the utilitarian principle is general happiness, which is a powerful principle in human nature. "The

---

[37] Ibid., 137.

social state is at once so natural, so necessary, and so habitual to man…this association riveted us more and more, as mankind is further removed from the state of savage independence."[38]

J. S. Mill's social philosophy presupposes that the interests of all are to be consulted and regarded equally in society or in the state of civilization except an absolute monarch. Happiness morality maintains that social bond and its health growth provide each individual with a stronger personal interest, thus the harmony between individual interest and the welfare of others is recognized as the ethical standard.

Mill frames individual liberty on utilitarian considerations, despite his disagreement with Bentham's principle of utility. He expresses the spirit of the utilitarian position in the sense that the utilitarian or happiness theory consists in appreciating instrumental value as good. For example, insofar as the medical skill or the art of music conduces to health or pleasure, it is proved to be good.[39]

Whatever else is good refers to a mean rather than an end. This position has little to do with deontology nor with teleology. If a means becomes instrumental in creating pleasure or happiness as the purpose, or the end, the end may justify the means. The useful means or utility becomes a test or a criterion of ascertaining what is right or wrong for the end.

As J. S. Mill writes about his creed of the greatest happiness principle, "actions are right in proportion as they tend to promote happiness, wrong as they tend to produce the reverse of happiness."[40]

This perspective takes up pleasure with the degree of virtue, which is conducive to pleasure; it cultivates the disinterested love

---

[38] "Utilitarianism," in *Classics of Moral and Political Theory*, 1011.
[39] Ibid., 997.
[40] Ibid., 998.

of virtue for the sake of protection from pain. If we desire money or fame in a disinterested way, such virtue is desired as a means or instrument for attaining the end itself.[41]

However, this instrumentalist view tends to elevate the end by justifying the means as a part of the end. Reason is at the disposal of the instrument rather than becoming critical in matters pertaining to the way money or fame would be acquired. In the struggle of existence for survival regarding money or fame, the reality of the disadvantaged is undermined for the sake of improvement, progress, and happiness among the fittest, though the equality of members of society is formally established.

In the utilitarian principle, the notion of justice varies in different persons according to preference and utility. "No one has a moral right to our generosity or beneficence, because we are not morally bound to practice those virtues towards any given individual."[42]

J. S. Mill's religious character can be seen in his interpretation of the golden rule and the command of love of the neighbor for becoming constitutive of the ideal perfection of utilitarian morality. He maintains that conduciveness to the general happiness is the essence of the criterion of God that God approves; the ultimate sanction of all morality is utility in connection with the subjective feeling of humankind, or conscience. In the Golden Rule of Jesus of Nazareth, he reads "the complete spirit of the ethics of utility."[43] "To do as one would be done by, and to love one's neighbor as oneself, constitute the ideal perfection of utilitarian morality."[44]

But the utilitarian rule seems to be easily degenerative, because who judges what is pleasure and happiness? Mill's reluctance to

---

[41] Ibid., 1013.
[42] Ibid., 1020.
[43] Ibid., 1003.
[44] Ibid.

people's sovereignty tends to prefer the role of the fittest or elitists. If a society decides the greatest good or pleasure for the rest of society, entailing the removal of a minority population, would its consequence be bound to maximizing the pleasure and happiness of a bigoted, racist, or fascist majority?

On the other hand, Mill does not countenance the Christian ethical teaching as the guidance, but other ethics must coexist in order to generate the moral regeneration of humankind. "The exclusive pretension made by a part of the truth to be the whole, must and ought to be protected against."[45]

Mill's reading of the New Testament sounds in Calvinist flavor in his argument that "the gospel always refers to a pre-existing morality"[46] in the Old Testament. He argues that St. Paul even gives an apparent sanction to slavery in Roman society, but he is silent about Paul's universal meaning of the gospel in inclusion without discrimination.

In Hegel's account of the theory of utility, a human being finds a useful means in reason in order to restrain the self-transcendence or preserve him/herself. The utilitarian form of the enlightenment merges all the manifold relationships of people into the single principle of usefulness without considering the dialectical movement and mediation. It consists in knowing only finitude; the knowledge about finitude is conceived of as the truth to be the highest knowledge attainable.[47]

In this sense Hegel characterizes the utilitarian relation to religion in the commercial sense through profitableness; "Godliness is profitable unto all things (1 Tim iv. 8)."[48]

---

[45] Mill, "On Liberty," Ibid., 961.
[46] Ibid., 960.
[47] Hegel, *Phenomenology of Mind*, 331.
[48] Ibid., 331.

Against Hegel's interpretation Gustafson maintains that similarities are found between utilitarian ethics and some forms of Christian ethics; the teaching and life of Jesus and the biblical notion of the kingdom of God on earth.[49]

Gustafson concurs with J. S. Mill who affirms: "If so, happiness is the sole end of human action, and the promotion of it the test by which to judge all human conduct; from whence it necessarily follows that it must be the criterion of morality…"[50]

There are good and realistic grounds for the deepest despair such as incurable pain and suffering of body and spirit, the bleakness of continuous poverty and unemployment, the loss of human dignity, no possibility of relief or hope. Gustafson consents to the death of such a person in the deepest despair, in which "neither moralists nor God ought to be their judge."[51]

Should the deepest despair be accepted as the pretext for justification to kill the poor, depressed, and disabled? Such despair cries must not be excused for death, but for hope and justice.

Indeed, utilitarianism has been accused of its consequentialism, because it is difficult to achieve consensus of consequences in various realms of public policy, pluralist societies, or in internal affairs. It represents the interest of those in the middle class.

According to Marx, the utility relation derives beneficence for oneself by doing harm to someone else, because such relation implies that of exploitation. The category of utilization is undertaken in the social intercourse with other people, such that it embodies the bourgeoisie principle of competition, which is the driving force for freer development of the individual. It characterizes "the consciousness of mutual exploitation as the

---

[49] Gustafson, *Ethics from a Theocentric Perspective* II: 115.
[50] Cited Ibid., 106.
[51] Ibid., 209.

universal mutual relation of all individuals"⁵² in which theory of utility is identified with exploitation.⁵³

Utilitarianism and Colonialism

J. S. Mill emphasizes the significance of the genius as the salt of the earth, which saves the members of the society from a mass politics of the government, collective mediocrity. Democratic government, except for the popular sovereign, could not rise above mediocrity. Mill's appeal to the genius—although he argues against hero-worship—tends toward elitist politics, because "many have let themselves be guided...by the counsels and influence of a more highly gifted and instructed One or Few... The honor and glory of the average man is that he is capable of following that initiative."⁵⁴

This perspective would be vulnerable to the tyranny of the exceptional individuals or political genius which is allowed for exercising despotism if it does not produce the worst effects but cultivate the individuality as well-developed human beings.⁵⁵ A sort of despotism is allowed in the name of individuality and social progress especially seen in his countenance of colonial rule.

Bentham had a close friendship with the Mill family, and he was in charge of John Stuart Mill for education. In 1823 Mill worked as a clerk for the East India Company, where his father, James Mill (1773–1836) was a high official. J. S. Mill is known at age 11 to proofread many volumes of his father's *History of British India*. The publication of these massive volumes in

---

52 Marx, "Utilitarianism," in *Karl Marx Selected Writings*, 186.
53 Ibid., 188.
54 Mill, "On Liberty," in *Classics of Moral and Political Theory*, 969.
55 Ibid., 967.

1818 enabled his father Mill to have an important post at the East India Company. He rose to the head of the office in 1830 and continued there until his death. His son, J. S. Mill was also later employed by the East India Company and rose to be Chief Examiner in his last year. He also remained working as a member for Westminster in Parliament until 1868.

On Liberty (1859), J. S. Mill deals with social liberty, which means "protection against the tyranny of political rulers."[56] He comprehends the French Revolution to be "a sudden and convulsive outbreak against monarchical and aristocratic despotism." However, he doubts that "self-government" would express "the power of the people over themselves" in the genuine sense. In the form of self-government, abuse of power occurs through the tyranny of the majority.[57]

Thus, Mill gives a restriction to the legitimate interference of collective opinion with individual independence while allowing for such interference with the liberty of the members of society only through self-protection, in other words, to prevent harm to others.[58]

However, he argues that the progressive principle is based on liberty and improvement, and it is antagonistic to the dominion of the custom. "The greater part of the world, properly speaking, no history, because the despotism of Custom is complete. This is the case over the whole East. Custom is there, in all things, the final appeal; justice and right mean conformity to custom."[59]

For social improvement Mill challenges a society that reinforces its members to conform to custom and convention. As J. S. Mill continues, "we are progressive as well as changeable:

---

[56] Ibid., 936.
[57] Ibid., 938.
[58] Ibid., 940.
[59] Ibid., 971.

we continually make new inventions in mechanical things, and keep them until they are again superseded by better; we are eager for improvement in politics, in education, even in morals...we are the most progressive people who ever lived.... Europe is, in my judgment, wholly indebted to this plurality of paths for its progressive and many-sided development."[60]

Imbued with a Eurocentric view, Mill defended the idea of colonial dominion in which non-liberal practices are justified toward non-Western societies; the despotism of custom stands as a hindrance to human progress. He defends colonial intervention, in which despotism is defined as "a legitimate mode of government in dealing with barbarians, provided the end be their improvement and the means justified by actually effecting that end."[61]

If the means are justified in the degree of attaining the purpose, this utilitarian political principle may affirm the purpose rationality in which the means becomes instrumental in effecting the purpose. In fact, the purpose justifies the means as its instrument. Thus utilitarian reason or rationality would be easily exposed to its distortion by the expediency of the purpose (obviously seen in the utilitarian justification of colonial rule).

The principle of utility turns into buttressing a logic of colonialism. A principle of nonintervention applies to only relations among civilized nations rather than relations of them with uncivilized or barbarous people. The latter violates the law of nations and the sacred duties, thus barbarians have no rights as a nation. The race in the backward states of society is regarded to be in its nonage.[62]

---

[60] Ibid., 971-2.
[61] Ibid., 941.
[62] Ibid.

British rule in India was not in violation since its civilized tutelage aimed at reforming India for the improvement. Rule by a good despot is required as "the ideal rule of a free people over a barbarous or semi-barbarous one."[63]

A Eurocentric discourse of civilizing mission becomes a foundation of justifying biopolitical sovereignty of the metropolis to regulate and kill the population of the periphery. Colonial racism is clothed in the biopolitical mode, which is based on the political discourse of freedom, sovereignty, and power; it justifies colonizing genocide.

J. S. Mill does not share with Bentham's dictum of equality; "everybody to count for one, nobody for more than one."[64] Mill's utilitarian principle of progress was seen in many respects to be influential upon social Darwinism while anticipating post-war social scientific approach to development and modernization after the World War II.[65]

In a like manner, Spencer regards Bentham's utilitarian scheme as his first principle, but disproves this principle "to be a sufficient guide to right."[66] However, Spencer remains in the confines of utilitarianism, comprehending "happiness as the ultimate end of morality." J. S. Mill concurs with Spencer in that "in ethics, as in all other branches of scientific study, the consilience of the results of both these processes, each corroborating and verifying the other, is requisite to give to any general proposition the kind and degree of evidence which constitutes scientific proof."[67]

Herbert Spencer (1820-1903) coined the term "survival of the fittest." He was influenced by Darwin's *Origin of the Species*

---

[63] Mill, *Considerations on Representative Government*, 79.
[64] Mill, "Utilitarianism," in *Classics of Moral and Political Theory*, 1026.
[65] McCarthy, *Race, Empire, and the Idea of Human Development*, 176.
[66] Ibid., Footnote 4.
[67] "Utilitarianism," in *Classics of Moral and Political Theory*, 1027.

(1859), and justified the laissez-faire capitalism of J. S. Mill. He incorporated Darwin's account of natural selection and laissez-faire liberalism into the framework of social Darwinism.[68] If human history is the story of the survival of the fittest at the expense of the others, governmental intervention is not required to protect the weak and help the needy. "The whole effort of nature is to get rid of such, to clear the world of them and to make room for better...It is best that they should die."[69]

Worldly success and progress remain crucial in assessing moral superiority. Survival of the fittest together with competition becomes the universal moral principle underlying belief in progress. The survival of the fittest provides nature with blood "red in tooth and claw" (Alfred Lord Tennyson's poem of 1850) and struggle for existence underlying rampant capitalism and excessive individualism remains central in competition and progress, in which the European race is at the apex of development in comparison with the inferior race. God's intention can be seen in humanity's evolution culturally over time in development from ignorant savage stages to the intelligent and morally civilized European Christian culture. The civilizing mission becomes a white man's burden and its manifest destiny. It is unfortunate to see that J. S. Mill's principle of liberty turns into justifying colonization of primitive societies and elitist imperialism by Europeans reinforcing the theory of social Darwinism.

Basically, biological theory in an evolutionary context in the nineteenth century is linked to the laissez-faire capitalism and political discourse of nationalism and power prestige to dominate and kill population and civilization in the periphery.

---

[68] In the fifth edition of *Origin* (1869) Darwin adopted the phrase "survival of the fittest."

[69] Spencer, *Social Statics*, 414-15.

The utilitarian receives strong critique in the circle of deontologists who emphasize duty and political prudence. The utilitarian way of thinking is based on the moral of cost-benefit analysis, integrating it with the moral calculus; it tends to translate all values into monetary terms, which is morally seen to be obtuse. There is no adequate weight on human dignity and individual rights in Bentham's principle of greatest happiness.[70]

John Rawls critiques Bentham's classical utilitarian theory because it does not take in earnest the distinction between persons, in which different people have different needs and goals.[71] There are other good things besides pleasure. Justice is more than impartiality since it treats people fairly and in proportion to both their needs and merits. It is morally wrong to use a person only as a means for the beneficial consequence of the community.

2. Morality, Market, and Colonialism

In taking issue with utilitarian theory, it is important to examine Adam Smith (1723-1790) in critical reference to utilitarian theory, laissez-faire capitalism, and colonialism. He made substantial contributions to political economy, and moral conviction remains at the core of his thinking in order to improve society in a just way. Under the influence of the Scottish Enlightenment, Smith is grounded on the individual right with political and social liberty that creates a just society. The enlightened self-interest would bring society to an equilibrium level, which government action could never achieve.

In his *Theory of Moral Sentiments* (1759), human action is described to rest heavily on the human emotion of sympathy, compassion, and empathy. Sympathy was the center of Smith's

---

[70] Sandel, *Justice*, 45; 48.
[71] Rawls, *A Theory of Justice*, 187.

initial moral thinking. It was a desire to see our feelings, which are echoed in other people. As social creatures, we follow a moral path. His moral theory of sentiments is influenced by David Hume, who affirms that sympathy, the greatest virtue, is the chief source of morality. In terms of pity or compassion, we feel sympathetic for the misery of others, when we see it.[72]

However, in dealing with the economic field, Smith conceptualizes the enlightened self-interest in *Wealth of Nations* (1776). It is an innate interest, but not selfish greed. The former drives us towards doing works unconsciously for the greater good, for happiness, and for greater utility. A theory of sympathy is to be expressed through the invisible hand, which is involved in regulating human self-interest in the economic realm through the division of labor. He takes a step further in advancing Hume's theory of utility through enlightened self-interest in the economic field in terms of the division of labor, competition, and market. For Smith "*the division of labor arises from a propensity in human nature to exchange,*" because "*this propensity is found in man alone.*"[73]

His well-known phrase "invisible hand" is first expressed in his moral theory to describe the apparent benefits to society of people behaving in their own interest. The rich consume little more than the poor and in spite of the natural selfishness and avarice, they divide all their improvements with the poor. "They are led by an invisible hand to make nearly the same distribution of the necessities of life."[74]

People interact in markets, and such an economic system is regulated on their own accord, which does not require government intervention. Every individual intends only his/

---

[72] Smith, *Theory of Moral Sentiments*, I. i. 1. 1.
[73] Smith, *The Wealth of Nations*, 22.
[74] Smith, *Theory of Moral Sentiments*, 265.

her own gain and security, and in many cases, he/she is "led by an invisible hand to promote an end which has no part of his [her] intention."⁷⁵ Human nature is grounded in the activity of exchange in the market place, because the human propensity to truck, barter, and exchange is common to all men; it is not found in other race of animals.⁷⁶

However, a question is raised whether the moral sentiment of compassion would come to terms with self-interest and competition through division labor. Should the division of labor become the moral basis for harmony between compassion and self-interest? Isn't it countenancing competition and greed through it by producing injustice in the life of the laborer?

In Smith's argument, an invisible hand advances the interest of society through exchange and competition, because every individual continues to search for his/her own advantage by "find[ing] out the most advantageous employment for whatever capital he can command."⁷⁷Human propensity to exchange which is driven by self-interest leads to the division of labor, thus the market arises in an inevitable manner by use of money. Labor is the real measure and universal standard of exchangeable value in an exchange of commodities.⁷⁸

The market becomes the destiny of human life and civilization in which the invisible hand regulates competition and exchange through the division of labor. If the market is the destiny of human product to exchange, where is the role of the state in eliminating anarchy of competition and greed in the realm of the market?

---

75 Smith, *The Wealth of Nations*, 572.
76 Ibid., 22.
77 Ibid., 569.
78 Ibid., 31; 52.

Granted every individual does not violate the laws of justice, Smith holds, every individual as the sovereign has three duties: (1) the duty of protecting the society (by means of a military force) from violence and foreign invasion; (2) the duty of protecting every member of the society from the injustice and oppression from another member of the society (by means of administration of justice and by the introduction of property); the liberty of every individual is grounded in the impartial administration of justice; (3) the sovereign has the duty of erecting and maintaining certain public works and institutions for the defense of the society and the administration of justice.[79]

Within the framework of duty, Smith elaborates the role of enlightened self-interest and the role of specialization through the division of labor and competition in promoting the good of the society and efficiency of capital accumulation. His concern for the poor does not go unnoticed in his defense of commercial society. The market economy should be a place of liberty and regulation in protecting individual members and the common good through the sovereign, administration of justice, and social institution.

This perspective may provide a basis for Smith's critique of the colonial trade economy. He observes that the policy of Europe associated with mercantilism and colonialism produced much of the economic inequality in eighteenth-century Europe. As he writes, "the discovery of America, however, certainly made a most essential one. By opening a new and inexhaustible market to all the commodities of Europe, it gave occasion to a new division of labor and improvements of art…The savage injustice of the Europeans rendered an event, which ought to have been beneficial to all, ruinous and destructive to several of

---

[79] Ibid., 879; 901; 916.

those unfortunate countries."⁸⁰ Smith's critique of the colonial economy is far removed from the libertarian reasoning of the economic system of nonintervention.

Libertarian Argument and Universalist Reasoning

The libertarian principle affirms individual rights in a powerful and far-reaching significance and requires a minimal state in protecting people against force, theft, and fraud and enforcing contracts for guarding individual rights. It reinvigorates laissez-faire capitalism against state intervention. For example, if the rich are taxed by the government to help the poor, or social welfare for the common good, such policy is unjustified because of its coercion.

Libertarian idea finds prominent expression in Friedrich A. Hayek (1899-1992) and his pupil Milton Friedman (1912-2006), who reacted against state intervention for greater economic equality; it would result in the ruin of a free society. In a philosophical context, Robert Nozick in *Anarchy, State and Utopia* (1974), defends the libertarian principle against distributive justice.

As Nozick argues, "only a minimal state, limited to enforcing contracts and protecting people against force, theft, and fraud, is justified. Any more extensive state violates persons' rights not to be forced to do certain things and is unjustified."⁸¹

The libertarian principle argues against distributive justice because distribution from a free market is just regardless of whether it turns out to be equal or unequal. If those in initial holdings or transfer are beneficiaries of past injustice,⁸² for example, from the enslavement of African Americans or the

---

⁸⁰ Ibid., 563.
⁸¹ Nozick, *Anarchy, State, and Utopia*, IX.
⁸² Ibid., 149.

exploitation of Native Americans, the injustice can be remedied through taxation, reparation, or else simply to redress past wrongs.

What matters is to maintain the idea of self-ownership including one's labor and their entitlement to its fruits. There is a moral continuity in the libertarian argument; from taxation (from one's earnings) to forced labor (in the sense of taking one's labor) to slavery (in denial of one's own self).[83]

Freedom of choice in the libertarian context according to self-ownership remains central in free-market philosophy, which is indebted to the economic principle of unfettered markets and anti-government regulation. "No harm principle" against the individual is excessively elevated over against common good in society based on redistribution of wealth. The government must not violate individual freedom regardless of the employer's discrimination against the employee regarding race, religion, gender, sexual orientation, or else.

This libertarian principle is not concerned with Smith's protection of the poor, state intervention in public policy, and critique of the European colonial system. Against the libertarian interpretation of Smith, Reinhold Niebuhr argues that Smith acknowledges a religious guarantee of the preservation of the community, which is guided by human self-interest (with an invisible hand). The latter is to promote an end of human life and its well-being that is not intended. This invisible hand can be understood as a harmony of nature, in other words, the power of a pre-established social harmony in transmuting conflicts of self-interest into mutual service.

Smith retains the universalist assumption, requiring moral demands for us to contribute to the wider interest of community

---

[83] Sandel, *Justice*, 65.

through self-sacrifice.⁸⁴ It is not denied that Smith is interested in protecting the right of workmen in relation to masters. "Whenever the legislature attempts to regulate the differences between masters and their workmen, its counselors are always the masters. When this regulation, therefore, is in favor of the workmen, it is always just and equitable; but it is sometimes otherwise when in favor of the masters."⁸⁵

According to Smith, "the wise and virtuous man is at all times willing that his own private interests should be sacrificed to the public interest of his own particular order of society—that the interests of this order of society be sacrificed to the greater interest of the state, He should therefore be equally willing that all those inferior interests should be sacrificed to the greater interests of the universe, to the interests of that great society of all sensible and intelligent beings, of which God himself is the immediate administrator and director."⁸⁶

Given this, Niebuhr emphasizes a real universalism in Smith, but Smith's creed has been misused in the direction of turning the economic freedom of the individual into the ideology of capitalism in expanding its unfettered power over the world without recognizing moral demand or political regulation.⁸⁷

In Niebuhr's moral reasoning, the utilitarians of the eighteenth and nineteenth centuries sought to establish an identity between the individual and the general interest in terms of the principle of "the greatest good of the greatest number." This principle is framed with a hedonistic analysis of morals and remains a collective egoistic view of life, lacking a logical

---

84 Niebuhr, "The Children of Light and the Children of Darkness," in *The Essential Reinhold Niebuhr*, 173.
85 Smith, *The Wealth of Nations*, 195.
86 Cited in Niebuhr, "The Children of Light and the Children of Darkness," in *The Essential Reinhold Niebuhr*, 173.
87 Ibid., 174.

assumption of obligation for the minority. The utilitarian concept of the wise egotist would be allied with Smith's theory of the harmless egotist. Jeremy Bentham, a devotee to Smith, was more constantly attached to a laissez-faire principle unleashing unrestrained greed in industrial capitalism.[88]

Unlike Niebuhr's evaluation, however, Bentham turned around from his Smithian philosophy toward state interventionism, even unleashing a slippery slope to the utilitarian model of state despotism. Furthermore, Smith does not sufficiently manage to take into account the invisible hand in terms of the ability of the government in intervening to cut through the conflicts of interests, not to mention the protection of the poor against the privilege of the strong.

What matters in his idea of public works and policy is to facilitate commerce in general, while including the administration of justice for the benefit of the whole society. Of special significance is his insistence for the state to consider the education of the common people more than people of rank and fortune.[89]

Nonetheless, Smith's democratic vision for social harmony was plagued by the tragic realities of the class conflicts that he himself went unnoticed, because of his excessive, yet naïve belief in the invisible hand as secularized providence. His theory has been disseminated as the representative of the natural harmony of interests with decreased government intervention in the economy. In Smith's reliance on the goodness of the rich, they could trickle down to the poor. The libertarian argument is, in fact, about unfettered greed and unregulated capitalism.

---

[88] Ibid., 176.
[89] Smith, *Wealth of Nations*, Book V. Ch. 1. Part 3. 989.

3. Adam Smith, Colonialism, and Biopolitics

It is of significance to differentiate Smith from Mill and social Darwinism concerning colonialism. Actually, Smith had a strong critique of Spanish mercantilism of early capitalism in the colonial context of America. Smith comprehends the global logic of capital which is the logic accumulation in connection with foreign commerce.[90] In Smith's view of the colonialism of the New World, he takes into account the discovery of America and the passage to the East Indies by the Cape of Good Hope, which are regarded as the two greatest and most important events in history. None could foresee what benefits or misfortunes would ensue from these events.

The superiority of force on the part of the Europeans committed every kind of injustice in the colonies with impunity and all the commercial benefits were sunk and lost in dreadful misfortune. They engaged in "the folly of hunting after gold and the injustice of coveting the possession of a country."[91]

It established the chimera project. Smith already sees a "Christian character" of capital accumulation and colonialism in Columbus' discovery, in which there plays a significant role in converting indigenous people to Christianity by sanctifying the injustice of the colonial project. The Council of Castile was attracted by the gold and it justified a method of plundering defenseless natives in favor of finding treasures of gold in a thirst.[92]

In his strong critique of the colonial economy, we see that his moral philosophy remains an undercurrent in guiding his economic and political views. Mercantilism was a system of state-regulated exploitation through trade in the age of colonialism and became the dominant school of thought from the sixteenth

---

[90] Ibid., 474.
[91] Ibid., 747; 794.
[92] Ibid., 711-12.

to the eighteenth century. It established notorious trade patterns such as the triangular trade in the North Atlantic in which raw materials from colonies were imported to the metropolis and then processed and redistributed to other colonies; the slave ship from a European port with a cargo of manufactured goods to Africa, then the slave ship sold its cargo for slaves; ships sailed from Africa to the New World in which slaves traded on the plantation in exchange for a cargo of raw materials; finally, it returned to Europe, its homeport to complete the triangle.[93]

The trading-capitalist phase of mercantilism in the seventeenth and eighteenth century was based on monopolistic trading companies supported by powerful national states such as Holland, England, and France. Settler colonialism, capitalist slavery, and economic nationalism remained ingredients in furthering mercantilism. In England, mercantilism reached its peak during the Long Parliament (1640-1660).

The Dutch India Company (1602) had arisen in the defeat of the old Genoese and came in competition with the new British high finance. It occupied a leading role in the European world economy from around 1610-20 to around 1730-40. Holland brought the colonial system and enjoyed the heyday of commercial greatness in 1648. The East India Company charted under Elizabeth I (1600) began its rule in India through military victory at Plassey in 1757 and lasted until 1858.

This colonial economic system paves the way to the industrial revolution (1760-1830) in which major technical changes, along with transport systems, were brought to increase the productivity of labor in agriculture, manufacturing, and mining; in fact, the industrial revolution along with its capitalist accumulation cannot be adequately comprehended without considering the historical phase of primitive accumulation as well as the British

---

[93] Franck, *Dependent Accumulation and Underdevelopment*, 14-17.

colonial rule (1858-1948). After the fourth Anglo-Dutch War (1781-84), Amsterdam was replaced by London "as the financial entrepot of the European world economy."[94]

The principle was to regulate colonial trade and to exploit a dependent colonial system through the carrying off of the surplus produce of the colonies and labor. Its slogan is: "Buying cheap and selling dear."[95]

The constitutional-institutional model of political sovereignty finds its biopolitical power to kill for economic profit in the mercantilist colonial setting through military and natural scientific advances. Colonialism, its political nationalism, and racism justify the death-function in the political economy of biopower in terms of docile bodies, discipline, surveillance, regulation, and control, as transposed into the regime of savage, bare life of the dominated. The mercantilist model of state sovereignty and biopolitics imply the first phase of necropolitics in a historical context. "Indeed, the slave condition results from a triple loss: loss of a "home," loss of rights over his or her body, and loss of political status."[96]

If we see the slavery system as one of the first instances of biopolitical experimentation, it must be sought in economic motivation for capital accumulation embodied in the very structure of the plantation system and its aftermath; a state of exception is fabricated to uphold economic gain and profit.

The colony, considered from the standpoint of the European judiciary system, represents the site or zone where sovereignty consists fundamentally in the exercise of a power outside the law; necropolitical power occurs in colonial occupation embedded with the European judiciary system of sovereignty; it is defined

---

[94] Arrighi, *The Long Twentieth Century*, 143.
[95] Dobb, *Studies in the Development of Capitalism*, 209.
[96] Mbembe, "Necropolitics," in *Biopolitics*, 169.

as the power to decide on the violence of the state of exception in the name of civilizing missions.[97]

This political economy of the sovereignty of metropolis has continued to back up the industrial revolution, exercising its hegemony in the world economy and colonialism in India and China. It has developed in the form of imperialism and its war and ended up producing Nazism and Stalinism while ushering to a new form of local wars, apartheid, and Palestine through the biopolitical strategy in late modern capitalism.

Smith defines monopoly as "the sole engine of the mercantile system."[98] He was not ignorant of triangular trade, in which British merchants were able to establish an advantageous carrying trade between the plantations and foreign countries. In the development of triangular trade and shipping and shipbuilding, the slave and sugar trade turned Bristol into the second city of England in the eighteenth century.

Since 1731 "Great Britain and her colonies still continue to almost the sole market for all the sugar produced in the British plantations."[99] Rum was a very important article in the trade and carried on by the Americans to the coast of Africa from which African slaves were brought back in return.[100]

The capital was accumulated by Liverpool from the slave trade which fertilized the energies of Manchester. Manchester goods for Africa were taken to the coast in Liverpool slave trades. Great Britain would become the center of emporium.[101] The surplus produce of the colonies was the original source of all increases of enjoyment and industry in Europe, and the monopoly was

---

[97] Ibid., 172.
[98] Smith, *The Wealth of Nations*, 800.
[99] Ibid., 733.
[100] Ibid., 734.
[101] Ibid., 735.

the principal badge of the dependence of the colonies upon the mother country.[102]

It is not surprising that Marx concurs with Smith's critique of colonialism and argues: "at the Peace of Utrecht, England extorted from the Spaniards, by the Asiento Treaty, the privilege of being allowed to ply the slave trade, not only between Africa and the English West Indies, which it had done until then but also between Africa and Spanish America. England thereby acquired the right to supply Spanish America until 1743 with 4,800 Negroes a year.... Liverpool grew fat on the basis of the slave trade. This was its method of primitive accumulation."[103]

In Smith's critique of mercantilist monopoly and colonialism, surplus produced from colonies forms a negative, irrational side of mercantile capitalism in precipitating underdevelopment in terms of external factors between metropolis and the periphery. "*The policy of Europe has done nothing for the prosperity of the colonies.*"[104]

Smith's moral critique can be expressed in his claim that Great Britain should voluntarily abandon all authority and dominion over the colonies, leaving them to elect their own magistrates, and enact their own laws.[105] All the commercial benefits have been sunk and lost to the natives in the dreadful misfortunes, while the superiority of force commit injustice with impunity on the part of the Europeans.[106]

Accordingly, Marx incorporates Smith's notion of the previous accumulation into his theory of the primitive accumulation in which this accumulation forms the point of departure for the capitalist mode of production because it refers to the pre-history

---

[102] Ibid., 752.
[103] Marx, *Capital* I: 924.
[104] Smith, *The Wealth of Nations*, 747.
[105] Ibid., 782.
[106] Ibid., 794.

of capital in which the mode of production corresponds to capital.[107]

Marx comprehends the colonial system as the genesis of industrial capitalism in terms of "the Christian character of primitive accumulation," in which Spain, Holland, and England were denounced for their slave trade, massacre, and bribery. This is what Marx characterizes about the Christian colonial system in his dealing with the chief moments of primitive accumulation: "the discovery of gold and silver in America, the extirpation, enslavement and entombment in mines of the indigenous population of the continent, the beginnings of the conquest and plunder of India, and the conversion of Africa into a preserve for the commercial hunting of black skins..."[108]

Marx's discourse of the Christian character of capital accumulation implies that the juridical-institutional model of the state intersects with and includes the biopolitical model of power, which is philosophically, biologically, scientifically, and religiously backed up. The state puts biological life at the center of its calculations, surveillance, discipline, and control while bringing to light the secret alliance or bloc of uniting political power of colonizing genocide with the bare lives of the people.

This refers to the extreme form of biopolitical governance of colonizing genocide, which features *homo sacer* as deprived of all rights, as someone to be killed; the colonizer is regarded as the murderer, such that necropolitics engenders a reality of innocent victim buried underside of modern history. "The inclusion of bare life in the political realm constitutes the original-if concealed-nucleus of sovereign power."[109]

---

[107] Marx, *Capital* I: 873-5.
[108] Ibid., 915.
[109] Agamben, "Introduction to Homo Sacer," in *Biopolitics*, 138.

Division of Labor and Its Problem

However, Smith's idea of division of labor becomes questionable, forming a target of critique. On the positive side, a division of labor would affect a great increase in production through the great increase in the quantity of work. Human skill and dexterity ensue in every working individual in saving time. Finally, labor was so much facilitated and abridged by the invention of all the machines.[110]

Furthermore, Foucault draws attention to biopolitical strategies in articulating the connection between the body and capitalism. In the system of capitalism, the controlled bodies are inserted into the machinery of production, and the phenomena of the population are adjusted to economic processes. As Foucault writes, "the adjustment of the accumulation of men to that of capital, the joining of the growth of human groups to the expansion of productive forces and the differential allocation of profit, were made possible in part by the exercise of bio-power in its many forms and modes of application."[111]

In fact, for Smith the division of labor appears to be greater, because it brings up and effects "the greatest improvement in the productive powers of labor, dexterity, and judgment."[112] He is concerned with the relation between the division of labor and application of proper machinery, which facilitates an abridged labor.[113]

In the praise of the division of labor, Smith undermines the negative side accompanied by the division of labor in which one's dexterity in performing simple operations can be acquired only at the expense of one's intellectual and social virtues.

---

[110] Smith, *The Wealth of Nations*, 14.
[111] Foucault, *The History of Sexuality* I: 141.
[112] Smith, *The Wealth of Nations*, Bk. 1. Ch. 1.
[113] Ibid., 16.

However, in the "satanic mills" of the new industrial age, human individuals are stultified and disfigured, and their capacities are atrophied in the industrial system. "Under the slack and scrap heaps vomited forth from the satanic mills," "a veritable abyss of human degradation" occurred in the social condition and economic sphere in the period of the industrial revolution (1760-1830).[114] The workers are cogs in a vast productive apparatus and line of production. This reality of social misery and its pathology flew in the face of Smith's universalist tone.

In Marx's critique of the division of labor, however, he does not sidestep Smith's attention even to the harmful effects of the division of labor in the *Wealth of Nations* Book V. Chapter I. For Smith "[t]he man whose whole life is spent in performing a few simple operations...has no occasion to exert his understanding... He generally becomes as stupid and ignorant as it is possible for a human creature to become.... It corrupts even the activity of his body and renders him incapable of exerting his strength with vigor and perseverance in any other employments than that to which he has been bred. His dexterity at his own particular trade seems in his manner to be acquired at the expense of his intellectual, social, and marital virtues. But in every improved and civilized society, this is the state into which the laboring poor, that is, the great body of the people, must necessarily fall."[115]

According to Marx, it is by technology and machinery that the industrial revolution of the eighteenth century began through a universal technical application because the machine replacing the worker is the point of departure for the industrial revolution in the instruments of labor.[116]

---

[114] Polanyi, *The Great Transformation*, 39.
[115] Cited in Marx, *Capital* I: 483.
[116] Ibid., 497.

In fact, Smith's wealth of nations is undertaken at the expense of the worker. It increases the socially productive power of workers for the benefit of the capitalist by crippling the individual worker, creating the domination of capital over labor, and accelerating the accumulation of the capital.[117]

The moral degradation occurs in the capitalist system in its exploitation of the labor of women and children under 13 years, who were sold in Great Britain by their parents, in places where "freedom of labor" still prevails despite legislation.[118]

In the discussion of the social division of labor, I am concerned with the moral significance of public theology, which steers between Charybdis of total alienation in the Marxist sense and Scylla of laissez-faire economics. It cannot be denied that social division of labor becomes a driving force in the process of rationalization, specialization, and differentiation in society. But its pathology must not be sidestepped in social stratification colonizing civil society in the life-world. Smith's reliance on the division of labor must be critically renewed in enhancing its moral dimension through structural transformation toward the common good and distributive justice.

---

[117] Ibid., 486.
[118] Ibid.

Chapter 3
Social Contract

This chapter investigates the philosophy of the social contract and civil society in dealing with Thomas Hobbes and John Locke. The first part is a study of Hobbes' political theory, and his *Leviathan* finds its significance in Carl Schmitt's political theology and total state in National Socialism. Foucault's theory of biopolitical sovereignty comes into critical focus. Revolting against this totalitarian stance, a new political theology has emerged in the aftermath of Auschwitz. A theological appraisal can be undertaken within the context of the Calvinist theory of resistance and Confessing Church concerning Hobbes's political theory and Carl Schmitt's political theology.

In the second part, I examine John Locke's contribution to liberal democracy, individual rights, and property. In a controversial debate on Locke, slavery and colonialism are taken into account, while critically renewing some limitations of his political theory and social contract.

Finally, I take on the significance of social contract and teleological reasoning in regard to John Rawls' theory of justice. The latter is critically involved in Aristotle's notion of justice while renewing the setbacks of Locke and advancing the difference principle in a social-democratic direction.

1. Hobbes and Political Theory

Thomas Hobbes (1588-1679) begins his social contract theory by taking issue with Aristotle, as seen in chapter 46 of *Leviathan*. What is central in Aristotle's moral philosophy is his articulation of human action for telos, a goal-directed action for human flourishing in the cultivation of virtue, or prudence. Aristotle seeks to attain "finer and more godlike...for a nation or "for city-states."[1] Political science exists only by convention in accordance with a rational principle, because it "aims at and what is the highest of all goods achievable by action."[2]

On the contrary, Hobbes' view of the human being is framed in a materialist flavor, comprehending a human being as a machine, who is not concerned with goal direction and cultivation of virtue for human flourishing in ethical relation with the other. Hobbes is concerned with art which creates an artificial man called the commonwealth, the great *Leviathan* imbued with greater stature and strength than the natural.[3]

What is crucial in Hobbes is his concept of power in embracing both natural (e. g. strength, prudence, arts, eloquence, liberality, nobility) and instrumental (or original; as means and instruments to acquire more than natural power); "reputation of prudence in the conduct of peace or war, is power."[4]

A human being is not virtue-directed, but power-directed, which would cause a war against the other. It is the passions that incline human beings to peace, and this perspective implies that fear of death becomes necessary to living; guided by reason, human beings are drawn to an agreement for articles of peace, which are

---

[1] "*Nicomachean Ethics*," in *A New Aristotle Reader*, 364.
[2] Ibid., 365.
[3] "The Introduction of Leviathan," in *Classics of Moral and Political Theory*, 552.
[4] "Leviathan," Chapter 10. Ibid., 579.

called the laws of nature.⁵ To avoid the evil of war, Hobbes sets out to consolidate the great of human powers united by people's consent into one person, "the power of a commonwealth."⁶

Everyone in War against Everyone

Hobbes was born in England when the Protestant Reformation was in full swing. Based on a picture of individual egotism as basically selfish, aggressive, and quarrelsome, he argues that human life in a state of nature would be "solitary, poor, nasty, brutish, and short."⁷ Assuming that "nature hath made men so equal,"⁸ there are three principal causes of quarrel in human nature; competition for gain, diffidence for safety, and glory for reputation. Human beings are in the condition of war, "as is of every man, against man."⁹

Morality can be established and developed in a social solution of practical problems arising from self-interest and competition, to the degree that we want to live in a peaceful and cooperative way through social contract. As a moralist, Hobbes writes that a law of nature is a precept or general rule of reason, which seeks to avoid destruction of life and secure peace (the first law); the second law, which is the sum of the right of nature as liberty, is to defend ourselves by all means. Endeavoring peace is derived from self-defense: "*whatsoever you require that others should to you, that do ye to them.*"¹⁰ This refers to the law of the Gospel, in which the fountain and origin of justice consists.

---

5   "Leviathan," Ch. 13. Ibid., 593.
6   "Leviathan," Ch. 10, Ibid., 577.
7   "Leviathan," Ch. 13. Ibid., 592.
8   Ibid., 591.
9   Ibid., 592.
10 Ibid., 594.

In the *Nichomachean Ethics* Aristotle differentiates the contemplative life (bio) of the philosopher (via contemplative) from the life of pleasure and the political life (via activa). In Greek, there is no single term that expresses the word life. There are two terms, one refers to *zoe* (expressed in the simple fact of living common to all living beings, for example, animals, men, or gods, the other denotes bios (expressed in the form or way of living proper to an individual or a group). In this categorization natural life as such is undermined for the sake of a qualified life of the cultivated person, engaged in a particular way of life of the polis.[11]

Only the realm of human affairs is explicitly denoted in Aristotle's concept of the *bios politikos* because it accentuates the action, praxis, which is required to establish and sustain human affairs in a political city-state. "Neither labor nor work was considered to possess sufficient dignity to constitute bios at all, an autonomous and authentically human way of life."[12]

Accordingly, it is necessary for Aristotle to act in accordance with the right reason as a common principle. The excellence of human beings is concerned with a choice that consists of a mean or intermediate as determined by reason. Aristotle defines the virtue of justice as a feature of a state and comprehends justice as the arrangement of political association. Human beings would be worst of all if they are separated from law and justice.[13]

Moral excellence is seen as a result of habit, and "legislators make the citizen good by forming habits in them."[14] What strikes in the active life of a statesman is to be cut off from all external influences for the contemplative life.

---

[11] Agamben, "Introduction to Homo Sacer," in *Biopolitics*, 134.
[12] Arendt, "Selections from the Human Condition," Ibid., 107.
[13] "Politics," in *A New Aristotle Reader*, 510.
[14] Ibid., 376.

On the contrary, Hobbes does not comprehend the law of nature in terms of divine commandment nor virtue (or purpose)-oriented, but it is based on a general rule of reason for convenient articles of peace through social contract. Nature does not precede the sovereign, but we transformed nature, even human nature, and created the sovereign as an artificial nature through art.

The true doctrine of the laws of nature is the true moral philosophy because moral philosophy is the science of what is good. The laws of nature (e. g. justice, modesty, equity, mercy), which are not disagreeable to reason and common life, are moral virtues. These are dictates of reason but improperly called the laws, because the laws are the conclusion of self-preservation and defense. But laws, properly called, command over people by right.[15]

If justice is to give to everyone his/her own, it should keep valid covenants. By mutual contract, human beings acquire the propriety that they abandon in recompense of the universal right. "The validity of covenants begins not but with the constitution of a civil power, sufficient to compel men to keep them: and then it is also that propriety begins."[16]

This perspective characterizes Hobbes' moral theory in terms of the sovereign through social contract. The core of Hobbes's moral philosophy can be seen in his attempt to elaborate on the characteristics of the law of nature to ensure peace through social contract.

"It is also a law of nature, *that all men that mediate peace, be allowed safe conduct*. For the law that commandeth peace, as the *end*, commandeth intercession, as the means; and to intercession, the means is self-conduct."[17]

---

[15] "Leviathan," Ch. 15, in *Classics of Moral and Political Theory*, 604.
[16] Ibid., 598.
[17] Ibid., 602.

To overcome the state of nature in amoral, solitary, and brutish life, he develops his theory of civil government and social contract, which is framed within the moral aspect. This perspective remains an undercurrent in his *Leviathan*, which is created as an immortal god by the art of human being, called a commonwealth, or state (*civitas* in Latin).

Natural Law, Sovereign, and Foucault's Critique

Hobbes' political philosophy was embedded with the political crisis which resulted from the English Civil War (1642), the reason of which was Charles' calling for a meeting of parliament for his war against the Scottish rebels (1640). Charles I's conflict with Parliament (with support of Presbyterian people and Puritans) led to civil war, the result of which was regicide.

Associated with the king, Hobbes in fear for his life fled to France, remaining there until 1651-52. His book *Leviathan*, which was published in London in 1651, appeared as his most influential and famous book, establishing the foundation for Western political philosophy and moral theory. We need a stable and cooperative society or state to prevent the state of nature through a social contract for ethical life.

In chapter 14 Hobbes expounds on the right of nature (*jus naturale*) in terms of liberty for the preservation of human life. Liberty is comprehended as the absence of external impediments. A law of nature (*lex naturalis*) is a precept or general rule (obligation) of reason, which forbids the human being to end a life. With the law of nature, everyone ought to endeavor peace and follow it. From this comes the second law of nature; self-defense, liberty against other people, as long as all people are in the condition of war of everyone against everyone. The third law of nature is justice by which to make covenants for peace. To break these is unjust, while their performance is just. "The mutual transferring of right is that which men call CONTRACT."[18]

Peace is a means to live because we are all endowed with natural rights or moral rights to life and the desire for self-preservation and protection as a moral entitlement. The moral rights in appreciation of life are seen as the source of human dignity and worth.

Nevertheless, Hobbes considers the value or worth of an individual from the standpoint of power rather than an end in the Kantian sense of categorical imperative. The value or dignity would be given and even measures according to the use of power; it is one's price, not absolute, "but a thing dependent on the need and judgment of another."[19]

Hobbes' understanding of power is not reduced to the economic sphere but displays many diverse realities. His moral philosophy is more grounded in seeking the means to peace in appreciation of value and dignity of life through the commonwealth than human dignity itself in a liberal, democratic sense. The commonwealth may provide protection from invaders, yet it doesn't appear to protect the individual from the power of the commonwealth. A person seems to be allowed to survive in the social contract, but he/she outside the contract doesn't appear to be entitled to much else.

In his understanding of human nature, everyone in the state of nature has the restless desire and a right for assurance and power until power ceases only in death. This inevitably leads to conflict, called a war of everyone against everyone (*bellum omnium contra omnes*).

In this condition, the only way for security is to establish a common power by conferring all the powers and strengths

---

[18] "Leviathan," Ch. 14. Ibid., 595.
[19] "Leviathan," Ch. 10. Ibid., 579.

upon one assembly of people. A commonwealth (*civitas* in Latin) implies that the multitude is united in one person in the generation of the Leviathan or the immortal god under whom we owe our peace, defense, and security.[20]

In dealing with the rights of the sovereign by institution, all the rights and faculties of human beings are derived and conferred to the sovereign power through people's consent; for example, property, punishment, the power to coin money, or the command of the militia, the right of making war and peace with other nations, etc. If market society does not degenerate into the struggle of all against all, it requires a single sovereign to force which is indivisible and unlimited. Law cannot be limited by appeal to the law of nature, the church, or the voice of conscience, but it must be obeyed concerning the command of the sovereign. The great authority is annexed to the sovereignty "in respect of the miseries, and horrible calamities, that accompany a civil war."[21]

Insofar as the absolute, unlimited power of the sovereign is to be instituted, there is a dimension of representative democracy through the covenant of people; assembly of people is given by the major part, in other words, it refers to the right to present the person of them all, or their representative through universal suffrage; everyone authorizes all the actions and judgments of the sovereign state for peace and protection of the individual life. Thus, sovereign power is conferred by the consent of the people who are assembled.[22]

Nascent European democracy began battling against the political absolutism of monarchy, but Hobbes' political philosophy of power retains an implication of natural life of human being (*zoe*; the bare, anonymous life) against Aristotle's

---

[20] "Leviathan," Ch. 17. Ibid., 608.
[21] "Leviathan," Ch. 18. Ibid., 612.
[22] "Leviathan," Ch. 18. Ibid., 608.

notion of the qualified life of the citizen (bio), by taking the former into the sovereignty. What is strengthened in Hobbes' modern democracy is to include the body of *homo sacer*, in other words, bare life through political inclusion of human life and body.

In dealing with political sovereignty and the human body, Michel Foucault investigates the process of the relation between politics and human bodies or population at the beginning of the modern age and defines the meaning of biopolitics, in which human natural life is incorporated into the mechanism and calculations of political power.

At the end of the first volume of *The History of Sexuality*, Foucault writes in brief: "For millennia, mankind remained what he was for Aristotle: a living animal with the additional capacity for a political existence; modern man is an animal whose politics calls his existence as a living being into question."[23]

In the passage from the ancient to the modern world, Foucault argues, the individual has been brought to objectify and constitute his/ her own self as a subject and, while he/ she binds him/ herself to the political power of external control.

A political animal turns into an animal seeking power in Hobbes's project of modern democracy to preserve natural life and its dignity. Biopolitical sovereignty is encroached and exercised in the field of human bodies and population as an entire social body

Nonetheless, Foucault gives up the juridical notion of sovereignty in order to undertake an analysis of power relations in the specific regime of its technology. The juridical model of sovereignty conceptualizes the individual in terms of a subject of natural rights or original powers while seeking to explain the ideal

---

[23] Foucault, *The History of Sexuality* 1: 143.

genesis of the state. What strikes in this model is to make the law into the fundamental manifestation of political power.[24]

On the contrary, Foucault's genealogical approach to the sovereignty through power relations cuts across limitations of the juridical constitution of sovereignty, and begins with the general model of war as a primary and fundamental state of things; his position considers all the phenomena of social domination, antagonism and struggle between individuals and groups, differentiation, and hierarchization as secondary.[25]

A society, once pervaded by warlike relations, Foucault holds, was slowly transformed into and replaced by a state, which is equipped with military apparatus and institutions backed up by a historical-political discourse of society and war. In this genealogical framework, war is made "the permanent basis of all the institutions of power."[26]

This perspective takes issue with the juridical-philosophical discourse of universal subject with the general right while rejecting the latter as an illusion and trap. Foucault problematizes Hobbes' notion of the war of all against all because he regards the latter as a game of representations rather than based on a real historical war. Sovereignty is established by a calculation to avoid war, rather than by an act of bellicose domination. It is non-war in Hobbes' political philosophy that grounds the state by giving it its forms.[27]

Foucault looks at the history of wars of religion as the womb of states, especially in the writings of Hotman related to France in the sixteenth-century Calvinist theory of resistance.

Against Foucault's assumption, however, Calvinist theory of resistance and democratic form of government cannot be

---

[24] Foucault, "Society Must be Defended," in *The Essential Foucault*, 294.
[25] Ibid.
[26] Ibid., 295.
[27] Ibid., 297.

adequately understood without considering the influence of religious ideas and their juridical-institutional-covenantal model. A real war model in the genealogical frame of force relations could not completely abandon the juridical-institutional model of sovereignty and natural rights of human beings.

But Foucault still seems to comply with the liberal democratic normative position of human rights and citizenship in confronting totalitarian governments. As he writes, "There exists an international citizenship that has its rights and its duties, and that obliges one to speak out against every abuse of power, whomever its author, whomever its victims. After all, we are all members of the community of the governed, and thereby obliged to show mutual solidarity."[28]

In fact, Foucault is not far removed from Hobbes's juridical-institutional model of sovereignty. Hobbes considers a possibility of disobedience against the sovereign if the latter commands the subject to kill, wound, or maim him/her; or not to resist those that assault him/her. The subject has the liberty to disobey for the right of nature (self-preservation and defense). It grounds an absolute right on the part of the governed against the injustice of people's suffering to stand up and speak out against those who are in power.[29]

Market Economy and Politics

There is an economic foundation for Hobbes' political theory in which the competitive market plays a major role. A theory is proposed in characterizing England at Hobbes' time in terms of

---

[28] Foucault, "Confronting Governments: Human Rights," in *The Essential Foucault*, 65.
[29] "Leviathan," Ch. 21. Ibid, 623.

market society in its bourgeoning stage, in which human labor becomes a commodity.[30]

In chapter 24 of *Leviathan*, Hobbes regarded human labor as a commodity that is exchangeable for benefit; it is recognized that colonial trade belongs to the commonwealth, selling the products from raw materials, which were brought in from other places. In the economic distribution, Hobbes continues, justice is defined by "*distributing* to every man his own."[31] This justice in assigning a portion to everyone is in the act of the sovereign consisting in the law. The observance of the equal distribution to each individual is called distributive justice (equity), which is enjoyed in common.[32]

Nonetheless, his sense of equity as honorable is problematically expressed in his appreciation of covetousness of great riches and ambition as honorable, a sign of power.[33] Furthermore, it is difficult to find a critical attitude toward colonial policy in the relation between metropolis and colonies. Hobbes remains silent about the cruel reality and injustice inflicted against the colonized as well as the British slave trade.[34] The latter took place in 1562 under the reign of Elizabeth 1 (1533-1603) and lasted until the abolition of the slave trade in 1807.

It is generally agreed upon that British mercantilism reached its heyday during the Long Parliament (1640-1660). The English East India Company had received its charter in 1600 and engaged in colonial expansion. Hobbes' idea of *Leviathan* would fit into the absolutist power of the state in mercantilist terms, in which the market economy was subordinated to the fusion of state and capital. The British East India Company (1600-1708) brought a

---

[30] Macpherson, *The Political Theory of Possessive Individualism*, 48.
[31] "Leviathan," Ch. 24. In *Classics of Moral and Political Theory*, 634.
[32] "Leviathan," Ch. 15. Ibid., 602.
[33] "Leviathan," Ch. 10. Ibid., 581.
[34] "Leviathan," Ch. 24. Ibid., 636.

return on investment through plunder and tribute from India. The English metal industries rapidly expanded its growth during the Genoese-led financial period of the late sixteenth and early seventeenth centuries.[35]

This is the picture of English society, which was similar to Hobbes' time. The international market system would become crucial in developing market society in England, yet without full-scale development of the bourgeois class. The enclosure movement, a revolution of the rich against the poor, began as early as the thirteenth century and had culminated in England by about 1780; as a result, it replaced the class of independent peasants with capitalist farmers who worked with wage labor. The Enclosure Acts began to take effect after 1760 and its wholesale years were between 1760 and 1820, driving the poor peasant off from the land, making them a landless working class, and providing their labor required in the new industries in the north of England. It contributed to the facilitation of the industrial revolution.[36]

Hobbes remains restrained in predicting such a bourgeois society fraught with crisis, exploitation, and colonialism in the world market. The self-perpetuating sovereign allows for the economic competition for wealth and power in a non-violent manner, and it may intervene or even abuse market relations for the sake of the interest of sovereign authority.

Hobbes, Calvinism, and Political Theology

Hobbes' *Leviathan* (1651; in Latin 1668) can be seen in the political tradition of Europe in comparison to the Calvinist theory of resistance. In the Massacre of St. Bartholomew of

---

[35] Arrighi, *The Long Twentieth Century*, 209-10.
[36] Beaud, *A History of Capitalism 1500-1980*, 64.

1572 under the conspiracy of Catherine de Medici, the leading Huguenots and their followers were massacred en masse, in particular, Admiral de Coligny was murdered. Since then, the polemical writings of the monarchomachists and their idea of the right to resistance began to lay out a modern constitutional government against the monarchy and its political absolutism.

Earlier on, John Calvin (1509-1564) in his letters to Huguenots justified political resistance in the framework of the established law of France, the law of the estates in contrast to the absolutism of the French monarchy.

Calvin himself draws attention to estates (called *ephori*) within a commonwealth for the constitutional defense of the people's freedom. He encourages the Huguenots to do their duty in intervening against a tyrannical ruler for the sake of the liberty of the people. Calvin sought so much to secure and order liberty in opposition to tyranny and anarchy, that civil government was established in 'a system compounded of aristocracy and democracy;'[37] he was so much convinced of the moral law as a testimony of natural law and conscience which was engraved and prescribed by God upon the human mind.[38]

Deliberate civil disobedience remains crucial in his thinking, which was not convinced of popular sovereignty and the use of violence. But he approved a constituted magistracy in the sense of *populares magistratus* to protect the liberties of people, the historical example of which would be found in the ephors of Sparta, the tribunes of Rome, and the demarchs of Athens; these were elected to office by the annual popular or general vote in accordance with liberty.[39] Furthermore, Calvin still left space for

---

[37] II. Ch. XX. 8. In Calvin, *Institutes of the Christian Religion* 2.
[38] II. Ch. XX. 16. Ibid.
[39] II. XX. 31. Ibid. footnote 54.

open resistance in emergency situations such as war, which took place in France intermittently from 1562 to 1598.

Escaping the massacre, Francois Hotman (1524-1590), Calvin's friend, defended the right of the estates to resist, and his *Franco-Gallia* (1573) has the inclination to stand for a democratic form of the state emphasizing the right of resistance and political authority for the people. This political model of political sovereignty is grounded in the Calvinist idea of covenant and law, which finds its powerful material interest in its historical course of time. This Calvinist position does not make war into the permanent basis of all the institutions of political power, but resistance and democratic government in light of the biblical idea of the covenant. Real wars and battles do not preside over the birth of states nor "laws are born in the middle of expeditions, conquests, and burning cities."[40]

On the contrary, the Calvinist idea of resistance and popular sovereignty incorporates the juridical notion of the individual into a subject of natural rights through the biblical idea of the image of God in the universal sense. The ideal genesis of the state is grounded in God's natural law and order, in which constitutional law is privileged as a manifestation of God's natural law and order. It is necessary to constitute the judicial institution of sovereignty in accordance with natural law, individual freedom, and democracy.

This religious-judicial notion of sovereignty and universal subject in the Calvinist framework can be in no way criticized as illusion and traps, which Foucault misjudges for his historical-political discourse of bellicose domination.[41] Rather, war is seen as inevitable self-defense, or just war coming as consequence from power struggles and resistance; such resistance is founded

---

[40] Foucault, "Society Must be Defended," in *The Essential Foucault*, 295.
[41] Ibid., 296.

on self-interest, but on the religious source it implies the site of the immanent critique regarding the political structure in the medieval French Catholic context.

Theodore Beza (1519-1605), Calvin's successor in Geneva, was involved in the first religious war of 1562-1563 in France and defended such a right against a tyrannical rule in terms of the rights of the people. In *The Right of Magistrate* Beza was indebted to Hotman, maintaining that people are not created for the rulers, but the latter for the people. Beza considers the resistance of the private citizen against the usurper. There is an emphasis on the legal right of the parliament to check the king through ephoral power in Hotman and Beza.

As further seen in the Scots Confession (1560), it was a significant part to protect the life of the innocent in resistance to tyranny and in support of the oppressed. The poor are protected against the greed of landlords, such that a notion of "Christian socialism" would be formulated.[42]

The famous *Vindiciae contra tyrannos* (*A Defense against Tyrants*) appeared from 1579 onwards, and gaining in prominence in the history of political theory; it was reprinted and spread (in English translation 1648 and 1689), and the authors of the joint work would be assumed to Hubert Languet and Philip du Plessis-Mornay (1549-1623), one of the significant leaders, who was active in resistance after the massacre. In this writing, a concept of a federalist, democratic state is deployed in which the theological idea of the covenant was employed to justify the right of resistance.

It is unfortunate that Hobbes would undermine these writings in their critique concerning tyranny and power. In fact, the theory of contract is grounded in the Old Testament in dealing with the double covenant in regard to God's law and the people of Israel;

---

[42] McNeil, *The History and Character of Calvinism*, 300.

the first covenant was undertaken with the people of Israel on Sinai through the Decalogue. The second covenant ensued with the king before God for the contract of rule. The king and the people are seen as "joint underwriters of a promise."[43] "Thus kings must always remember that they are indeed kings by God's grace but that they rule through the people and for the people."[44]

A notion of popular sovereignty occupies a central place within the framework of the federal theology (originated in Heinrich Bullinger), and a notion of covenantal contract in the Old Testament continues to live on in the New Testament rather than superseded. In American political history, a new colony was begun in 1628-30 at Massachusetts Bay. John Winthrop (1588-1649), the first governor and the chief figure among the Puritans, appealed to 'America: A Covenanted Nation' before the Massachusetts Bay Company in 1630.[45] In the American Declaration of Independence (1776), a political idea of the covenant is expressed: "*We hold these truths to be self-evident, that all men are created equal, that they are endowed by their Creator with certain unalienable rights, that among these are life, liberty, and the pursuit of happiness.*"[46]

This reformed tradition of political theology, resistance right, and popular sovereignty contradicts Hobbes' negative anthropology in the *Leviathan*. Given this political history, it is important to examine the significance of Hobbes' *Leviathan* which appeared in 1651, two years after the execution of Charles I. The event of the latter can be seen in the light of the Calvinist theory of the state and its resistance.

---

[43] *Constitutionalism and Resistance in the Sixteenth Century*, 143.
[44] Cited in Moltmann, *God for a Secular Society*, 28.
[45] Ibid., 30.
[46] https://www. britannica. com/topic/Declaration-of-Independence/Text-of-the-Declaration-of-Independence

However, Hobbes takes a different form toward the sovereign will and social contract within the framework of natural law, in which all humankind moves in a perpetual and restless desire of power after power. This striving for power ceased in death. But to avoid the miserable condition of the war people find it necessary to make covenants by transferring their freedom and power to a sovereign; the civil society or the state has come into existence, such that generates the great commonwealth by an institution (covenant), or Leviathan in the sense of the immortal God. The state sovereign possesses all power and authority in worldly and spiritual matters.

Although Hobbes grew up in a Presbyterian house, he does not merely consider a biblical notion of the divine covenant, instead, his reading of the Bible focuses on the sovereign power of God whether in monarchy, or in one assembly of people, or in popular and aristocratic commonwealths.[47]

His concern is with proposing a social contract among human beings to put an end to the perpetual war of everybody against everybody. If human beings are wolves by nature in their struggle against each other, it would be a logical consequence for the Leviathan to become a tyranny to stop anarchy, which is defined by the tyranny itself. The "good" Leviathan (Job, 41:24) is contrasted with the "wicked" Behemoth, the English parliament.

It was Carl Schmitt, a conservative jurist and member of the Nazi party that drew attention to the *Leviathan* by introducing the term "political theology" for political sovereignty. The modern theory of the state implies a secularized theological concept, to the degree that political theory of the state is analogously seen in the theological discussion of God. He identifies God of Calvinism with Leviathan, the immortal God of Hobbes.[48]

---

[47] "Leviathan," Ch. 20. In *Classics of Moral and Political Theory*, 620.
[48] Schmitt, *The Leviathan in the State Theory of Thomas Hobbes*, 32.

In *The Leviathan in the State Theory of Thomas Hobbes: Meaning and Failure of a Political Symbol* (1938), Schmitt is concerned with the mutual relation between protection and obedience in Hobbes' construction of the state, standing in favor of obedience at the expense of protection. "The state... guarantees me the security of my physical existence [and] in return it demands unconditional obedience.... All further discussions lead to a "pre-political" condition of insecurity, where ultimately one can no longer be certain of one's physical security..."[49]

Schmitt attacked the distinction between spiritual and political power as Judeo-Christian while arguing Hobbes' position as contrary to the Jewish Christian doctrine of the distinction between religion and politics. In Schmitt's account, "Hobbes regarded Jews as the originators of the revolutionary state-destroying distinction between religion and politics...The distinction between the secular and the spiritual power was, according to Hobbes, alien to the heathens because religion was to them a part of politics."[50]

According to Giorgio Agamben, Carl Schmitt defines that "Sovereign is he who decides on the state of exception,"[51] although it has the limited concept of the doctrine of law and the State on the sphere of human life. Political reflection of human life, bare life, and the social body remains crucial in the political community, as articulated in *Leviathan* or *The Social Contract*.

In *De homine*, Hobbes distinguishes the human natural body from the political body: "Man is not only a natural body but also a body of the city, that is, of the so-called political part." The body can be killed in reference to the natural equality of men and the necessity of the Commonwealth.

---

[49] Ibid., 45.
[50] Ibid., 10.
[51] Agamben, "Introduction to Homo Sacer," in *Biopolitics*, 42.

"If we look at adult men and consider the fragility of the unity of the human body (whose ruin marks the end of every strength, vigor, and force) and the ease with which the weakest man can kill the strongest man, there is no reason for someone to trust in his strength and think himself superior to others by nature. Those who can do the same things to each other are equals. And those who can do the supreme thing—that is, kill—are, by nature, equal among themselves." (*De cive*, p. 93)"[52]

Agamben reads the body of Leviathan as formed out of all the bodies of individuals in this direction. Its capacity to kill the body of the subject constitutes the new political body, which has advanced in the Western democratic development of sovereignty. In his diagnosis, parliamentary democracies in the twentieth century were able to turn into totalitarian states.

Nazism and fascism transformed the decision on bare life into the supreme political principle, which continues to remain with us. Modern democracy has produced decadence and gradual convergence occurred with totalitarian states in post-democratic, spectacular societies.[53]

Agamben attempts to articulate the politicization of life in terms of contiguity between democracy and totalitarianism. Here, Hobbes' Leviathan is made a bulwark for the totalitarian state imbued with biopolitical sovereignty, without further ado.

But Schmitt takes issue with Hobbes' reservation of the right to religious freedom in the private sphere. In the freedom of thought and faith in private life, Hobbes allows for the free rights of the individual in the liberal constitutional system; in fact, such reservation leads to Jewish undermining of the state through castration of the Leviathan.[54]

---

[52] Agamben, "The Politicization of Life," Ibid.,151.
[53] Ibid., 147.
[54] Moltmann, *God for a Secular Society*, 39.

Unlike Schmitt, however, it is of special importance to examine the religious dimensions in Hobbes' political theory. Hobbes develops his theory of the kingdom of God in terms of God's sovereign power underwriting the dictates of natural reasons, revelation, and faith. He articulates the natural dictates of right reason under God's universal reign, in which Hobbes conceptualizes the significance of common consent. The laws of nature under divine laws reinforce moral virtues such as equity, justice, mercy, and humility.[55]

Through the dictate of natural reason, we have rational worship of God in terms of "prayers, thanksgiving, offerings and sacrifice."[56] The laws of the divine worship consist in obedience to divine law (or the laws of nature), in which natural reason dictates this divine law to private persons, because "obedience is more acceptable to God than sacrifice."[57]

Based on the natural kingdom of God and divine natural laws, Hobbes considers a commonwealth in the act of common consent or contract to be public worship. Leviathan would become good to the degree that it serves God's justice and moral laws.

Theological Critique of Totalitarian State

In the resistance of the Confessing Church Karl Barth challenged German Christians supporting National Socialism and played a major role in issuing The Barmen Declaration (1934); here it is written: "We repudiate the false teaching that the church can and may, apart from the ministry, set up special leaders (*Führer*) equipped with powers to rule." (Thesis 4)

---

[55] Leviathan, Ch. 31. In *Classics of Moral and Political Theory*, 673.
[56] Ibid., 675.
[57] Ibid.

"The state is defined as having "the responsibility to provide for justice and peace in the yet unredeemed world." "We repudiate the false teaching that the state can and should expand beyond its special responsibility to become the single and total order of human life, and also thereby fulfill the commission of the church." (Thesis 5)[58]

Helmut Gollwitzer, a member of the Confessing Church, championed against the persecution and extermination of the Jews together with Dietrich Bonhoeffer. Gollwitzer draws attention to "justice and peace" in the fifth thesis of the Barmen Declaration and advocates it for a better, socialist order; the state has to care for law and order because we are the state in the sense of the sovereignty of the people. If "the constitution secures the sovereignty of the people" and "implies the free codetermination and cooperation of all in the processes of decisions in society, this constitution is the state, in which and through which we all provide for 'law and peace.'"[59]

A new political theology after Auschwitz (Moltmann and J. B. Metz) has emerged and championed against Hobbes and Schmitt. It sought to make public use of the Christian faith and practice it in secular society. It transcends the problems of Schmitt's political theology which confines religion to the realm of political sovereignty. However, it is difficult to confine Hobbes' theological, public thinking only to Schmitt's version of political theology and the total state.

According to Schmitt, what matters in Hobbes is to restore the unity of politics and religion in light of the totalitarian state. In *The Concept of the Political*, Schmitt writes: "The state as the decisive political entity possesses an enormous power: the possibility of waging war and thereby publicly disposing of the

---

[58] *Creeds of the Churches*, 521.
[59] Gollwitzer, *An Introduction to Protestant Theology*, 203.

lives of men. The *jus belli* contains such a disposition. It suggests a double possibility: the right to demand from its own members the readiness to die and unhesitatingly to kill enemies..."[60]

Critical Reflection

It is widely taken that Hobbes represents secular absolutism or monarchical absolutism, but his position is still framed within people's consent or social contract buttressing the modern state; it runs counter to the pre-modern declaration: "I am the state" (*L'état, c'est moi.* Louis XIV, 1638-1715).

The modern system of European states began to emerge through the Treaty of Westphalia (1648), signed three years prior to the publication of *Leviathan*. Ending the thirty years' war (1568–1648), the Treaty affirms the principle in the Peace of Augsburg (1555): *Cuius regio, eius religio* (whose realm, his religion; the religion of the ruler is to dictate the religion of the ruled). The individual sovereign state is elevated to become the highest level of authority against the universalist claims of the Holy Roman Empire. Although the state is characterized as "god" in Hobbes' theory, this characterization does not share in Schmitt's clumsy identification of it with the time of Louis XIV.[61]

Rather, Hobbes displays a side of modern liberalism in the sense of representative democracy that the sovereign is the source of the law for the safety of the people; it is based on justice and equality, requiring the concord and obedience on the part of the people. Without the latter, people cannot flourish.

For Hobbes, all individuals equally are free by nature, and sovereignty by an institution is seen by a covenant of everybody. Every subject has the liberty to disobey when the sovereign

---

[60] Schmitt, *The Concept of the Political*, 46.
[61] Schmitt, *The Leviathan in the State Theory of Thomas Hobbes*, 32.

violates the individual rights by "frustrate[ing] the end for which the sovereignty was ordained."[62]

Such disobedience can only happen en masse under the power of a sovereign. The only real way would be for people to exercise their liberty against the sovereign through a revolution in a prophetic or secular sense.

For the safety of the people, Hobbes continues that "justice [must] be equally administered to all degrees of people." "And whereas many men…become unable to maintain themselves by their labor; they ought not be left to the charity of private persons, but be provided for …by the laws of the commonwealth."[63]

Morality comes to terms with the state whose purpose is to secure human beings in economic life as well as by making social morals feasible. The state enforces the rules and laws by which to ensure moral life. For Hobbes, the primary purpose of government is to protect humans in the exercise of their equal rights. Thus, people enter into a social contract in order to preserve their own rights. The passions inclining people to peace are because of fear of death, such that reason suggests convenient articles of peace for agreement. As he writes, "these are the laws of nature, dictating peace, for a means of the conservation of men in multitudes; and which only concerns the doctrine of civil society."[64]

The right of nature consists of the liberty to preserve one's life, while laws of nature consist of general rules or obligations of reason in which everyone ought to seek peace and then defend themselves. Justice or injustice depends on whether the covenants are to be performed or not. Right is given priority over duty, and the individual finds its liberty and dignity within the sphere of the

---

[62] "Leviathan," Ch. 21. Ibid., 624.
[63] "Leviathan," Ch. 30. Ibid., 668.
[64] "Leviathan," Ch. 5. Ibid., 603.

law. Moral autonomy implies the individual's right to judge the requirements of natural law using his or her right reason because of the dictates of reason (the requirements of natural law).

According to Hobbes, the liberty for the ancient Greeks and Romans is not the property of the individual, but the liberty of the commonwealth; "every commonwealth had an absolute liberty," and "their representative had the liberty to resist or invade other people."[65] They are taught to hate the monarchy on the basis of collective or common good rather than any particular individual. But the liberty for the modern lies in the predetermination of the sovereign in the law regulating their activities and also in their act of submission, obligation, and duty. For the safety of the people's justice is required to be "equally administered to all degrees of people."[66]

Thus, Hobbes leaves space for rebellion. If people are judges of what is lawful and unlawful not by the law itself, but by their own conscience and private judgments, it is lawful to rebel when they accuse the dominant as tyrants.[67]

This perspective runs counter to Schmitt's political theology for a total sovereign with excessive emphasis on the immortal "god," as seen in National Socialism or in socialist Leviathan. In Schmitt's account, furthermore, we read: "Western liberal democrats agree with Bolshevist Marxists that the state is an apparatus that the most varied political constellations can use as a technically neutral instrument."[68]

Despite its leaning toward absolutist government, Hobbesian democracy may entail characteristics of liberalism in people's consent to the sovereign power of the State through universal

---

[65] "Leviathan," Ch. 21. Ibid., 622-3.
[66] "Leviathan," Ch. 30. Ibid., 667.
[67] "Leviathan," Ch. 30. Ibid., 664.
[68] Schmitt, *The Leviathan in the State Theory of Thomas Hobbes*, 42.

suffrage, as the state intervenes accordingly by exercising its power to the law.

However, Hobbes has too much faith in the "good" Leviathan and little faith in the people. The Hobbesian variant focuses on the constitution of the supranational sovereign entity on the contractual agreement but concentrated on the political sovereign ruling over life and death, the Hobbesian God on earth. This constitutes the right of nation-states and secures the international system, which would overcome the anarchy that nation-states would produce.[69]

Alternatively, if the individual supposedly has the liberty to disobey the sovereign, which infringes on their rights, the individual belongs to God. The sovereign is also subject to God. If the individual is imbued with this God-knowledge of individual rights and justice, then how can the individual have a default disposition of kill or be killed and therefore need the sovereign? This perspective finds its significance in Locke's concept of civil society and constitutional democracy as to contest the figure of power.

2. Divine Workmanship and Natural Law

John Locke (1632-1704) expanded and defended the concept of natural rights such as rights to life, liberty, and property against the government when the latter misuses its power in violating our natural rights. John Locke, a classic Republican, contributed a groundwork to the enlightenment and liberalism, and he developed political liberty, representative government in rebellion against tyranny, religious tolerance, and a model of separation between church and state.

---

[69] Hardt and Negri, *Empire*, 6.

He wrote the *Two Treatises of Government* to defend the Glorious Revolution of 1688, as he counters the absolutist philosophy of Thomas Hobbes. The Stuart regime under James II had collapsed in 1688 by the English political elite in its relinquishment to William III of Orange, who was to be in possession of England, Scotland, and Ireland. With the Bill of Rights (1689) underwriting regular parliament, free election, freedom of speech in parliament, a Catholic monarchy or absolutist monarchy was stamped out. The religious policy was quite tolerant, under the condition that the dissidents must not conspire against the sovereign. Presbyterianism became the official religion in Scotland with its doctrinal norm of the Westminster Confession.[70]

Of special significance was Locke's joining in the household of Lord Ashley of Shaftesbury, who was hostile to Charles II. Locke returned to England from exile in Holland. In his two treatises, he set out to justify King William on the basis of the consent of the people.

The *Two Treatises* entails political revolution, which refers to a restoration of natural rights against tyranny and monarchical absolutism; such rights reside in every private citizen, alone as well as collective underlying an idea of tyrannicide.[71]

However, in his earlier position, Locke remained restrained in a liberal, democratic direction. What was characteristic in the seventeenth-century absolutist idea was the work of Sir Robert Filmer, *Patriarcha, or the Natural Power of Kings* rather than Hobbes' *Leviathan*. In Filmer's argument, we are born unfree and unequal, such that political society is rooted in the ordination of

---

[70] Gonzalez, *The History of Christianity* II: 209.
[71] Locke, *Two Treatises of Government*, XXXV. Locke finds biblical support for tyrannicide in Ehud's slaying of King Eglon, as seen analogously in the execution of Charles I after Civil War.

God revealed in the natural order of patriarchy. The original power of monarchs can be seen in Adam's rights as father and husband.[72]

In the first treatise, Locke mounted an attack on Filmer's position of patriarchy based on God-given rulership through Adam. Locke stands for God's workmanship in which all people are regarded as the workmanship or property of God without subordination among them.[73] It undercuts masculine potency and patriarchal domination. His position dethrones the power of the prince by divine right, which is based on the natural unfreedom of human beings by birth.[74]

In the first treatise (ca. 1679-81), however, Locke does not claim for a right of resistance or insurrection. What drove Locke to the revolutionary position in the second treatise (1681-1683) was "the treason trials, the City coup, and the persecution."[75]

His political theory is based on the social contract and people's consent rather than the contract between king and people; thus, rulers are merely servants and officials, such that the executive power is ministerial and subordinated to the legislative and responsible for it.[76]

He opposes the tyranny obscuring public good and dissolving government; the right of revolution is vested with the agent of revolution entitled with the private or collective citizen. It is a way of restoration of natural right "for the preservation of property, peace, and unity amongst themselves"[77] in a state of war against rebellion by the tyrant, who is denounced as "beasts of prey, those dangerous and noxious creatures."[78]

---

[72] Ibid., XVIII-XIX.
[73] Locke, *The Second Treatise* (=II). Ch. 2; 6.
[74] Locke, *The First Treatise* (=I). Ch. 1; 5; 6.
[75] Locke, *Two Treatises of Government*, XXI.
[76] Locke, II. Ch. 13; 152.
[77] Locke, II. Ch. 19; 226.
[78] Locke, II. Ch. 3. 16.

Natural reason dictates what the law is because the law of nature or reason is written or implanted by God in the hearts of Adam and all humankind, thus it is necessary for parents to preserve, nourish and educate their children as the workmanship of God, not as theirs.[79] "God and nature" is linked with "reason and revelation," which stands in the tradition of God and natural law.[80]

However, reason in the state of nature is apt to force or to fraud, running into a state of war. To avoid the state of war, it is necessary for reason to form civil society by an act of consent of every individual in constituting a social contract or original compact. Its purpose is to secure a property that is to be regulated by the laws of the society for the common good; an individual becomes both person and possession under government in the form of perfect democracy.[81]

This perspective cuts through the limitations of Hobbes' negative anthropology regarding perpetual war among human beings in the state of nature. For Locke, a human being is a property-acquiring animal, which is grounded in God's workmanship.

The task of the social contract is to create an external formal order, politico-juridical order, in which political power implies a right of making laws to regulate and preserve property.[82]

He furthers to conceptualize the first function of the law in theological tradition in which God has appointed civil government to restrain the partiality and violence of people (Rom

---

[79] Locke, II. Ch. 6; 56.
[80] However, Locke's natural law position in its realism or essential contradicts with experience position in his *Essay Concerning Human Understanding*, in which the mind at birth is a tabla rasa, thus knowledge comes only from experience. This contradiction is irreconcilable in Locke's philosophy.
[81] Locke, II. Ch. 8. 120; Ch. 10. 132.
[82] Locke, II. Ch. 1. art. 3.

13: 4); it implies the proper remedy for offenders and criminals within "the inconveniences of the state of nature."[83] The task of the State is to regulate and control the antagonistic and mutually exclusive spheres in individual life, which tend to the dissociation and competition of real interests.

The legislative power receives a delegated power from the people who can appoint the form of the government by constituting the legislative. The legislative is sacred and unalterable. It is limited to the public good of the society, designed just for the good of the people.[84] The government is limited and can be dissolved, but not the civil society. We do not enter into civil society in order to be devoured by a lion. This is characteristic of the revolution in the political sense of Locke, which can be seen in the 1989 overthrowing of Marxist states in Eastern Europe.[85]

In Locke's view, in the natural condition of humankind (the Law of Nature), there is no civil authority; nor is it a state without morality. This condition presupposes equality to one another in a state of perfect and complete liberty, free from the interference of others. The Law of Nature as the basis of all morality, which is granted to us by God, commands us not to harm others.

But in the state of nature, the enjoyment of natural rights and property is very uncertain, unsafe replete with fears and continual dangers, because it is constantly exposed to the invasion of others, offense, and violence. In the state of nature, there are many things to be desired. The great and chief purpose for government is to

---

[83] Locke, II. Ch. 2. 13.
[84] Locke, II. Ch. 11. 134; 135.
[85] Locke, *Two Treatises of Government*, XXXVI. His political philosophy and social contract theory considerably influenced Thomas Jefferson, author of the American *Declaration of Independence* (1776), which stands in the natural law tradition. Ibid., XXV.

preservation through common consent the mutual preservation of their lives, liberties, and estates, generally speaking, property.[86]

Consent, Moral Reasoning, and Resistance

Out of the state of nature, people enter into civil society to preserve lives, liberties, and estates (or property) through the social contract (an act of consent) between citizens; the powers of the government are delegated and represented by the people. By their consent, the legislative power is established to preserve society and its members. As the supreme power of the society, the legislation must not be arbitrary over the lives and fortunes of the people, because nobody has absolute arbitrary power over oneself or others. The legislative power "is limited to the public good of the society."[87]

Locke separates three distinct functions of government (legislative, executive, and judiciary) and seeks to enhance liberty by balancing one another. Tyranny inevitably occurs to the point where the executive power subordinates the legislature to itself, or where the judiciary is perverted by the executive power. It leads to a state of war with people who have a right to remove the political force, and reinstates the legislative in the exercise of their power.

As Locke writes, "the power of assembling and dismissing the legislative, placed in the executive, gives not the executive a superiority over it, but is a fiduciary trust, placed in him, for the safety of the people..."[88]

---

[86] Locke, II. Ch. 9. 123; 124.
[87] Locke, II. Ch. 11. 135.
[88] Locke, II. Ch. 13. 156.

Rational people agree with each other in following and respecting the rules and the laws. The morally binding rules facilitate a harmonious life and collaboration in social beings.

Locke's idea of consent entails a dimension of resistance because no government can have a right to enforce people without consent. Power returns to the community as a whole body of the people which establishes any form of government. Social contract theory does not justify a civil law or institution in enforcing racial segregation, because it violates citizens' rights in terms of liberty and rights. To avoid the state of war, people have to quit the state of nature, entering into the civil society, but when violence is used and injury is done by hands in the administration of justice, the only remedy is left to "an appeal to heaven;" in other words, revolution, is based on conscience as "the supreme judge of all men."[89]

Against the theory of social contract theory, some critics argue that there would be a lack of fairness or a flaw in the consent because neither Black people nor women were included in the Constitutional Convention. Michael Sandel makes a charge against the principle of consent in the name of fairness.[90]

However, the point of departure in the social contract is the fairness or equity on the basis of individual freedom, sovereignty, and economic right of property. This political principle includes resistance or a possibility of revolution against the authority's coercion and injustice excluding the consent of the people as citizens through voting.

According to Locke, society can be made by the consent of every individual. Otherwise, the "original compact would signify nothing, and be no compact…"[91] This refutes a constitution that elevates the political society to the Leviathan.

---

[89] Locke, II. Ch. 3. 21.
[90] Sandel, *Justice*, 143.
[91] Locke, II. Ch. 8. 97.

Civil Disobedience and Social Contract

The problem of civil disobedience is an essential part of the social contract theory and its human rights. Morality can be nourished and sought in social justice because moral individual beings can be threatened by the system of an immoral society.

The Jim Crow laws are the case test for determining the social contract theory. If racial segregation is legalized as a collection of laws lasting from the post-civil war era (as early as 1865 after the abolition of slavery) until 1968 in the civil rights movement, it was meant to marginalize African Americans; it denies them the right to vote, hold jobs, and receive education or other opportunities.

In the context of public theology, it is James Cone that draws attention to the meaning of the cross in connection with black people crucified in the lynching tree; it underwrites a critical and political dimension of God's reconciliation as an alternative to white supremacy. His public theology in the struggle for freedom remains pivotal in mobilizing the civil rights movement against Jim Crow laws.[92]

Given this, public theology can be articulated in terms of God and natural rights in which no inalienable rights of all is violated; injustice and immorality of racial segregation must be challenged and require people's consent, especially from the side of the victims.

We may find such an aspect in Locke's political theory. For him "the constitution of the legislative is the first and fundamental act of society" "by the consent and appointment of the people."[93] Contrary to the latter, no one can have the authority of making laws, thus people are not under obligation to obey them. The

---

[92] Cone, *The Cross and the Lynching Tree*, 71-3.
[93] Locke, II. Ch. 19. 211.

power of the people which provides for their safety anew by a new legislative is the best defense against rebellion.[94]

"But if [people] have set limits to the duration of their legislative, and made this supreme power in... assembly, only temporary: or else when by the miscarriages of those in authority, it is forfeited; ...it reverts to the society, and the people have a right to act as supreme and continue the legislative in themselves, or erect a new form, or under the old form place it in new hands, as they think good."[95]

A fair term of social collaboration and mutual benefits has to be judged according to human liberties, free consent, and resistance, in which civil constitution has a moral character in serving the people for "the preservation of property, peace, and unity amongst themselves."[96]

Locke's idea of consent seeks to maintain the benefits of a government. He limits the legislative power only to preserve the society, against "a right to destroy, enslave, or designedly to impoverish the subjects."[97]

Locke takes a step further in conceptualizing a just revolution based on the principle of consent against tyranny. He would refute David Hume (1711-1776) who states: "Can we seriously say that a poor peasant ...has a free choice to leave his country, when he...lives from day to day by the small wages which he requires?"[98]

In fact, Locke frames property rights around the rights of personality, and every rational being is entitled to it. For the right of subsistence, it is significant to feed the impoverished: our duty to the needy. The holding of property entails stewardship in such

---

[94] Locke, II. Ch. 19. 223.
[95] Locke, II. Ch. 19. 243.
[96] Locke, II. Ch. 19. 228.
[97] Locke, II. Ch. 16. 184.
[98] Cited in Rachels, *The Elements of Moral Philosophy*, 94.

a way that private property is allowed for the common good. For making substance available for all, the legislature intervenes. God "has given his needy brother a right to the surplusage of his goods; so that it cannot justly be denied him when his pressing wants to call for it. And therefore, no man could ever have a just power over the life of another...God wants [every person] to afford to the wants of his brother."[99]

Given this, how would Locke comprehend and develop the social contract position in dealing with the relation between slavery and colonialism?

Slavery and Colonialism

Locke declared in the opening line of his *First Treatise*: "Slavery is so vile and miserable an estate of man, and so directly opposite to the generous temper and courage of our nation; that 'tis hardly to be conceived, that an Englishman, much less a gentleman, should plead for it.'"[100]

However, "Of Conquest" (chapter 16) in the second treatise Locke regards the power of the conqueror in a just war as that of having despotic rights over the captive: "[H]e has an absolute power over the lives of those, who by putting themselves in a state of war, have forfeited them; but he has not thereby a right and title to their possession."[101] Against the conqueror, the conquered people under the yoke of constraint "have always a right to shake it off," setting themselves from the usurpation, or tyranny.[102]

What is at stake in Locke is his theory of consent, because nobody or no government can have a right to obedience from

---

[99] Locke, I. Ch. 4. 42.
[100] Locke, I. Ch. 1. 1.
[101] Locke, II. Ch. 16. 180.
[102] Locke, II. Ch. 16. 192.

those with no free consent; it is true to the extent that "the conqueror in a just war has a right to the estate, as well as power over the person of the conquered."[103] As Locke asks, "Can anyone say, the king, or conqueror, after his grant, may by his power of conqueror, take away all, or part of the land from the heirs of one, or from the other, during his life, he paying the rent?"[104]

In so doing, the grants and promises of people in power are just mockery and conspiracy as seen on the parts of the conquered. Locke's argument strikes me, because the conqueror in a just cause has a despotic right over the conquered, while he has no lawful title to dominion over the conquered regarding their wife and children by way of conquest.

On the other hand, however, Locke justifies colonial exploitation, when it comes to the unproductive "wastelands" of the Native Americans. Locke argues that a king of a large and fruitful territory in the rich land of Americans "feeds, lodges, and is clad worse than a day-laborer in England."[105] For Locke, "God gave the world to men in common; but ...it cannot be supposed he meant it should always remain common and uncultivated. He gave it to the use of the industrious and rational, (and labor was to be his title to it;) not to the fancy or covetousness of the quarrelsome and contentious."[106]

The idea of God's "workmanship" provides a basis for justifying colonial exploitation, to the degree that those capable of cultivating America fruitfully possess a better right to own it.

It can be argued that there is no property in durable objects, such as lands and houses because they pass from hand to hand;

---

[103] Locke, II. Ch. 16. 193.
[104] Locke, II. Ch. 16. 194.
[105] Locke, II. Ch. 5. 41.
[106] Locke, II. Ch. 5. 34. In later American history, the Two Treatises was used (or misused) in the courtroom to uphold colonial exploitation against native land rights. Locke, *Two Treatises of Government*, XI.

in some period, they must have been founded on fraud, violence, and injustice, as seen in colonial times.

That being the case, shouldn't Locke have clarified that the relation between the colonizer and the colonized was based upon mutual consent, rather than justifying colonial exploitation through the principle of God's workmanship? If the native Indians of America lived in the state of nature, capable of having mutual trust and binding contracts, does not Locke acknowledge that they "freely act in the choice of their governors and forms of government" through the mutual agreement of the people?[107]

If Locke defines property to be involved in one's life, liberty, and religion, shouldn't it be reframed within universal right to work imbued with its distinctive moral feature in terms of God's handwork and solidarity with the impoverished for the common good?

Taken all together, Locke's ambivalent position in the *Two Treatises* (1689) causes confusion and controversy, accusing himself of justifying slavery, as further seen in his coauthored document of the *Fundamental Constitutions of Carolina* (1669), in which a hereditary aristocracy is constructed.[108]

Acting as a political advisor to Lord Ashley of Shaftesbury, Locke took the opportunity to have information of commercial and colonial matters in the Americas; he invested in slave-trading companies and served as secretary to the Council of Trade and Plantations. Assisting the Lord's Proprietors of Carolina, he fascinated Shaftsbury in drafting *The Fundamental Constitutions*

---

[107] Locke, I. Ch. 8. 102.

[108] Locke, in the later revision of the Constitutions did not alter the slavery article. He was a shareholder in the Royal African Company charted in 1672, which sought to monopolize the English slave trade. McCarthy, *Race, Empire, and the Idea of Human Development*, 167.

of Carolina. An Essay on Toleration (1667) marked a decisive change of his mind.[109]

Given this, Locke's position concerning slavery is expressed: "For, it is evident, the person sold was not under an absolute, arbitrary, despotical power. For the master could not have the power to kill him, at any time, whom, at a certain time, he was obliged to let go free out of his service; and the master of such a servant was so far from having an arbitrary power over his life, that he could not, at pleasure, so much as maim him, but the loss of an eye, or tooth, set him free (*Exodus* 21)."[110]

Therefore, Locke's defense of property may entail a communitarian dimension in contrast to a libertarian and anti-statist vision, granted that he safeguarded unlimited property in the legitimacy of the capitalist ethic in its financial and commercial stage. The consenting citizens may choose to include a degree of egalitarianism and a share for the disadvantaged through the social contract and divine workmanship. Property is organized around the rights of personality through a universal right to work, because we are an expression of God's workmanship, and respect the needs of others, who are also God's workmanship.

On the other hand, it is noteworthy that Locke defends enclosure of common lands for greater productivity (seen analogously in Adam Smith) through the principle of consent[111] and unequal property relations of his time; with respect to resources in America, he argues that "now of those good things which nature hath provided in common, everyone had a right… to as much as he could use, and had a property in all that he could affect with his labor."[112]

---

[109] Locke, *Two Treatises of Government*, XVII.
[110] Locke, II. Ch. 4. 24.
[111] "No one can enclose or appropriate any part, without the consent of all his fellow commoners." II. Ch. 5. 35.
[112] Locke, II. Ch. 5. 46.

However, Locke seems to be vulnerable to only a finite amount of land. In his context, did not Locke know about the Nine Years' War in America (1688-1697) and the contentious fur trade? European agricultural expansion was pressured on territory acquired from the Native Americans.

To protect property does not necessarily mean to accumulate legitimate fortunes or enlarge possession in a rampant and unlimited manner as injuring to anyone. Locke is still cautious: "He wasted not the common stock; destroyed no part of the portion of goods that belonged to others.... ; the exceeding of the bounds of his just property not lying in the largeness of his possession, but the perishing of anything uselessly in it."[113]

In a nutshell, civil liberty becomes a constitutive part of moral liberty in affirming human dignity. The end of the law in political relation of ruler-citizen established by consent is "to preserve and enlarge freedom."[114] This aspect contradicts the sub-political relation of master-slave, which is based on absolute, arbitrary, irrational, and coercive power of the master.

Social Contract and Teleological Reasoning

In the tradition of the social contract theory, John Rawls (1921-2002) in his *Theory of Justice* deals with justice as fairness for its primacy. He considers Aristotle's sense of justice in which an idea of refraining from *pleonexia* (greed or covetousness) remains crucial; it is refraining from gaining some advantage for oneself, or it refrains from denying a person that which is due to him/her. Aristotle provides an account of what properly belongs to a person and of what is due to him/her.[115]

---

[113] Ibid.
[114] Locke, II. Ch. 6. 57.
[115] Rawls, *A Theory of Justice*, 9.

Rawls comprehends that such entitlements are derived from social institutions, the idea of which would accord to Aristotle's sense of social justice. This perspective characterizes the justice of the basic structure.[116]

Aristotle distinguished two types of economy in terms of the oikonomic form (*oikonomike* needed to satisfy basic needs in households and polis) and the chrematistic economic form for acquisition (chrematistic used to increase monetary property for its own sake). The former assumes a natural form of economy in which money is used as a means of exchange for vital goods. But human desire is embodied in the second form of unnatural chrematistic economy in monetary mechanisms for unlimited accumulation of money. Political prohibition together with ethical education is required to protect the common good of the polis.[117]

According to Aristotle, justice is of teleological character in consideration of the purpose or end of the social practice in question as well as relevant to virtues of honor and reward or moral desert. Accordingly, justice implies giving the individuals what they deserve, giving each person his or her due. The relevant grounds of merit or desert or a person due depends on what is distributed.

However, Aristotle defines the equals in terms of the virtues which are relevant or conditional to what we are distributing (for example, flutes). In the case of flute playing, the relevant merit is the capacity of playing well; it has little to do with wealth, nobility of birth, or physical beauty, or chance, although "birth and beauty may be greater goods than the ability to play the flute."[118]

---

[116] Ibid., 10.
[117] Duchrow and Hinkelammert, *Transcending Greedy Money*, 91.
[118] Aristotle, *The Politics*, Bk. III. Ch. XII [1282b]

Accordingly, justice may entail an aspect of discrimination in accordance with merit, because the best flute player deserves his/her due in the distribution of the best flute; that is what the best flute is for, to be played well—the telos of flutes is to produce excellent music or to maximize the greatest happiness for the greatest member. Inquiry into the telos determines the way just distribution of goods is undertaken rather than utility principle and private interest.[119]

Any police or political association must devote itself to the purpose of encouraging goodness; otherwise, the law becomes a mere covenant rather than becoming a rule of life by which to render the members of a society to be good and just.[120]

Democracy is based on the citizenship and political authority of the majority by misconstruing the purpose of political society because the latter has no preference for the rule of the majority. It undermines the purpose of cultivating the virtue of citizens, which is the highest end of political association. "The end and purpose of a polis is a good life, and the institutions of social life are means to that end."[121]

Although acknowledging the significance of Aristotle's moral theory and economic justice as social justice, however, Rawls grounds the theory of justice in the philosophical tradition of a social contract (Locke, Rousseau, and Kant), which is termed fairness based on the original agreement. What matters in this tradition is the original position of equality which corresponds to the state of nature in a hypothetical sense.

In a like manner, Rawls conceptualizes the principles behind a veil of ignorance, in which no one is advantaged or disadvantaged. Simply, we do not know anything at all in the veil of ignorance

---

[119] Sandel, *Justice*, 188.
[120] Aristotle, *The Politics*, Bk. III. Ch. IX [1280b].
[121] Ibid.

regarding class or gender, race or ethnicity, political opinions, or religious convictions.

Given the circumstances of the original position, two principles of justice would emerge from the hypothetical contracts; the first offers equal basic liberties (freedom of speech and religion) for all citizens. In this hypothetical consent, the law is taken to be just as it would be agreed upon by the public as a whole. It is to be clarified in terms of a veil of ignorance.

The second principle is concerned with social and economic equality for the life of the disadvantaged, granting that there are social and economic inequalities. The primary social goods (housing, food, judiciary protection, public health care, and education) are to be arranged against natural disadvantage in order to bring advantage to everyone, while nonessential goods remain intact in seeking liberty and enjoyment by opportunity in their own term.

Rawls articulates the state of nature in the tradition of a social contract in terms of the identity between justice and fairness, thus a society satisfying this principle of justice is called a fair society. Institutions are to be regulated in accordance with the principles of justice in all subsequent criticism and reform since we would have contracted into the general system and rules of the civil society.[122]

The original position in a veil of ignorance is based on an original position of equality without advantage or disadvantage between human beings as moral persons, capable of doing good and right. It is extended to apply to the basic structure of society. It includes a reflective equilibrium in revising the existing judgment in dealing with the discrepancy between the original position and correct distribution of wealth and authority.[123]

---

[122] Rawls, *A Theory of Justice*, 12-3.
[123] Ibid., 18.

In this process, we avoid conflict of judgment and adjust until residing in equilibrium. His method of reflective equilibrium is of hermeneutical relevance, correlating the epistemological with the motivational, moral in dealing with the human sense of justice in an appropriate manner; this procedure is undertaken in terms of appreciation of moral beliefs, revision of these, and semantic retrieval of moral judgment in a given context. The reflective equilibrium deals with the social world and its moral complexity, coming to terms with the principle of appropriateness; the principle of universalization (you shall not kill the innocent) should be adjusted and revised in a particular situation that would violate the principle of universalization.

We read such an aspect of distributive justice already in Kant's moral philosophy: "Although we may entirely within our rights, according to the laws of the land and the rules of our social structure, we may nevertheless be participating in general injustice, and in giving to an unfortunate man we do not give him a gratuity but only help to return to him that of which the general injustice of our system has deprived him."[124]

In regard to property and other social goods, people should pursue their own interests or good in order to benefit the disadvantaged in society. In Rawls' basic statement it reads: "We see then that the difference principle represents, in effect, an agreement to regard the distribution of natural talents as a common asset."[125] His difference principle is so radical because the pursuit of property and other social goods is faced toward the other.

Rawls can fit in with the Aristotelian economic position for *oikonomia* against chrematistic acquisition in unrestrained accumulation and considers restraining practical reason to ethical

---

[124] Kant, *Lectures on Ethics*, "Duties Toward Others" (1779). Cited in Boss, ed. *Ethics for Life*, 331.
[125] Rawls, *A Theory of Justice*, 101.

self-understanding in the sphere of the good in which *phronesis* is defined against episteme within a deontological framework. But Rawls argues against teleological reasoning based on natural fitness in regards to slaves or women as ruled by a master or a husband. Consent and the freedom to choose remain critical against the telos and the fit.

Critique and Difference Principle

Rawls' theory of justice also integrates Locke's political theory and social contract reasoning within his deontic framework, while cutting across some limitations and setbacks of Locke.

However, a critique can be raised to Rawls from the standpoint of Foucault's genealogy which undercuts the familiar enlightenment metanarrative of universal principle and reason. Foucault's method of problematization facilitates a method of reflective equilibrium in drawing attention to power/knowledge interplay in analyzing what is taken for granted as accepted ideas and principles of practical reason; it also enhances the reflective equilibrium by way of inclusion of what has been excluded and deviant.

In reality, many forms of injustice and inequality such as race, ethnicity, sexuality, and women remain in place— "deeply entrenched in the beliefs and values, symbols and images, practices and institutions, structures and functions of national and global society,"[126] though these forms have been eliminated legally.

We may choose to be behind a veil of ignorance because we do not know different people with different interests and motivations in economic situations, ethnic stratification, race,

---

[126] McCarthy, Race, *Empire*, and *The Idea of Human Development*, 30.

gender, or religion. This reality in a veil of ignorance would lead us to adopt an original position of equality built upon a hypothetical agreement, thus it rejects utilitarianism as well as a laissez-faire, libertarian principle.

Rawls refines the social contract theory in terms of a principle of equal basic liberties for all citizens (including the right to liberty of conscience and freedom of thought) for social democratic direction. Rawls integrates the rights and liberties with a notion of democratic equality, arguing for "the principle of fair equality of opportunity and the difference principle."[127] These two principles, particularly the difference principle features justice as fairness in its liberal, or social-democratic orientation to cut through the limitations of a teleological theory of politics and ethics.

According to the difference principle, "[t]he naturally advantaged are not to gain merely because they are more gifted, but only to cover the costs of training and education and for using their endowments in ways that help the less fortunate as well... But it does not follow that one should eliminate distinctions... The basic structure of society can be arranged so that these contingencies work for the good of the least fortunate."[128]

This perspective implies the egalitarian position in contrast to the meritocratic theory of justice in which the free market is provided with fair equality of opportunity. Although the distribution of wealth and income is determined by the natural distribution of abilities and talents, a free market society with equal educational opportunities does not necessarily engender a just distribution of income and wealth.

Rawls takes issue with the meritocratic position according to which people deserve the rewards their talents can bring with

---

[127] Rawls, *A Theory of Justice*, XII.
[128] Ibid., Sec. 17.

effort. "That we deserve the superior character that enables us to make the effort to cultivate our abilities is also problematic; for such character depends in good part upon fortunate family and social circumstances in early life for which can claim no credit. The notion of desert does not apply here."[129]

This perspective in which justice is fairness rejects the conception of justice as happiness according to virtue in the tradition of Aristotle. The primary purpose of the law is for Aristotle to cultivate the habits for good character. "Legislators make the citizens good by forming habits in them, and this is the wish of every legislator, and those who do not effect it miss the mark, and it is in this that a good constitution differs from a bad one."[130]

Agents in acting morally take a mean between extremes, considering what is appropriate to each occasion and discern the particular features of situations for a precept or a rule.

What is at issue in moral conduct and question does not consist in fixity, but appropriate deliberation under the circumstances; it requires practical wisdom concerned with particulars concerning how to act with respect to the human good. Practical wisdom, a moral virtue, has political implications in seeking the highest human good for fellow citizens.[131]

Those with the qualities of character and judgment who are greatest in civic virtue are identified with the common good. The purpose of the political society exists to honor and reward civic virtue, such that public recognition of those with civic excellence becomes the pedagogical role of the good society. The laws form good character setting us toward civic virtue. The citizens exercise capacities for practical wisdom and appropriate judgment,

---

[129] Ibid.
[130] Aristotle, *Politics*, Bk. III. 1003b.
[131] Sandel, *Justice*, 199.

cultivating their human nature for the good life. The moral desert becomes crucial in Aristotle's combination between the teleological notion of justice and its honorific one (honor and virtue).[132]

This meritocracy is based on an elitist political system, standing for those who contributed most to the community as those deserving the most in return, when it comes to distributive justice.

However, the resources of the society and economic opportunities are unjust in the social arrangement of capitalist society; it has been created in natural endowment (natural lottery) and historical circumstances by creating disadvantages for certain people. Against this, an idea of fair argues for compensating disadvantaged people for their past inequality through reparation, welfare, and charity.

Critical Conclusion

Rawls does not consider the moral desert as the basis for distributive justice. For instance, affirmative action of racial and ethnic diversity in college admission brings disadvantage to high SAT scores of those who morally deserve. In the case of distributive justice, it has less to do with rewarding virtue or moral desert. The difference principle, which is in contrast to the moral desert, facilitates the purpose of the political society in promoting the good life and common good through distributive justice in an egalitarian manner.

If we are able to realize our nature in the sense of a political or social animal, there is a reality and structure of inequality and injustice in social stratification in a hierarchical and discriminatory manner. Moral life in political society is not adequately performed

---

[132] Ibid., 194-5.

without considering the principle of equality and difference in the protection of those on the margins of society.

The difference principle should also be taken in full in the context of property-owning democracy (or of a liberal socialist regime): it is a principle of reciprocity, or mutuality according to the appropriate division of social advantages because society is seen as a fair system of cooperation among free and equal citizens from one generation to the next.

For example, there is certain inequality between the medical doctor and bus driver for their wage. But the advantaged works for the benefit of the disadvantaged by taxing the former to provide the latter with education, health, and welfare. Inequality can be overcome through the difference principle. The property-owning democracy works with its system of competitive markets, carrying out the idea of society as a fair system of cooperation among citizens as free and equal persons for dispersing the ownership of wealth and capital.

The unfairness must be undertaken and overcome in terms of the difference principle, which takes issue with the libertarian theory of justice imbued with formal equality and competition in a free market. The latter is expressed in Milton Friedman, a staunch defender of the laissez-faire principle: "Life is not fair… But it is also important to recognize how much we benefit from the very unfairness we deplore."[133]

In Rawls' argument, justice as fairness includes a right to personal property, but no natural right of private property by birth. The injustice of the libertarian system "is that it permits distributive shares to be improperly influenced by the factors so arbitrary from a moral point of view."[134]

---

[133] Milton and Rose Friedman, *Free to Choose*, 136.
[134] Rawls, *A Theory of Justice*, sec 12.

The difference principle facilitates correcting the unequal distribution of wealth, talents, and endowments while affirming their advantage for the community as a whole. Rawls' strategy, which is grounded in equal respect for the free and equal moral person, stands for the construction of a realist utopia in the sense of kingdom of ends.

Given this, a question arises whether justice as fairness is best realized by property-owning democracy or by a liberal socialist regime. It "is left to be settled by historical conditions and the traditions, institutions, and social forces of each country."[135]

This position should be met with a political theory of general will in Rousseau, who reinforces the priority of civil society against the state with emphasis on the solidarity principle.

---

[135] Ibid., XVI.

Chapter 4
General Will

In the tradition of social contract theory, we observe that the political principles of Hobbes and Locke find their significance in *Second Discourse* by Jean-Jacques Rousseau (1712-1778).[1] Social contract approach runs counter to the political theory of Aristotle and the medieval inheritance of Thomas Aquinas; church, king, and nobility are so allied one another that Christian teaching sanctioned divine character of monarchy.

Against this synthesis of religion and the state, a profound critique was raised on the part of the Enlightenment, which focuses on the significance of education, sound reasoning, and progress for enlightening the masses. This enlightening project was seen in Diderot's massive work of *Encyclopedia*.

However, Rousseau begins with a serious critique of the growing faith in enlightenment and progress (seen in Diderot's *Encyclopedia*), which is read in his *Discourse on the Sciences and Arts* (the *First Discourse*). In his famous response to the question of Dijon academy for a prize dissertation (1750)–"*Has the restoration of the sciences and arts tended to purify morals?*"—we read that the sciences and the arts have always been harmful to morality because of their decomposition of the natural virtue of the human heart.

---

[1] Rousseau, *The First and Second Discourses*. The full title is *Discourse on the Origin and Foundations of Inequality Among Men*, which was written for another prize competition of the Academy of Dijon.

This chapter is a study of J. J. Rousseau's social contract and popular sovereignty in which general will plays a normative role in regard to liberty, justice, and solidarity. I examine Hegel's critique of Rousseau and Kant while undertaking a response to Hegel from the standpoint of Rousseau and Kant. Then, the totalitarian aspect of Rousseau should be critically reviewed, while a comparison is made between Rousseau and Hugo Grotius (Aristotle included) regarding slavery and colony. Finally, a theological assessment is to be made in dealing with distributive justice in Dietrich Bonhoeffer, while reviewing Barth's appropriation of Rousseau's political philosophy and civil society for his public theology in taking on significance between church and state.

Rousseau and Enlightenment

In his sudden inspiration on the question of Dijon, Rousseau confesses that a human being is naturally good, but it is by "all the contradictions of the social system and all the abuses of our institutions" that human beings become wicked.[2]

His ethical concern is expressed in the *First Discourse*. "Our souls have been corrupted in proportion to the advancement of our sciences and arts toward perfection."[3] Rousseau favors virtue and patriotism of the ancients like Sparta and republican Rome, such that can be mirrored in his native city of Geneva.

Ancient political thinkers talked about morals and virtue constantly, but Rousseau lamented that modern time talks only of business and money.[4] Enlightenment and modernity have produced wealth and luxury which are fatal to sound morals as

---

[2] Rousseau, *On the Social Contract*, 8. [Hereafter SC]
[3] "First Discourse," 39.
[4] Ibid., 51.

well as political power. Luxury has a necessary consequence in dissolving morals and leading to the corruption of taste. "One cannot reflect on morals without delighting in the recollection of the simplicity of the earliest times."[5] Sparta was moral while Athens was corrupt. Although the Roman Empire devoured all the wealth of the world, it became the prey of Bavarian people.[6]

A paradox is seen in Rousseau's bitter critique of the arts and sciences and his praising of ignorance by contributing to a famous academy of Dijon. Such paradox or contradiction is what Rousseau seeks to reconcile. In fact, Rousseau favors integrity and virtue than erudition and science, because Enlightenment in the spread of the arts and sciences has corrupted human life and society as seen in all times and in all places.[7]

His critique of modernity and progress is performed in terms of the political tradition of Hobbes and Locke (included classical authors with great significance) challenging the most traditionalists in the eighteenth century. Rousseau is not merely of romantic or pre-modern profile in his character and orientation; but a stance *ad fontes* (return to the natural liberty, sympathy, and equality in the state of nature) provides him with a resource in elaborating his social contract theory and popular sovereignty to transcend origin and progress of inequality and domination in subsequent historical contexts. This perspective resonates with Rawls' original position.

Rousseau's argument against the Enlightenment, progress and modernity is further seen in his answer to a prize question by the Dijon (1754)— "What is the origin of inequality among men; and is it authorized by natural law?" His position is elaborated in

---

[5] Ibid., 53-4.
[6] Ibid., 51.
[7] Ibid., 34; 40.

dealing with liberty, goodness, and equality in the primitive state of nature.

State of Nature and Inequality of Possession

Rousseau envisions the state of nature in which a human being is by nature good: "wandering in the forests, without industry, without speech, without domicile, without war, and without liaisons, without need of his fellow-men, likewise with no desire to harm them."[8]

Natural "man" outside of society was a stupid yet self-sufficient, peaceful, good animal that is guided by self-preservation and compassion, not by innate reason. Rousseau's notion of the state of nature is not supposed on Hobbesian assumptions of war among people, in which "man is naturally intrepid and seeks only to attack and fight."[9]

Against this assumption of negative anthropology, Rousseau conceptualizes the state of nature in terms of "hypothetical and conditional reasoning" rather than historical truth.[10] Unless self-preservation is threatened, the human-animal is not wicked, but he is driven by "the inner impulse of commiseration."[11] Commiseration or pity, the most virtuous is a natural sentiment like a gentle voice, which moderates the activity of self-love in each individual, replacing laws, morals, and virtue, and "contribut[ing] to the mutual preservation of the entire species."[12]

---

[8] "*Second Discourse*," 137.
[9] Ibid., 107.
[10] Ibid., 103.
[11] Ibid., 96.
[12] Ibid., 133.

The human being in the natural state is affirmed as a free agent, which distinguishes itself in an act of freedom from the other beasts. "[Savage man] is free to acquiesce or resist, and it is above all in the consciousness of this freedom that the spirituality of his soul is shown."[13]

Self-preservation and well-being, anterior to reason, are the most appropriate for the human race, and they do not require the principle of sociability.[14] However, violating the positive anthropology of humanity in the state of nature, inequality of possessions has taken place; it is in the violent competition for the material means of existence at the evolutionary scale, in other words, war of all against all in the sense of Hobbes.

Or in the axiom of Locke, *where there is no property, there is no injury*.[15] The warlike situation leads to the foundation of civil society by transforming possession into a lawful right to property through the social contract for civil security and liberty.

Natural pity prevents a savage man from harming anyone, and inequality is barely perceptible in the primitive state of nature. However, at the evolutionary scale of development, war of all has arrived, accompanying brute force and violence. Hence mere possession is transformed into a right of property through law and order. In hypotheticals, he insists on the right to property through law and order, but it implies that law and order are created to prevent the annexation and acquisition of private property.

In the progress of inequality in the different revolutions, the law and the right of property is established as the first stage, while the institution of the governments becomes the second; the third changes legitimatize power into arbitrary power which

---

[13] Ibid., 114.
[14] Ibid., 95.
[15] Ibid., 150.

establishes unjust, tyrannical rule as the last stage of inequality.[16] The last stage in a war of all against all and its moral corruption must be overthrown by revolution with complete justice.

Inequality begins with society itself in which there is the potential of unfreedom, tyranny, and slavery. Civil society corrupted the original liberty of human beings in the state of nature, and history is seen as decay rather than as progress. The faithful *amore propre* means greed and evil passion, which is in opposition to the natural, innocent, and good love of the self.

The latter, together with commiseration in sympathy with the suffering, helps to sustain the mutual preservation of the entire species. Rousseau's anti-Eurocentric position is expressed in his appreciation of the dignity of savage man; "as the Caribs…which until now has departed least from the state of nature, are precisely the most peaceful in their loves and the least subject to jealousy, even though they live in a burning hot climate…"[17]

Rousseau's position to *Revenon a la nature!*[18] is based on his conception of human beings in the state of nature. It does not imply the return to the pure state of nature in a Romantic sense in order to live as a beast, because the right of the strongest or inequality existed still in the state of nature. Instead, it implies as a conjecture a need to ground the proper ordering of civil society on the natural law as the ideal of natural liberty (free agent) and equality by combining and uniting "all their will with and into a single one."[19]

---

[16] Ibid., 177.

[17] Ibid., 136.

[18] Barth remains suspicious of the catchphrase which belongs to Rousseau himself. Barth, "Rousseau," in *Protestant Theology*, 168. Voltaire argues against Rousseau because the former is against the human race for a return to the forests. "Introduction" in *The First and Second Discourse*, 20.

[19] "*Second Discourse*," 169.

However, in the context of the second discourse, the concept of general will does not appear, which remains central in the *Social Contract*. But two writings are consistently connected rather than inconsistent.[20]

According to Rousseau's conjectures, the natural man had received in potentiality perfectibility, social virtues, and the other faculties, such that inequality between domination and servitude is barely perceptible.[21]

His thought experiment of original position for "hypothetical and conditional reasonings"[22] in the state of nature becomes a political basis for liberty, equality, and individual rights by which to cut across problems of civil society based on the division of labor and progress.

His perspective counters that a savage man is naturally cruel and needs civilization for him/her to be made gentler, because "nothing is so gentle as man in his primitive state, when, placed by nature at equal distances from the stupidity of brutes and the fatal enlightenment of civil man..."[23]

The colonial notion of progress and civilizing mission is no longer tenable in all subsequent historical development because progress is unveiled as a step toward the ruin and decrepitude of the human species. Through human labor, the cultivation of the land and its division followed, and the first rule of justice comes, once the property is recognized; labor produces continuing possession, transforming it into a property. The division of land produced the right to property which is different from natural law.[24]

Rousseau gives an account of the first effect of property as the inseparable consequence of nascent inequality: "in a word,

---

[20] Durkheim, *Montesquieu and Rousseau*, 135.
[21] "*Second Discourse*," 140.
[22] Ibid., 103.
[23] Ibid., 150.
[24] Ibid., 154.

competition ad rivalry, on one hand, opposition of interest on the other; and always the hidden desire to profit at the expense of others."[25] Property, a basis of political society, is subject to profound critique, because it causes "crimes, wars, murders, miseries, and horrors."[26]

It stifles natural pity, and destroys equality in which a human being is made "avaricious, ambitious, and evil." There occurs a perpetual conflict among all, "the most horrible state of war," which ends in fights and murders, as Hobbes envisions.[27]

Social Contract, Popular-legislative Model, and Rights of Property

To avoid the horrible situation, in which the possessions become burdensome, people are led to institute regulations of justice and peace by gathering into one supreme power. In Rousseau's account, "the origin of society and laws…gave new fetters to the weak and new forces to the rich; it "destroyed natural freedom for all time, and established forever the law of property and inequality;" it "changed a clever usurpation into an irrevocable right, and for the profit of a few ambitious men henceforth subjected the whole human race to work, servitude, and misery."[28]

His principle of solidarity with the poor is impressively expressed in the second discourse: "Do you not know that a multitude of your brethren die or suffer from a need of what you have in excess and that you needed express and unanimous

---

[25] Ibid., 156.
[26] Ibid., 141.
[27] Ibid., 157.
[28] Ibid., 160.

consent of the human race to appropriate for yourself anything from common subsistence that exceeded your own."[29]

Rousseau argues that government should not begin with arbitrary power, and such power must not serve as a foundation for the rights of society with instituted inequality. But the body politics is established as a true contract between the people and those chosen by them for themselves. By a contract, the two parties are under obligation to observe laws as stipulated as forming the bonds of their union. Since "the law...constitutes the essence of the State, everyone would return by right to his natural freedom."[30]

This perspective characterizes Rousseau's position in terms of popular, legislature approach to the State, in which he takes issue with the limitation of a parliamentary system. Sovereignty in the sense of general will cannot be represented, because they are the agents or deputies of the people rather than their representatives. During the election of members of the parliament, people are free to choose, but they are no longer free thereafter.[31]

In his concept of sovereignty Rousseau differentiates a citizen from the bourgeoisie. The name "people" is taken collectively, while they are called citizens individually as participants in the sovereign sovereignty. They as subjects are subject to the laws of the State.[32]

Sovereignty is not defined as receptacle or representative, which is transferred to it by the people (in the case of Locke). A Representative system is based on a social compact to secure freedom of property as the basic right of human beings, such that society is established for the protection of property through

---

[29] Ibid., 158.
[30] Ibid., 170.
[31] SC, Book III, Ch. XV.
[32] SC, Book I, Ch. VIII.

formal equality. For Locke equality appears only formal or free before the law, because all have the right to be free to dispose of the property freely. This formal quality tends to sidestep the social reality of inequality of property and exploitation, which is incompatible with freedom.

The formal quality, which tends to political or moral inequality, depends on a bad convention, which is established by the consent of people, yet with authorization of different privileges.[33] In Rousseau's account, the origin of society and laws in the mask of benevolence provides new fetters to the weak and new forces to the rich. It destroyed natural freedom through competition and rivalry while having "the hidden desire to profit at the expenses of others" by establishing the law of property and inequality. "All these evils are the first effect of property and the inseparable consequence of nascent inequality."[34]

Unlike Locke's possessive individualism and formality of representative system, Rousseau's critique of social inequality and exploitation remains an undercurrent in his approach to popular sovereignty, general will, and economic justice. Sovereign is a commission, or employment, a mere executive organ, in which the rulers are mere officials of the people. Since the law is only the declaration of the general will. Rousseau argues that people cannot be represented in the legislative power but in the executive power. Those in the executive power are "not the masters of the people, but officers; people can establish and depose them when it pleases."[35]

This perspective implies Rousseau's critique of representative or parliamentary government through popular sovereignty in the sense of direct or participatory democracy. However, it cannot

---

[33] "*Second Discourse*," 101.
[34] Ibid., 156.
[35] SC, Book III, Ch. XVIII.

be identified with the Marxist position of abolition or withering away of the state, as Lucio Colletti speculates.[36]

What matters in Rousseau's popular-legislative position is to establish a city-state in the sense of republic through the social contract and general, which engenders people as state citizens in terms of "civil freedom and the proprietorship of everything he possesses."[37] To this is moral freedom added, while civil freedom is restrained by the general will. Pure democracy implies government without government, in other words, it refers to the removal of the government, a complete absence of domination (anarchy), which is identified as the final state of a classless society.

As Iring Fetscher writes correctly, "the Hobbesian State serves to produce security of the bourgeois ...for Rousseau freedom is reproduced for the human being who is transformed into a (State) citizen. What is at stake is the problem of legitimate order of domination (republic)...not loss of domination or limitation of domination as such."[38]

Rather, Rousseau's limitation can be seen in his lack of conceptual clarity in dealing with the independent existence of judiciary system or jurisdiction between the State and citizen as the third force.[39]

In the popular-legislative approach to the city-state, Rousseau is concerned with civil freedom and equality. No citizen should be so opulent in regard to wealth. Moderation is assumed "in goods and influence on the part of the upper classes," while "moderation in avarice and covetousness on the part of the lower classes."[40]

---

[36] Colletti, *From Rousseau to Lenin*, 184.
[37] SC, Book 1, Ch. VIII.
[38] Fetscher, *Rousseaus politische Philosophie*, 103.
[39] Ibid., 107.
[40] SC, Book II, Ch. XI.

In dealing with the progress of social inequality Rousseau finds it important to explicate the establishment of the law and the rights of property as the first stage in which the status of rich and poor was authorized; the institution of the magistracy as the second stage in which the status of powerful and weak was authorized; as the third and last stage legitimate power changes into arbitrary power in which the status of master and slave was authorized as the last degree of inequality. New revolution dissolves the government by bringing it closer to the legitimate institution.[41]

In *Social Contract* Rousseau argues that "to renounce one's freedom is to renounce one's status as a man, the rights of humanity, and even its duties."[42] The natural right precedes civil society, while the latter presupposes the natural right and confirms it as civil liberty through people's consent in the social contract and general will imbued with popular sovereignty.

What strikes in Rousseau's analysis of the relationship between the state of nature and the social origin of inequality can be seen in his attempt to restore natural liberty and equality through social contract reasoning and general will; it culminates in his construction of civil society and republican democracy.

General Will, Citizen, and Solidarity Principle

In the famous opening of Book I, chapter 1 of the *Social Contract*, we read: "Man was/is born free, and everywhere he is in chains." This position implies a revolutionary impulse against all existing institutions and social progress, while at the same time

---

[41] "*Second Discourse*," 172.
[42] SC, Book I, Ch. IV.

he maintains that "the social order is a sacred right that serves as a basis for all the others."[43]

In a shift from natural freedom to the slavery of the civilized society at an evolutionary scale, Rousseau is concerned with the elaboration of social order as a sacred right through a social contract based on principles of political right and freedom.

Individual freedom cannot be properly understood without the general will by which to sustain the city-state. It is in a positive law that freedom is ensured as freedom; the latter establishes and guarantees the law. Rousseau holds that *"each of us puts his person and all his power in common under the supreme direction of the general will, and in a body, we receive each member as an indivisible part of the whole."*[44]

In taking part in general will, one stands for all (public person by their union more than the sum of every individual), while all stand for one. The individual of all completely transfers the rights to the community as such, as the public person by virtue of the consent.

If social contract transfers the total alienation of each associate with all his rights to the whole community, should it imply violating the inalienable rights of the individual, resulting in totalitarian direction as seen in Hobbes? Rousseau finds a flaw in an idea of "the inalienable rights," because "if some rights were left to private individuals…the association would necessarily become tyrannical or ineffectual?"[45]

He seeks to find a proper relation between the individual and the community under the supreme direction of the general will. This act of association produces a moral and collective body, which now takes the name of City, Republic, or body

---

[43] SC, Book I, Ch. 1.
[44] SC, Book I, Ch. VI.
[45] Ibid.

politic or State. When passive, it is Sovereign, but when active, it is Power.[46]

Sovereignty, which is an attribute of the entire body politic, is represented by a moral and collective body in the assembly rather than any individual or group or the sum of every individual. A Republic is governed by an assembly in which citizen has a right to vote because the general will is in the common interest of the majority.[47]

The exercise of political power by individual leaders must be subordinated to the freely expressed will of the people as sovereign. The general will thus presupposes an egalitarian community, which is enacted by vote and law affecting every citizen equally. "The law is a public, solemn act of the general will, and since everyone has subjected himself to this will through the fundamental compact."[48]

The logic of the general will for the common good or the principle of political right transforms the traditional concept of the common good into popular sovereignty based on people's consent. Thus, every legitimate government is republican as ruled by laws.[49]

This perspective distinguishes a citizen from a mere bourgeois by virtue of the Republic in the embodiment of the general will. Individuals are united in the state or as sovereign in their own rights as the people; they are citizens by sharing in the sovereignty as well as subjects to the laws of the state.[50]

Rousseau distinguished political economy or public economy (called government) from the supreme authority (called sovereignty). The body politic is a moral being with a general will

---

[46] Ibid.
[47] SC, Book IV, Ch. III.
[48] SC, "Geneva Manuscript," Book II, Ch. IV.
[49] SC, Bk. II, Ch. VI.
[50] Barth, "Rousseau," in *Protestant Theology*, 175.

that tends toward the preservation and welfare of the whole and of each part. It is not supposed to act in a way detrimental to the subjects, but only in their favor through freedom, human rights, and property rights. The citizen is subordinated to a sovereign for the sake of generality. General will in favor of the common good is "the source and supplement of all the laws."[51] General will, based on common interest, is greatly differentiated from the will of all, which considers private interest, "only a sum of private wills."[52]

Virtue or patriotism is based on the conformity of the private will to the general will which makes virtue reign.[53] The duty in following the rules and laws set aside the self-interest in favor of the society which makes duty and virtue come together. Rousseau focuses on the significance of the general will and its lawful embodiment in which duty and virtue become effective with regard to the disadvantaged.

He establishes the general will as the first principle of public economy, supporting the public economy as justice for all. It "especially [protects] the poor against the tyranny of the rich."[54] For Rousseau, "it is, therefore, one of the government's most important tasks to prevent extreme inequality of wealth, not by taking treasures away from those who possess them, but by removing the means of accumulating them from everyone; nor by building poorhouse, but by protecting citizens from becoming poor."[55]

Rousseau furthers: "these are the most obvious causes of opulence and indigence, of the substitution of private interest for the public interest, of the mutual hate of citizens, of their indifference to the common cause, of the corruption of the

---

[51] "Discourse on Political Economy," SC, 216.
[52] SC, Bk. II, Ch. III.
[53] Ibid., 217.
[54] Ibid., 221.
[55] Ibid., 221-2.

people, and of the weakening of all the mechanisms of the government."⁵⁶

"Nothing is more dangerous than the influence of private interests on public affairs... either luxury is the result of wealth, or it makes wealth necessary. It corrupts both rich and poor, the one by possessing, the other by coveting. It sells out the homeland to indolence and vanity; it deprives the State of all of its citizens by enslaving some of them to others and all of them to opinion."⁵⁷

Rousseau's argument from public affairs over private interest is characteristic of civil society and economic justice. This principle of solidarity reinforces the distributive justice among members, which characterizes the common good underlying the relation between the individual and the community in a more egalitarian manner.

In fact, Rousseau does not deduce the state or civil society from the abstract principles of liberty and equality of the individual, but from the general will imbued with the solidarity principle; he cuts across Hegel's assumption of the general will as the sum or common element of the individual will. Hegel's critique of Rousseau and Kant deserves attention.

1. A Critical Reflection: Hegel and Political Philosophy

For Hegel, philosophy is not concerned with the instruction of the world about what it ought to be, but it is reality as reflected and apprehended in its concept. Its critical function consists in correcting the employment of philosophy for political action in a false, ideological manner; but it does not direct against the institution of the state, nor does it present any guideline for revolutionizing praxis. The theory has an *ex post facto* (retroactive

---

⁵⁶ Ibid., 222.
⁵⁷ SC, Bk. III, Ch. IV.

force or effect) character in relation to praxis. But it is not always consistent, because he grants the critical role for philosophy to prepare for a revolutionizing praxis during his Frankfurt period.[58]

What matters in his political philosophy is to transform or transfer the classical concept of the polis to the state with the establishment of authority and power over the citizens. His political philosophy, despite its connection with Thomas Hobbes, takes issue with the political theory of social contract, especially Kant and Rousseau.

According to Hegel, the Kantian doctrine of the right maintains that "the highest factor is a limitation of my freedom or caprice, in order that it may be able to subsist alongside every other individual's caprice in accordance with a universal law."[59]

The definition of right in the Kantian sense, Hegel holds, undertakes the view of Rousseau. In the tradition of Kant and Rousseau, Hegel holds, there is neither the absolute and rational will nor the true spirit; rather "the will and spirit of the particular individual in their peculiar caprice are the substantive and primary basis."[60]

Hegel rejects the principle of caprice as a mere external and formal because the latter is devoid of the universal or the speculative thought in the dialectical method. In Hegel's account, Rousseau's contribution can be seen in his search for the general will as the principle of the state. Unfortunately, Rousseau comprehends "the will only in a determinate form as the individual will," by regarding "the universal will not as the absolutely rational element in the will, but only as a "general" will."[61]

---

[58] Habermas, *Theory and Practice*, 179-80.
[59] Hegel, *Philosophy of Right*, para. 29.
[60] Ibid.
[61] Ibid., para. 258.

Hegel argues that Rousseau sees the general will as proceeding out of the individual will in its caprice. Such perspective has a detrimental consequence because Rousseau reduces the union of individuals in the state to a contract; something based on the arbitrary wills of all individuals, their opinion, and their capriciously given express consent. Universal will is not regarded as the absolute reasonable will, but only as the common will; "it proceeds out of the individual will as conscious. Thus, the union of individuals in a state becomes a contract, which is based upon caprice, opinion, and optional, explicit consent." According to Hegel, Rousseau "destroy[s] the absolutely divine, and its absolute authority and majesty."[62]

Hegel is convinced that the civil society is fraught with conflict and antagonism in the sense that everyone is in the state of war against everyone else (*bellum omnium contra omnes*), but the state as a moral universe is rational and final, and the rule of the law is the adequate form of regulating social contradiction within modern society; it also safeguards each individual and transforms the modern society into a rational society.[63] Social contract philosophy is wrongly assumed because the state and society in the context of the contract is made to be the arbitrariness in governing private interests.[64]

Accordingly, such an experiment of social contract theory came to the maximum frightfulness and terror in the context of the French Revolution. Hegel's critique of Rousseau can be seen in this regard because the latter turns "the will and the spirit of the particular individual in his particular caprice" into "the substantive and primary basis" for society.[65]

---

[62] Ibid.
[63] Marcuse, *Reason and Revolution*, 182-3.
[64] Ibid., 185.
[65] Hegel, *Philosophy of Rights*, para. 29.

Rousseau and Kant in Response

In effect, Rousseau does not equate general will with the will of all as only a sum of private wills based on a public decision, which considers private interest. In the differentiation of the general will from the will of all, general will considers only the common interest and is always right and inalienable, tending to a public utility. "But it does not follow that the people's deliberations always have the same rectitude."[66]

Rousseau bases morality on the purity of the will, seeing its realization in the general will in the public life through the social contract and people's consent for common good. A social contract is built on individual freedom as a basic natural right, but the social contract is seen in bringing all the rights of each individual down to the whole community for the principle of solidarity.

The science of the legislator or maxims of politics is distinguished from the idea of the civil state. It is concerned with the actual friction between the general will and the will of the citizens in actual political life in regard to each specific circumstance and concrete situation.

In the perfect legislation, according to Rousseau, the private or individual will should be null; the corporate will becomes very subordinate; the general will becomes dominant and sovereign in ruling all the others.[67]

In the maxims of politics, Rousseau shows his preference for the ancient republican regime in ancient polis or city-states in which the friction or contradiction becomes less in the relationship between private interests and the common interest. Thus "the will of the people or the sovereign will, which is general

---

[66] SC, Bk. II, Ch. III.
[67] SC, Bk. III, Ch. II.

both in relation to the State considered as a whole and in relation to the government considered as part of that whole."[68]

Rousseau's preference for ancient political practice in the republican polis is differentiated from the political tradition of Hobbes and Hegel who tend to favor the authority of the state in regulating an expansionist commercial society of the middle class.

Rousseau's most important concept of general will comes to the picture in reference to popular sovereignty against tyranny. Under the supreme direction of the general will, his principle of political right is defined in terms of the idea of a civil state. What the individual gains here is "civil freedom and the proprietorship of everything he possesses... [the] civil freedom...is limited by the general will; and between possession, which is only the effect of force or the right of the first occupant, and property, which can only be based on a positive title. To the foregoing acquisitions of the civil state could be added moral freedom, which alone makes man truly the master of himself...and obedience to the law one has prescribed for oneself is freedom."[69]

Hegel's unqualified critique of Rousseau is not based on his meticulous reading of Rousseau's writings, but rather it is undertaken in his assessment of the logical consequence from the French Revolution upon the principle of Rousseau.

If Hegel blames Kant who is committed to empty formalism by purchasing radical autonomy at the cost of emptiness, he completely sidesteps Kant's political theory in connection with Rousseau.

Rousseau is distinguished from those advocates for the "pursuit of happiness" in unregulated and unfettered property rights. In his view, it is clear that private property is a sacred

---

[68] Ibid.
[69] SC, Bk. I, Ch. VIII.

individual right in a limited sense, morally justifiable with the theory of the social contract under the principle of the general will and solidarity with the poor. He is rather critical of an unlimited property right which would be the source and the means of exploitation and unfreedom.[70]

If Rousseau regards modernity and progress to be decadence and corruption, Hegel has confidence in the development of reason, in which the modern state becomes the symbol of reconciliation between an individual's need in multiplication and the universal through the social division of labor and co-operation and rationalization.

Hegel: Civil Society, State, and Democracy

Hegel articulates civil society as "a set of economic relations between individuals."[71] Here, a system of change satisfies, multiplying, and fulfilling the needs of the individual through division of labor, exchange, and rationalization; he takes sides with modern bourgeois economics such as James Steuart (1707-1780) and Adam Smith (1723-1790).

Hegel does not sidestep a detrimental reality of civil society which is characterized by a crisis of overproduction and the under-privileged. "It hence becomes apparent that despite an excess of wealth civil society is not rich enough, i. e. its own resources are insufficient to check excessive poverty and the creation of a penurious rabble"[72]

In civil society accumulation of wealth takes place, whereas impoverishment increases on the part of the working class. This refers to blind reality or anarchy of political economy in civil

---

[70] Macpherson, *The Life and Times of Liberal Democracy*, 16.
[71] Taylor, *Hegel*, 432.
[72] Hegel, *Philosophy of Right*, para. 245.

society, the problem of which is to be overcome in a state. Civil society is fraught with crisis, indignation, and alienation, but it is still guided by the "invisible hand" (Adam Smith) in serving as the instrument of the cunning of reason.[73]

According to Hegel, it is in the modern State that the civil society is incorporated, thus the State can be seen as a realization of rational necessity or self-articulation of the Idea, thus "the highest embodiment of *Sittlichkeit;*"[74] it is built upon the monarchy because ancient Greek *Sittlichkiet* was lost forever through progress and bourgeois civil society. It can be undertaken in terms of a representative monarch as served by bureaucrats.[75]

This refers to the totalitarian or better authoritarian side in Hegel's political philosophy because of its function to transcend the antagonistic contradiction of civil society. It is in the state that the perfect unity between the individual and the universal occurs while preserving and satisfying the genuine interest of the individual.

Given this, there is an affinity between Hegel and Hobbes, since the latter does not concern which form the sovereign state would assume either in democracy, oligarchy, or limited monarchy, if its authority is asserted in relation with other states as well as its citizen.

The universal (the state) as the objective reality must be imposed upon the particulars (civil society). In the government of discipline, Hegel elevates the state above civil society, which engenders the detrimental effect of contradiction and

---

[73] Taylor, *Hegel*, 433.
[74] Ibid., 428.
[75] Ibid., 443.

antagonism with the society; thus the sovereign state shapes itself as a disciplinary state.[76]

Hegel's political philosophy is of the reactionary profile, as seen in his pessimism on the English Reform Bill for the power of parliament weakening the monarchy. As the result of the July Revolution (1830), the Bourbons in France were overthrown and voting rights were undertaken in a democratic manner, and such electoral reform in England was in a heated discussion and was imminent for the strengthening of parliament.

Against the English Reform Bill, Hegel just before his death (1831) entails a severe critique of the bill and safeguards the authority and power of the monarchy by warning that the power of the people would mislead by "seeking its strength in the people and bringing about a revolution instead of a reform."[77]

Individual freedom in Hegel's system is overshadowed by the authority of the state vested in the universal for substantial power, as it comes to the course of contradiction, compulsion, and antagonism in the civil society. The State has its content in the universal spirit, which exists in art, religion, and philosophy in the form of pure free thought.[78]

The State exists in the development of world history and is actualized in "an unfolding of the spirit's self-consciousness and freedom." The State implies "the exhibition and actualization of the universal spirit."[79] The world mind, the unfathomable God materializes itself, striving to realize freedom and to be institutionalized only in the state. The right of the state is subordinated to that of the world mind and universal history.[80]

---

[76] Marcuse, *Reason and Revolution*, 172-5.
[77] Habermas, *Theory and Practice*, 189.
[78] Hegel, *Philosophy of Right*, para. 341.
[79] Ibid., para. 342.
[80] Taylor, *Hegel*, 134-5.

The main historical stages such as the Oriental (despotism), the Greco-Roman (democracy and aristocracy), and the German-Christian (monarchy) are schematized in the development of freedom, and the German nations in the monarchy as the source of real freedom were the first to attain the freedom of the mind as culminating in German Reformation with the principle of subjectivity through Christian freedom and human equality. It is expressed and embodied in the constitutional monarchy as "the consummation of the realization of freedom."[81]

Seen in this perspective, a universal principle of history makes use of individuals as its tool or agents of the world mind to serve universal interest concerning a higher purpose of freedom for a common good. Thus, history is necessarily universal history which unfolds itself through individual figures and cultural wholes.[82] Hegel turns away from a fundamental principle of the modern state, liberty, and universal direct suffrage, which is critiqued as an "atomistic and abstract point of view," because it underwrites the state as aggregate of individuals in the "elementary, irrational, barbarous and frightful" sense.[83]

Hegel's problem is seen in presenting what *is* as the *essence* of the state. Hegel's claim—the rational is actual—is contradicted precisely by an irrational actuality. Hegel does not search for an adequate actualization of the being-for-itself of public affairs, although Hegel does not "fail to note how pitiful and full of contradiction"[84] public affairs are. Hegel's logic of the universal and its content in various forms becomes a foundation for his metaphysical illusion of the state.

---

[81] Marcuse, *Reason and Revolution*, 237; 245.
[82] Ibid., 229-30.
[83] Hegel, *Philosophy of Right*, para. 303.
[84] Ibid., 58.

The right of the state is subordinate to the world spirit in universal history. In his conception of the world spirit, Hegel argues that the state has its real content in universal history, in which the particulars are "the unconscious tools and organs of the world-spirit."[85]

In Marx' critique of Hegel, Marx defends democracy with universal suffrage for the solution of the split between political society and civil society in agreement with the modern French: "In a true democracy the *political state disappears.*"[86]

It is not the constitution that creates the people, but the people create the constitution. "Democracy relates to all other forms of the state as their Old Testament. Man does not exist because of the law but rather the law exists for the good of man. Democracy is *human existence,* while in the other political forms man has only *legal* existence."[87]

In fact, Marx's idea of democracy may be implicated in Hegel's notion of freedom. Individual self-actualization is socially constructed in the sphere of ethical life along with the social institutional structures toward a common good. The sphere of ethical life embodies different forms of reciprocal recognition. Hegel's doctrine of freedom in an institutional-theoretical framework is of sociological relevance (Durkheim), becoming relevant to the political philosophy of the present.[88]

---

[85] Hegel, *Philosophy of Right*, para. 344.
[86] Marx, Critique of Hegel's *Philosophy of Right*, 32.
[87] Ibid., 31.
[88] Honneth, *The I in We*, 30.

Dialectical Thinking and Teleology

In fact, Hegel's philosophy of the state is grounded in his dialectical logic, into which he incorporates Aristotle's logic of relation between potentiality and the actuality, or the relation of matter and form (or its combination as hylomorphism).[89] Here, the development scheme is seen in potentiality in the germ for its constant actualization; a potentiality strives to realize itself in the actual course of development in the process of which Hegel regards a general law of history.

His dialectical view of history is grounded in the philosophy of the Enlightenment in its articulation of the human path in the rising middle class to progress, development, and maturity. Reason, as the sovereign of the world, is manifest in nature and comes to realization in history through the human mind as its driving force. The essence of the latter is freedom and realizes itself in the progress of the self-consciousness of freedom, which goes through interests, needs, and life, and battles among individuals toward the progress of historical reason.

If historical change implies development, there exists a latent destiny in the principle of development; a potentiality strives to realize itself through the self-conscious exercise of mastery over the whole process. The thinking subject is entitled to produce itself,

---

[89] Taylor, *Hegel*, 82. According to Aristotle, nature as a principle of change and alteration is twofold; nature as matter, while nature as form (or end). Everything else is for the end. In the process of becoming, *entelecheia* implies a continuous process of change or being-at-work in reference to the end *(energia)*. There is a relation between potentiality (matter; for instance, uncarved piece of wood as potential status) and actuality (a form; actual status or substance). Although the action is an actuality, incomplete actions are also the potentiality for further actions. "Hot in actuality, cold in potentiality.... the actuality of the potential, *qua* potential, is change." "Physics," Book II. Ch. 8, in *A New Aristotle Reader*, 112; 108.

expanding itself actually to what it always was potentially, while transforming it into a new condition. This process is manifested in history and progressed to real universality in the state, which is generated and maintained by reason and morality.[90]

In the scheme of world history, Hegel's German-centric position is unveiled in subordinating the Oriental despotism and the Geek and Roman world (democracy and aristocracy) embedded with the institution of slavery to the German nations under the influence of Protestant Christianity; it is in the German nations with a constitutional monarchy, that is consummated as the realization of freedom at the historical scheme of development.[91]

Nonetheless, it is difficult to credit Hegel as recommending Prussia as the fullest realization of the modern state against the civil society or Nazi's reclaim for the total state. In Hegel's deified State the civil society is ruled, while the direct totalitarian rule over the whole occurs in the fascist form; a civil society under Fascism rules the State, in terms of the totalitarian leadership of civil society.[92]

Against this, Hegel's notion of the State is based on government in terms of the standards of critical reason as well as universally valid law safeguarding the interests of every individual,[93] which replaces the Greek model of the polis. The State in the universe is the embodiment of concrete freedom and represents the identity between the general and particular will in terms of its authority for duty and obligation to citizens as well as recognition of their rights.[94]

---

[90] Ibid., 239-40.
[91] Marcuse, *Reason and Revolution*, 235; 237.
[92] Taylor, *Hegel*, 452; Marcuse, *Reason and Revolution*, 216.
[93] Marcuse, *Reason and Revolution*, 180-1.
[94] Ibid., 203.

2. Rousseau, General Will, and Economic Justice

Rousseau runs counter to Hegelian dialectical direction. But it can be argued whether Rousseau was a totalitarian thinker. In Book II, chapter IV, we read: "If the State or the City is only a moral person whose life consists in the union of its members, it must have a universal, compulsory force to move and arrange each part in the manner best suited to the whole."

If we discern a "totalitarian" element in this statement, the social compact provides the body politic with absolute power over all its members as directed by the general will. However, Rousseau does not deal with an act of the sovereign in terms of an order or a command given by a master to a slave, but he acknowledges a legitimate convention as a social contract between the body of the State and each of its members in an equitable, useful, and solid manner. Subjects are subordinated to such conventions by obeying their own will only: 'each to all and all to each.'[95] "Thus a citizen owes the State all the services he can render it, and the sovereign, for its part, cannot burden the subjects with any chain that is useless to the community."[96]

Rousseau's democratic republicanism reemploys social contract theory to construct and feature the general will, which proceeds from the alienation of the agreement among individual wills. The definition of sovereign power is framed in the popular, democratic sense, because "properly understood, all of these clauses [of the social contract] come down to a single one, namely the total alienation of each associate, with all his rights, to the whole community."[97]

One could easily read this position in a totalitarian manner. But on the other hand, when framed differently, one can hear

---

[95] SC, "Geneva Manuscript," Bk. I, Ch. VI.
[96] Ibid.
[97] Ibid., Bk. 1, Ch. 6.

echoes of an outline pushing toward democratic socialism, which is grounded in the liberty, private property, and solidarity principle. Citizens as political, moral subjects become crucial in taking civil initiative and movement for human rights, common good, and justice in civil society, which is not subsumed under a Hobbesian notion of immortal god on earth.

The State is built on general will and entails universal, compulsory force through people's consent and universal suffrage, while the State must be in service of the citizens' lives and rights. Civil society is not merely conflated with economic society beset by social strife and contradiction, but it is conceptualized in the sense of general will over against sum of private will. It becomes a foundation for the political society (the State), which ensures the life of citizens in terms of liberty, property, and solidarity. The point of departure is grounded on popular sovereignty and consent which is articulated in a social contract bound to the general will. Political society has its meaning in securing and fulfilling civil society.

Rousseau's concept of the civil state is featured as republican democracy, especially in promoting solidarity with the poor. If a law has been enacted by the legislative for public force and consented to by the vote of the people, it is binding on all. His democratic notion of civil society is differentiated from Hegel's synthesis of modern sovereignty with capitalist economic society; in his capitalist sovereignty, the state has the higher power and external authority as the metaphysical instance to which the particular interest of individuals is subordinate.

Freedom, Revolution, and Distributive Justice

What is crucial in Rousseau's thought is the great principle according to which "nature made man happy and good," "but society depraves him and makes him miserable."[98] If the Greek antiquity emphasized the significance of political order within which human beings becomes virtuous, Rousseau takes into account the state of nature by stressing freedom. In the *Social Contract* political society must protect civil liberty which is a substitute for the natural liberty previously in the state of nature.[99]

To the extent that the history of society passes through a stage of legitimate government under law, it terminates in the most extreme inequality as compared to "a war of all against all." In the *Second Discourse* Rousseau analyzes the progress of inequality in different courses. Law and the right of property were established because the status of rich and poor was authorized in the first stage. The institution of the magistracy or government belongs to the second stage in which the status of the power and the weak was established. The final stage refers to the fact that legitimate power is transformed into arbitrary power, in which the status of master and slave was authorized as the last degree of inequality. In the final stage, a new revolution would "dissolve the government altogether or bring it closer to its legitimate institution."[100]

If the magistracy and its rights are destroyed, "the magistrates would immediately cease to be legitimate." Then "the people would no longer be bound to obey them." Not the magistrate

---

[98] SC, 7.
[99] SC, Bk. I, Ch. VI-VIII. Rousseau, *The First and Second Discourses*, 21; 24.
[100] "*Second Discourse*," 172.

"but the law ...had constituted the essence of the State," therefore, "everyone would return by right to his natural freedom."[101]

The basic consistency between the *Social Contract* and the *Second Discourse* can be shown in this right to just revolution. However, Rousseau is highly skeptical of violent revolutions, which can be seen in politics of terror by Maximilian Robespierre. *Social Contract* does not imply the execution of the general will through the reign of terror. Instead, it supports civil freedom and the proprietorship of everything under the law. Moral freedom is added to the acquisition of the civil state.[102]

This perspective runs counter to Hegel who does not appreciate revolution as ushering to the modern State; Hegel was influenced under reform by the Napoleonic conquest, having an expectation for the Crown Prince, the future Fredrick William IV with outspoken reactionary politics, along with Bismarck's politics of nationalism.[103]

In natural liberty, according to Rousseau, a human being is threatened by survival of the fittest in which the strong is free to dominate the weak. Under civil liberty, humankind is free as each citizen pledges to protect the rights and liberties of all through the law. Without the right of community for all, there would be neither solidarity in the social bond nor real force in the exercise of sovereignty.[104]

Morality springs from a social contract, and the society secures moral life and solidarity with the poor and for the public good of the people. Rousseau locates *suum cuique* ("to each, his own" or "may all get their due") within private property and civil freedom which are the bases of the community. The

---

[101] Ibid., 169-70.
[102] SC, Bk. I, Ch. IX.
[103] Taylor, *Hegel*, 454.
[104] SC, "Geneva Manuscript," Bk. I, Ch, III.

principle of *suum cuique* "serves as the basis of all right of property."[105]

The Latin phrase *suum cuique* relates to an ancient Greek principle of justice in Plato's *Republic* (4. 433a). There is "justice when everyone minds his own business and refrains from meddling in others' affairs." It is necessary for everyone to do according to his/her abilities and capabilities in serving the country and the society as a whole. Therefore, everyone should receive his/her own not to be deprived of his/her own rights and property.

Rousseau argues that "the true principles of the just and unjust must, therefore, be sought in the fundamental and universal law of the greatest good of all, and not in the private relations between one and another."[106]

Rousseau comprehends *suum cuique* by taking private property and civil freedom as the basis of the community for the common good along with the general will. He further considers freedom and distributive justice in the protection of the poor in civil society and stands for a participatory theory of democracy in terms of universal suffrage; his position remains grounded in legal authority and execution through *suum cuique*.

What constitutes the common good consists of two principles: freedom and equality. Together with freedom of citizens, Rousseau defends equality, because "with regard to wealth, no citizen should be so opulent that he can buy another, and none so poor that he is constrained to sell himself." This principle of solidarity "presumes moderation in goods and influence on the part of the upper classes and moderation in avarice and covetousness on the part of the lower classes."[107]

---

[105] Ibid. Bk. II, Ch. IV.
[106] Ibid.
[107] SC, Bk. II, Ch. XI.

It is important for Rousseau to comprehend the principle of *suum cuique* in terms of the solidarity principle. Rousseau remains realistic, because "in the strict sense of the term, a true democracy has never existed and never will exist." "If there were a people of Gods, it would govern itself democratically. Such a perfect government is not suited to me."[108]

Rousseau's preference for the ancient republican polis is based on patriotism and virtue or the city-state in Sparta and early republican Rome.[109] He prefers a small community, a Greek polis in contrast to the larger State. Justice becomes possible when everyone minds his/her own business, according to his/her abilities and capabilities. Also, everyone should receive his/her own (rights), not be deprived of his/her own right and property.

Rousseau's Critique of Slavery and Hugo Grotius

Rousseau runs counter to Aristotle, who unfolded the principle of *suum cuique* in a teleological way of thinking; justice is to fit persons to the roles that deserve; the role enables a person to realize his/her nature. Giving a person his/her due implies giving him/her the office and honor which deserve him/her according to his/her nature. Teleological interpretation of the *suum cuique* undermines the principle of freedom to choose while justifying the system of slavery by nature.

For Aristotle, the just system of slavery is met with two conditions: necessary and natural. Since the polis requires a division of labor, slavery looks after the household during the

---

[108] SC, Bk. III, Ch. IV.
[109] For Rousseau, however, "Athens was not, in fact, a democracy, but a highly tyrannical aristocracy, governed by learned men and orators." "Political Economy," SC, 213.

activity of the citizens in the assembly for the common good. Furthermore, slavery is natural by birth to perform the role. A slave, by nature, fits its nature to be ruled by a master.[110]

Contrary to Aristotle, Rousseau argues that force does not produce right. The right of the strongest in the state of nature has degenerated into a state of war and such a right cannot produce legitimate obligation which is rationally binding by conscience. "Might does not make right."[111] Likewise, slavery cannot be natural nor a legitimate convention, "since no man has any natural authority."[112] Slavery does not belong to human nature and natural freedom.

France was heavily involved in the slavery trade (1721-30) in terms of Code Noir (1684; applied to the Black slaves in the colonies); Nantes was the major slaving port; French ships departed to Africa bringing the enslaved Africans to plantations in the Americas and the Caribbean. Despite the decree of the abolition of slavery (1794) through the French revolution, slave trading illegally continued between 1818 and 1831.

Hugo Grotius (1583-1645), a famous Dutch jurist and a father of international law stayed in Paris until 1631 after his escape from imprisonment (1621) under the patronage of Louis XIII). He published his masterpiece *De Jure Belli ac Pacis* (1625); *On the Law of War and Peace (in three books)* and proposed a general theory of law that would restrain and regulate war between various independent powers, including states.

In 1604 Grotius was employed by the Dutch East India Company and involved in legal controversy arising from Dutch capture of Portuguese ships in the Indian Ocean. He defended the legality of the Dutch seizure of the Portuguese ships on the

---

[110] Sandel, *Justice*, 202-3.
[111] SC, Bk. I, Ch. IV. 49.
[112] Ibid.

basis of Dutch natural law right against the Portuguese monopoly claim.[113]

In his rationalist position, seen within the Thomist tradition, the natural laws apply to all rational and social beings bound to the law of nature, if they are rational and social. The natural laws must be independent of the region and be applied to all people regardless of their religious beliefs (as if there is no God) "There is no God, or that the affairs of men are of no concern to Him."[114]

Thus, international society should be governed by common laws, actual laws, and mutual consent to enforce the laws; it finds concrete expression in the Peace of Westphalia (1648), putting end to the Thirty Year's War. European judiciary theory affirms that no state violates borders and interferes in the domestic affairs of the sovereign states. Under certain circumstances, war is justifiable in terms of self-defense, reparation of injury, and punishment.

Grotius conceptualizes social contract reasoning, in which human political authority derives fundamentally from the consent of the governed,[115] but he rejects the idea of the sovereignty of the people; he reinforces an idea of one's enslavement for private ownership of the ruler.

On the contrary, Rousseau counters that Grotius "spares no pains to rob the people of all their rights and invest king with them."[116]

The power of the State is, according to Grotius, based on such a result of the collective agreement that individual powers and rights are transferred to the ruler. It justifies slavery, following in Aristotle's reasoning of slaves by nature.[117]

---

[113] Grotius, *On the Law of War and Peace*, XVI.
[114] Ibid., XXV. Prol. 4.
[115] Ibid., Prol. 5.
[116] SC, II. 2.
[117] Grotius, *On the Law of War and Peace*, XXII.

For him, sovereignty is "that power... whose actions are not subject to the legal control of another."[118] It can be kept in view that those who hold sovereignty are necessarily superior to all others, implying that slavery and colony are compatible with a just society. The efficacy of the colony is established as a form of slavery and terror through the critical issue of just war as an instrument of right, even compatible with God's will. Things are necessary to attain in wars that are permissible.[119]

The equality of all civilized states was notably applied to the right to wage war (the taking of life) to support colonial expansion. To kill or to conclude peace was recognized as one of the preeminent functions of any state, which has the right of enslaving the loser.

However, Rousseau argues against Grotius' defense of monarch in which a private individual can enslave him/herself to a master. He takes issue with Grotius' justification of slavery (along with Aristotle), which derives from war. In Grotius' rationalization of slavery, Rousseau argues, "as the victor has the right to kill the vanquished, the latter can buy back his life at the cost of his freedom—a convention all the more legitimate in that it is profitable for both of them."[120]

Against this rationalization of slavery in defeated war, Rousseau maintains that war is a relation between State and State, such that private individuals become enemies, by accident, as soldiers in a war rather than as citizens. "Even in the midst of war, a just prince 'respects the person and goods of private individuals,' although taking away "everything in an enemy country that belongs to the public."[121] "With regard to the right

---

[118] Ibid., I. 3;7. 1
[119] Ibid., III. 1. 2.
[120] SC, Bk. I, Ch. IV.
[121] Ibid.

of conquest," Rousseau holds, "the law of the strongest 'cannot establish the right to enslave them.'"[122]

In the critical analysis of the progress of European society, Rousseau characterizes "honor without virtue, reason without wisdom, and pleasure without happiness" as the spirit of that society.[123]

He illustrates a story of a single Hottentot from infancy taken by Van der Stel, governor of the Cape of Good Hope; he was raised according to the Christian religion and educated in the practice of European customs. With great hopes, the governor sent him to the Indies with a general commissioner, and he was employed there in the affairs of the company. After the death of the commissioner, he returned to the Cape and paid a visit to some of his Hottentot relatives. Then he decided to divest himself of his European finery by clothing himself in a sheepskin. He made a speech: "*I renounce also for my entire life the Christian religion; my resolution is to live and die in the religion, ways, and customs of my ancestors...*"[124]

Although Rousseau is not involved in analyzing European colonialism and the global trade system of mercantilism as a basis for inequality of the property, his social contract reasoning in the framework of general will is a promising project for ushering to postcolonial inquiry in dealing with public affairs.

---

[122] Ibid.
[123] "*Second Discourse*," 180.
[124] Rousseau's Notes of "*Second Discourse*," 225-6.

3. Theological Reflection: Natural Right and Sovereignty

In the theological context, it is Dietrich Bonhoeffer who calls attention to the principle of *suum cuique* in elaborating the Roman law dictum and the ancient Greek principle of justice for the significance of theological ethical direction. The "one's own" belongs to each and every person, while at the same time it is different and unequal in every case. If there is a right naturally given as an innate right, it is not to be destroyed by any "unnatural" right from without. "The principle of *suum cuique*," Bonhoeffer holds, "recognizes the priority of the rights which are implied in the natural over all other rights. But …it preserves the natural from arbitrary and revolutionary outbursts by pointing to the right which is due to the other man and which is just as much a natural right as is my own."[125] Bonhoeffer's concept of freedom includes the double side in that God's grace in Christ is free for humankind, while we are free for God. "God enters into creation and so creates freedom."[126]

The theological principle of freedom characterizes the dimension of the *suum cuique* in contrast to Aristotle's notion of a slave by nature. In Bonhoeffer's account, however, the principle of *suum cuique* entails limitations of applicability, because conflicts between rights are rooted in the natural. The principle overlooks the conflict of rights inherent in nature itself, thus it requires positive rights to intervene from outside nature.

Bonhoeffer comprehends naturally given right with due honor in connection with God the Creator, even in a world involved in conflict. God has created the individual in God's image and God guarantees the individual rights as recognized. A human being as the image of God means that he/she is free for the worship

---

[125] Bonhoeffer, *Ethics*, 151.
[126] Bonhoeffer, *Creation and Fall*, 63.

of God. "Freedom is not a quality a human being has; it is not an ability, a capacity, an attribute of being that may be deeply hidden in a person but can somehow be uncovered."[127]

Thus, Bonhoeffer reinterprets the principle of rights as the penultimate in the sense that Jesus Christ gives to each one's own through the Holy Spirit. The penultimate, a thing before the last, is determined by the last thing, the ultimate.[128] The relationship between these two dimensions has a reality in the reconciliation of Jesus Christ until the world is ripe for its ultimate. Hence "the eternal life, the new life, breaks in with ever greater power into the earthly and wins its space for itself within it."[129]

On the other hand, Bonhoeffer maintains that the principle of *suum cuique* considers the individual to enter into the world with its own natural right. He takes issue with teleological reasoning in which a natural right of the individual is subordinated only to the community in the promotion of social eudemonism (or utilitarianism) in the curtailment of all the rights of the individual; "the individual becomes only a means to an end in the service of the community. The happiness of the community takes precedence over the natural right of the individual."[130]

Given this, social eudemonism attacks the natural life of the individual, and its consequence by despotism leads to chaos through the destruction of all individual rights. In resistance to social eudemonism, it is necessary to consider that God has created the individual in God's image and God guarantees the individual rights as recognized through freedom. "The principle of *suum cuique* is the highest possible attainment of a reason

---

[127] Ibid.
[128] Ibid., 152.
[129] Ibid., 132.
[130] Ibid., 152.

which is in accord with reality and which, within the natural life, discerns the right which is given to the individual by God (of whom reason knows nothing."[131]

In other respects, it is Karl Barth who draws attention to Rousseau's political philosophy. Rousseau grounds sovereignty in the general will; representatives of the people should be merely agents of the people because the law consists only in the declaration of the general will.

In Barth's account, a parliamentary system based on universal suffrage and popular sovereignty would be a possible form of government to which Rousseau tends.[132] It can be true that Rousseau implies democratic government joined in confederations (*Social Contract*, Book 3, Ch. 15). His popular-legislative theory is differentiated from modern constitutional theory in which Hobbes conceptualizes the Sovereign as representative of the body politics *(Leviathan*, Part 1, Ch. 16 and part 2. Ch. 18). But Rousseau considers representative government in the people of Poland.

In his seminal article "The Christian Community and the Civil Community."[133] Barth is not reluctant to assert that his political ethics is in affinity with Rousseau for the line of Christian political thought and action. Barth shares in his affinity with Rousseau's conception of natural law. As Barth says, "[w]e bear no grudge against anyone who may have been reminded of Rousseau…We need not be ashamed of the affinity."[134]

Barth also confirms that the polis is in the kingdom of Jesus Christ, in which the Christian community is in an affinity with the civil communities of the free people, the democracy.

---

[131] Ibid., 153.
[132] Barth, "Rousseau," in *Protestant Theology*, 177.
[133] "The Christian Community and the Civil Community (1946)," in *Karl Barth: Theologian of Freedom*, 265-96.
[134] These 28, Ibid., 290.

The democratic State comes to terms with social justice in the economic sphere, because Barth encourages the church to focus on the lower and lost levels of human society. "The poor, the socially and economically weak and threatened, will always be the object of its primary and particular concern, and it will always insist on the State's special responsibility for these weaker members of society."[135] Democracy and equality are expressed in the principle of solidarity with the poor in the public affairs.

Conclusion

Rousseau reacts against Hobbes' negative anthropology and considers pity as a natural sentiment in moderating the love of oneself in each individual. Rousseau favors the maxim of natural goodness – "*Do what us good for you with the least possible harm to others*"—over against the sublime maxim of reasoned justice: *Do unto others as you would have them do unto you.*[136]

His ethical subjectivism abides in the law of heart (sympathy, compassion, and forgiveness). Education should be mainly concerned with eliminating the negative influence of society upon natural development and innate goodness. Nonetheless, Rousseau does not forget that in natural liberty, a human being is threatened by a survival of the fittest, and vulnerable to brutal forces.

At this juncture, such ethical subjectivism is not extreme but bound to universal moral standards or common good in a social contract. According to Rousseau, "[a]ll justice comes from God; He alone is its source…There is, without doubt, a universal justice for man emanating from reason alone and founded on the simple right of humanity; but to be acknowledged, this justice

---

[135] These 17, Ibid., 284.
[136] Rousseau, *Second Discourse*, 133.

must be reciprocal...Therefore, there must be conventions and laws to combine rights with duties and to bring justice back to its object."[137]

The common good founded upon political society is the place of the norm where the law of heart intersects with a moral theory. It refers to communitarian moral reasoning which stands under legal and rational dominion rather than ethical subjectivism. "The body politic is thus also a moral being that has a will; and this general will, which always tends toward the preservation and welfare of the whole and of each part, and which is the source of the laws, is...the rule of what is just and unjust."[138]

Morality is nurtured and constituted by democracy, liberty, and economic justice in which a concern for the poor plays a major role. Property without solidarity with the others would be empty, while property imbued with moral character would be meaningful for community and justice.

In today's debate, social contract theory finds its theoretical elaboration in Rawls' theory of justice as fairness. His theory of original position articulates the dimension of social justice in the economic distribution in a liberal, socialist direction, taking a step further in elevating the public concern with the disadvantaged in the tradition of Locke and Rousseau.

Rawls' central definition of justice means fairness for a constitutional democracy as an alternative to utilitarian doctrine, which cannot "provide a satisfactory account of the basic rights and liberties of citizens as free and equal persons, a requirement of absolutely first importance for an account of democratic institutions."[139]

---

[137] SC, "Geneva Manuscript," Bk. II, Ch. IV.
[138] SC, "Discourse on Political Economy," 212.
[139] Rawls, *A Theory of Justice*, XII.

In the tradition of a social contract and constitutional democracy, I find the conception of civil society to be an important regime for public theology to engage in. Along with common good and solidarity (or difference principle), recognition of the other in the sense of co-humanity becomes crucial in safeguarding civil society in the spheres of ethical life. The anti-colonial aspect in Rousseau's thought can be appropriated to shape public theology in its significance of incomplete project of modernity.

In this direction, it is of special significance to articulate Rousseau's political theory by expanding its modern revival in different ways of life and culture in democratic pluralistic societies. His idea of popular sovereignty can be enhanced to satisfy the moral standard of egalitarian universalism, and it should be reconciled with the liberal democratic idea of constitution.[140]

As Habermas writes, "Democracy and human rights form the universalist core of the constitutional state that emerged from the American and French Revolutions in different variants. This universalism still has its explosive power and vitality, not only in Third World countries and the Soviet bloc but also in European nations, where constitutional patriotism acquires new significance in the course of an identity transformation."[141]

Rousseau's republican democracy finds its philosophical culmination in the Kantian theory of hospitality in his critique of colonialism and cosmopolitan principle. This perspective can be dealt with in the next chapter.

---

[140] Habermas, *Between Naturalism and Religion*, 274.
[141] Habermas, *Between Facts and Norms*, 465.

Chapter 5
Cosmopolitan Principle

This chapter is a theological, philosophical study of Kant's appropriation of Stoic morality by extending universal reason and human dignity to the cosmopolitan principle and his ethic of hospitality. First, I begin with an argument for the existence of God in Kant's moral philosophy. Kant's appropriation of the Stoic principle comes into focus since it characterizes a historical dimension in Kant's philosophy with social-political significance; a theological interpretation is cast upon Kant's idea of radical evil, and Kant's limitations in his teleological consideration of history are critically renewed in terms of Husserl's theory of life-world.

Second, I examine his project of the cosmopolitan principle, which shows a universal historical aspect of Kant and his threshold to world civil society. His idea of perpetual peace is imbued with his critique of slavery and colonialism. Kant's cosmopolitan constitution and its theoretical contribution to United Nations can be discussed in view of several critical and constructive proposals.

Third, I scrutinize several critical arguments against Kant and clarify his own position, while improving on his limitations. Critical arguments against Kant can be seen in terms of theodicy and the Kantian philosophical system of justifying victims in the progress of historical development (Thomas McCarthy). I undertake a theonomous interpretation (in accordance with Paul

Tillich) of Kantian chiliastic-ethical formation, in which Kant would run in threshold to theology and religious socialism.

1. God, Morality, and Philosophy of History

Kant includes the practical side of the existence of God. With an emphasis on the categorical imperative, he acknowledges the unconditional validity of the ethical command. He derives a concept of God in terms of a lawgiver and a guarantor, in which Kant coordinates morality and happiness from the ethical standpoint. In dealing with the argument for the existence of God, Tillich is convinced that Kant would share with Augustine "the unconditional element in every encounter with reality"[1]

Kant shares a biblical notion of radical evil with Augustine while avoiding a notion of original sin in an act of sexual propagation. Kant's deontology contrasts with Thomas Aquinas' (1225-1274) teleology.

Here, evil is regarded as unrealized human potential in a naturalist, teleological framework. It is caused by a defect of the will, by failing to realize human potential; it refers to a lack of understanding of the good. The Thomist position is differentiated from Augustine's notion of evil as the privation of the good, or absence of God.

Thomist moral theology contrasts with Kantian philosophy of religion and radical evil. Kant is concerned with God's immanence as the symbol of human ideals within practical reason and freedom. Kant makes room for faith pertaining to our practical, moral lives. It refers to the practical function of faith, which engages with our free will or assent; we are bound to morality in our free act of faith.

---

[1] Tillich, *Systematic Theology* 1: 207.

Kant may share in Augustine's idea of original sin which remains innate in the sense of radical evil, whereas we are responsible for sinful action. Kant identifies God with the eternal source of practical reason, that is the God of sanctification in theological parlance. Faith is feasible only within the limits of reason. However, we are inclined by nature toward evil, which is equated with a will not fully good. Perverse will is the worst form of evil, which might be seen in self-love in Augustine's sense. Concupiscence in the general anthropological sense, more than in sexual terms, can be manifested in the perversity of evil (hubris), which is the privation of the good. Evil does not exist in and of itself.

Kant and the Philosophy of History

Eventually, Kant conceptualizes fundamental principles of the metaphysics of morals in terms of a priori practical reason in contrast to any empirical motives or inclination. In a universal history with a cosmopolitan intent (1784), he provides a broader field for developing duty ethics in a historical, social, and political frame of reference. He presents the combination of law and right with politics and makes it into a limiting condition of politics.

Kant's duty ethics cannot be adequately comprehended without the republican form of government, in which Kant's philosophy of history plays a significant role in elaborating the evolutionary history according to its end. Kant's moral philosophy is framed within a universal history with cosmopolitan vision; it characterizes the comprehensive dimension of his duty ethics in relation to the social theory of the right and justice in republican democracy and the cosmopolitan ethics of hospitality.

Moral Politics and Political Ethics

In Kant's moral philosophy, the reality of evil is not simply seen in the individual passion but is socially bound. A human individual as a social being, when he/she is among persons, mutually corrupts each other's predispositions; he/she makes one another evil through "envy, the lust for power, greed, and the malignant inclinations."[2]

Kant develops his political ethics in terms of a notion of a moral politician, who finds his/her duty to remedy defects of the constitution in the idea of reason; this model is contrasted with a political moralist, who "thwarts the purpose of bringing politics into the agreement with morals."[3]

To counteract the tempting forces, Kant proposes a social moral ideal as an ethico-civil, or an ethical commonwealth in contrast to a juridico-civil. This special and unique principle of union would be called a kingdom of virtue, and humans have a duty to promote such kingdom of virtue as the highest social good. This concept has a strong social-political component.

Kant's political philosophy is differentiated from the libertarian principle concerned with self-ownership as the end rather than as means to the welfare of others. He is not convinced of an unlimited right of self-possession and the libertarian principle of laissez-faire capitalism, but he concerns the right of those left behind and safety network, which is not at the disposal of possessive individualism.

To understand duty ethics and its significance of rights in a social, political context, it is substantial to investigate Kant's view of the Stoic virtue ethics and social contract theory (especially

---

[2] Kant, "Religion within the Limits of Reason Alone," in *Basic Writings of Kant*, 85.
[3] Kant, "To Eternal Peace," Ibid., 465.

in reference to Rousseau), which reinforces his philosophy of universal history with cosmopolitan intent and perpetual peace.

The Stoic Principle

The Stoic insight remains crucial in characterizing Kant's own development in its distinguished manner for his universal history. The doctrine of the Stoics was a religious-metaphysical doctrine and comprehends the idea of God as the First Cause or the universal Law of Nature. Reason is the foundation of both humanity and the universe; therefore, the goal of life is to live according to Reason, in other words, Nature. A cosmos is pervaded by the *Logos* as the divine Principle of order, which controls the universe. Human beings, despite their corruption, reflect the same rationality of God, and they are received into the seminal reason (*logos spermatikos*) of the Universe.

The Law of Nature requires human life in conformity with the harmonious course of Nature, and the moral and religious freedom of the dignity of reason is united with God. This perfection of the moral life is not disturbed by any external happenings in the world of sense (*apatheia*). This idea was seen as part of the Golden Age in the past and lost. It is again undertaken by Kant in a new era of modernity with a fresh beginning.

The Stoic perspective is not far removed from Aristotle, who conceptualizes virtue as the basis of our happiness. Moderation in the acquisition and use of external goods is recommended to be used ethically. For the Stoic, only virtue is unconditionally good, becoming the only component of happiness without recourse to external goods. This view does not strictly reject all other goods in all circumstances, which includes Aristotle's external goods.

Stoic happiness is much more democratic than Aristotelian aristocracy (underlying Thomas' aristocratic monarchy).

Everyone has the same moral character and can be equal and happy, sharing with one another the same rational mind of God. The duty of the will is to learn to discern this Law of Nature by which to achieve the control of the external desires of sense and the personality hidden in God.

This individualism correlates with universalism because humans as rational beings are fundamentally equal in a reflection of the universal reason of God. All people are equally called to the same knowledge of God and in their surrender to the Divine law of Nature, thus they are united by an ethical bond.[4] This refers to a distinctive feature of the Stoic idea of universal natural law and its citizenship of the world in the cosmopolitan vision.

Kant appreciates the Stoic idea of universal natural law, cosmopolitan vision, and virtue. The Stoics called attention to the virtue concerning the conflict of the good with the evil principle within human life. Their watchword "virtue" signifies courage and valor in Greek as well as in Latin, and it presupposes the presence of the enemy. Virtue is sufficient for happiness, and to be free of passions (*apatheia*), it is substantial to follow the reason. Because the "*logos*" or universal reason is inherent in all things, the Stoics recognized the common reason and essential value of all people in an egalitarian manner rather than teleological-hierarchical reasoning. Living according to reason and virtue is to live in harmony with the divine order of the universe.

---

[4] Troeltsch, *The Social Teaching of the Christian Churches*, I: 65-6.

Kant's Critique of the Stoics and Theonomous Ethics

However, to become morally good, Kant holds, it is not enough to allow the seed of goodness implanted in us (*logos spermatikos*) in order to unfold without hindrance. Indeed, there is a presence of evil within us to be combatted and overcome.[5] Certainly, Kant regards the word "virtue" as a noble one. Natural inclinations are good when considered in themselves. When they are brought into harmony in a wholeness, it is called happiness. If reason accomplishes this, it is termed prudence. The Stoics regarded human moral struggle as a conflict with the inclinations, and the cause of transgression is located only in human failure to combat these inclinations.

In Kant's account, however, there is a lack of world renewal as opposed to the world and sin, because the Stoic attention was directed toward a Golden Age which has been irrevocably lost.[6] The Stoics did not call out wisdom against the wickedness of the human heart. For them, the universal ethical principle is derived from the dignity of human nature, whose freedom is regarded as independence from the power of inclinations. They derived the moral laws directly from reason because reason alone makes moral laws, and its command is absolute through these laws.

In the Stoic scheme of interpretation, each human being has an inherent capacity to reason, while human reason (*logos*) in each one of us, regardless of social rank, is connected with or attuned to the divine *logos*. Slaves, like the rest of us, could access the universal *logos* through their reasoning, while socially remaining slaves.

---

[5] Kant, "Religion within the Limits of Reason Alone," in *Basic Writings of Kant*, 395.

[6] Ibid., 396-7. See further Troeltsch, *The Social Teaching of the Christian Churches* I: 66.

In Tillich's explanation, there is the shared transcendent capacity, or universal *logos*, among all human beings. For the dialectic between individualization and participation, Tillich considers the encounter between the Stoic idea of universal reason and the Christian idea of individual dignity; each person, no matter his/her social status, is respected as an end in its relation to God. Reason and Christian love are encountered and combined in universal significance, which warrants individual human dignity.

As Tillich writes: "No process of emancipation was begun until the Stoic philosophers fought successfully for the doctrine that every human being participates in the universal *logos*. The uniqueness of every person was not established until the Christian church acknowledged the universality of salvation and the potentiality of every human being to participate in it."[7]

Eventually, Kant values the morality of the Stoics as an initiatory alliance for his philosophical theology. But specific principles of moral goodness ought to be present as maxims to combat evil. In their absence, all virtues would certainly be splendid frailties. Then the rebel would not be conquered or exterminated.[8] Kant complements an aspect of justice and morality for human dignity to highlight the interdependence between individualization and participation.

In his retrieval of the significance of the Stoic principle, Kant elaborates the dignity of morality in dealing with the empirical, historical stream, by distinguishing right from wrong; Kant's moral rationality in autonomy for self-legislation is different from purpose (or instrumental) rationality (heteronomy), which drives human reason in terms of means and calculation for the

---

[7] Tillich, *Systematic Theology* 1: 175.
[8] Kant, "Religion within the Limits of Reason Alone," in *Basic Writings of Kant*, 396, footnote 14.

end. For Kant moral progress is meaningful such that rationality is intertwined with moral meaning. Rationality is meaningful in its moral worth. This is a Kantian type of moral rationality imbued with the theonomous, which holds a distinctive place as duty and responsibility. It includes the virtue of prudence, which is classified as the theonomous rationality.

Practical reason, which governs our will for moral principle and law, comes to terms with his universal historical position; autonomy of the individual can be enhanced in terms of the universal law (theonomy) imbued with the kingdom of God.

We are not only instruments to pursue and realize the end in the sense of the heteronomy, but we are the author of moral legislation in treating persons as ends in themselves against any attempt to utilize them as the means or utility.

Kant's moral philosophy cannot be properly comprehended apart from his deliberation of radical evil. Kant argues that evil cannot be sought in the undisciplined natural inclinations, or unrealized potential in a Thomist sense, but it is an invisible foe hiding behind reason. Only what is opposed to the moral law is evil in itself, which is to be eradicated completely. Only reason teaches this truth and puts it into actual practice, thus it alone deserves the name of wisdom.

Kant calls attention to Paul's notion of an invisible enemy, which is known only through its effect upon us as evil spirits outside us. "We wrestle not against flesh and blood (the natural inclinations) but against principalities and powers—against evil spirits."[9] This refers to the conception of what is unfathomable for us.

In his basis of religion upon morality, Kant contrasts a reality of radical evil with human moral commitment to the kingdom of God; the latter is to be established on earth in resistance to evil. A "theological" side of Kant is associated with the concept

---

[9]   Ibid., 397.

of universal human dignity and the kingdom of God, in which "dignity must be defended in civil society as an intrinsic, unconditioned, incomparable worth or worthiness."[10]

His Enlightenment philosophy implies a maturing theology of social sanctification by combining the Greek notion of universal *logos* with Christian commitments to morality, virtue, and the kingdom of God. His moral philosophy has a theonomous character to the extent that practical reason and its autonomy do not reject biblical moral command. Its theonomous quality is still dependent upon the theological subject matter of the kingdom of God, ultimate concern, by realizing its moral concern in civil society and the world.[11]

Nature and Teleological History

Kant finds it substantial to incorporate the virtue-based approach in the Stoic stance into his moral philosophy, in which empirical considerations of interest, preference, or virtue can be undertaken to articulate the basis for universal moral principle in connection with universal history.

According to Kant, history considers the play of the freedom of human will, and its regular progression is to be discovered "as a steady, progressive, though slow, evolution of the original predispositions of the entire species."[12]

In Kant's social moral theory, the Stoic ethics is transformed into developing the social ethics of justice in which he takes on the significance of the social character of human life in regard to its interdependence in the natural world. Our natural desires and

---

[10] Kant, *Groundwork of the Metaphysic of Morals*, 36.
[11] Tillich, *Systematic Theology* 3: 267.
[12] Kant, "Idea for a Universal History with Cosmopolitan Intent," in *Basic Writings of Kant*, 119.

inclinations can be directed by rational activity and our exercise of self-determination to combat the reality of evil.

In Kant's teleological theory of nature, nature's course reveals a teleology, producing harmony from human disharmony. All natural dispositions of creatures are destined to unfold according to their end. It is considered in its usefulness through evolution. It requires trials, experience, and information in order to progress gradually from one level to another in transmitting its enlightenment to another.

In the employment of its means to its end, nature gave humans reasoning and freedom of will based on reason, and this clearly shows nature's purpose in regard to human equipment. Humans are not led by instinct or instructed by innate knowledge, but their equipment and development together with all pleasures, insights, and intelligence should be achieved by their own work.[13]

Kant incorporates the Stoic idea of Nature by elaborating it in the evolutionary-historical scheme of development. It is not consonant with Aristotle's moral reasoning of the relation between potentiality and actuality in self-cultivation toward the end, which has no bearing on history and social change. The Stoic position is reinforced and reinterpreted through Kant's teleological view of nature and history in an evolutionary sense, in which nature's teleology does not contradict human reason. Natural grounds for duties and obligations to one another are based on interdependence and integrated with its teleological history in which the mutually social good of communities is an important part.

In fact, moral duty confers moral worth in human action, and it does not necessarily discard moral prudence or compassion for helping others; it has nothing to do with the moral misanthrope

---

[13] Ibid., 120-1.

because prudence or taking leisure in helping the other does not necessarily undermine the value of moral worth.[14]

The State of Nature and Antagonism

For Kant, the state of nature is characterized by the propensity to evil in which human beings are in mutual interdependence imbued with mutual antagonism, a condition of savagery; it belongs to animality, which is comprehended in terms of self-preservation, the propagation of the species, and community with other people (social impulse); these are called "vices of the coarseness of nature,"[15] in which no reason is required.

Kant's developmental scheme includes the predisposition to humanity which is termed under the self-love requiring reason; it desires equality, but jealousy and rivalry aroused in us to attain superiority over all through animosity against all. Nature uses the idea of such rivalry only as a drive to culture, thus these diabolical vices are called vices of culture. Finally, the predisposition to personality is the capacity to respect the moral law within us, in which reason dictates moral laws in an unconditional manner. It implies moral sentiment as the motivating force of the will, which is *"in itself a sufficient incentive of the will."*[16]

However, the propensity to evil in human nature (habitual craving, concupiscence) consists in the possibility of deviating the subjective maxims from the moral law. A natural propensity to evil in the human being is seen in the frailty of human nature, impurity, and corruption of the human heart.[17] It perpetuates in

---

[14] Sandel, *Justice*, 115.
[15] "Religion within the Limits of Reason Alone," in *Basic Writings of Kant*, 376.
[16] Ibid., 377.
[17] Ibid., 379-80.

the long passage through cultivation or culture to moralization or morality in the developmental scheme.

The civilized state (a glittering misery) is bound up with the development of the natural dispositions in human animality, and the end of nature makes us receptive to higher ends to transcend the animal condition toward morality. Compassion or altruistic action becomes a component of moral worth, though it does not replace the motive of moral duty.

Nature or Providence turns evil to good, and human beings would not be able to develop their excellent natural capacities without Nature, which fosters social incompatibility or antagonism.

By antagonism, Kant means the unsociable sociability of human beings, that is, the propensity of people to enter into society. This propensity is linked to a constant mutual resistance threatening to dissolve this society. This antagonism becomes the cause of a lawful order of this society in the end.[18] A human being finds in him/herself the unsocial disposition in which he/she wishes to direct everything merely according to his/her own propensity and selfish interest. Without the antagonism in competition and resistance, all the excellent capacities implanted in humankind by nature would not develop and unfold without the antagonism in competition and desire for power.

Because of this antagonism, human propensity seeks to enter into society with a law-governed social order. Through human inclination to associate with others and isolate (unsociable quality), in other words, the sources of unsociability and continuous resistance there occur so many evils. But the natural impulses drive humankind to a new exertion of their powers and development of their natural faculties.

---

[18] Kant, "Idea for a Universal History with Cosmopolitan Intent," Ibid., 122.

The first steps are achieved from barbarism to culture because a culture consists of the social value of humans. The basis is laid bare for a frame of mind through continuous enlightenment in the course of time. All the excellent natural faculties of humankind would forever remain undeveloped without their nature for quarrelsomeness, enviously competitive vanity, and insatiable desire to possess or to rule. Nature wants discord while raising humankind "out of lethargy and inactive contentment into work and trouble."[19]

Rousseau takes the state of nature as the basis for natural liberty and equality, transcending the war of everybody against everybody in civil society. But Kant takes into account the "history" in terms of development in morality and civil society. Civil society is that of progress through the development of human natural capacities, moving civilization forward.

If Rousseau finds the reality of evil built upon competition and inequality in a social, political, and economic context, Kant's understanding of radical evil incorporates the Stoic principle into his scheme of history in terms of moral rationality (interacting with moral sentiments and empirical reality). The state of nature and civil society should be framed and reinforced through the principle of reason, which stands in contrast to the reality of radical evil everywhere.

History Effect and Teleology

Kant's philosophical history is not to displace true empirical history by the idea of a universal history founded upon a principle a priori. In the latter pure reason acts through mere ideas which offer no object to experience, true empirical history.

---

[19] Ibid., 123.

On the contrary, in his philosophical history, he argues that reason should have power, but interact with the plan of nature in terms of disadvantage, failures, and resistance. The feckless condition of the savages equipped with all the natural predispositions of our species forced them to enter into a civil constitution. The evolution of the world is integrated into the end, the moral one that reason prescribes, and it promotes the concept of duty toward eternal peace.[20]

Kant's historical-rational anthropology is different from Rousseau's positive anthropology as well as Hobbes' negative anthropology requiring Leviathan. In *Fundamental Principles of the Metaphysics of Morals* (1785), Kant maintains that teleology considers nature as a kingdom of ends (a theoretical idea), while ethics becomes a possible kingdom of ends, or a kingdom of nature (a practical idea). It is substantial to comprehend Kant's moral theory in correlation with his philosophical history in bringing the kingdom of nature to the kingdom of ends at an evolutionary scale. His teleological history including nature reinforces his moral theory in a historical frame of reference actively involved in empirical reality.[21]

Kant appropriates the Stoic idea of Nature to the point of articulating the moral development, which has undergone discord, antagonism, and competition. However, Kant's philosophical notion of evolution cannot be misused as a biological-racial way of justifying Eurocentric supremacy.

Kant seeks to harmonize a possible kingdom of ends with a kingdom of nature through the complete characterization of all maxims; it is performed in terms of universal laws of nature as well as an end in itself through his philosophical history at a providential-evolutionary scale of moral development.

---

[20] "To Eternal Peace," Ibid., 451.
[21] "Fundamental Principles of the Metaphysics of Morals," Ibid., 193; 195.

However, the evolutionary process is not merely ruthless and competitive based on the struggle of the fittest, but it entails a purpose and an end that Kant formulates in his view on the teleological theory of nature. It differentiates him from laissez-faire capitalism or Social Darwinism because Kant is concerned with moral progress against the reality of radical evil in accordance with St. Paul.

In his idea for a universal history with cosmopolitan intent, Kant writes that *"the history of mankind could be viewed on the whole as the realization of a hidden plan of nature in order to bring about an internally—and for this purpose also externally—perfect constitution; since this is the only state in which nature can develop all predispositions of mankind."*[22]

History of effect is not separated from the realm of nature, because "what good is to praise the majesty and wisdom of creation."[23] The evolution of the world (or called providence) is directed toward a higher goal, in other words, the objective final end. The history of age is now composed of complexity, and our later generation is going to cope with the burden of history. Without a doubt, they will care for the history of the most ancient period from the perspective, in which to examine "what nations and governments have contributed toward world government or how they have damaged it.[24]

A pathologically enforced coordination of society finally transforms the raw natural faculty of moral discrimination into a moral whole. This evolutionary process implies the arrangement of a wise creator rather than on the hand of an evil spirit.[25] Kant credits the evolutionary development into divine providence,

---

[22] Ibid., 129.
[23] Ibid.
[24] Ibid., 451.
[25] Ibid., 123.

which can be seen in human development to civil society and human rights. The latest problem for humankind to seek is the achievement of a civil society that administers right generally.

According to Kant, the Jewish people in the time of the Ptolemies are advanced through the Greek translation of the Bible; it becomes an undercurrent in guiding the later history. Kant quotes David Hume who says that "the first page of *Thucydides* is the real beginning of history."[26] The Greek history has been preserved or at least certified. Thucydides, an Athenian historian in his *History of the Peloponnesian War* made a scientific, empirical report based on impartiality and evidence of historical analysis on the war between Sparta and Athens until the year 411 BC. His history of war made no reference to intervention by the deities.

We may trace its influence upon the formation and malformation of the body-politics of the Roman empire. The chain of influence is seen in the further development of the Barbarian under the Greek-Roman civilization. Through the enlightened nations, we will discover a regular procession of improvements in constitutional government which give laws to all other states eventually. Human history would open up a consoling vision of the future, because it works itself "up to the full development of the germs that nature has laid in it" and fulfills its vocation on earth.[27]

The historical perspective implies teleological significance in Kant's philosophy, in which human development at an evolutionary scale is in universal interaction and in connection with the effect of history and the life-world. Moral progress can be affirmed in the analysis of the process of rationalization and

---

[26] Kant, "Idea for a Universal History with Cosmopolitan Intent," Ibid., 131. Footnote 2.
[27] Ibid., 132.

social formation in each society and culture. Human history is a history of moral progress in the human struggle against evil, which cuts through the limitation of the Marxist notion of class struggle.

Critical Reflection: Life-world and Kant

Kant's attempt is to write a general world history, in which a plan of nature, considered almost in itself as divine providence, aims at a perfect civil association of humankind. This civil association expands the notion of the kingdom of ends into a social, political dimension. It is possible and even helpful to the intention of nature.[28]

Each state is interested in the maintenance of the whole, and this body-politics provides the hope that transformation will finally come about through and after many revolutions. The highest intent of nature is "a general cosmopolitan condition as the womb to which all the original predispositions of the human species will be developed."[29]

However, Kant remains restrained in clarifying the extent to which history would shape and condition diverse forms of human reason in different times and places. An imperative of morality can be sought and enhanced in interaction with a different history, society, and culture, in which Kantian history of teleology can be renewed in terms of democratic consensus and justice of recognition.

In fact, Kant's philosophy of universal history would be better located in the dialectical relationship between duty and inclination, autonomy and heteronomy, or categorical and hypothetical imperative through the notion of life-world and

---

[28] Ibid., 131.
[29] Ibid., 130.

its teleology. Each life-world has its uniqueness and validity in society, culture, and morality, while it remains a general framework for the norm and validity. Life-world is given as an endless and meaningful horizon of all known and unknown realities.

As Edmund Husserl writes: "...horizon can be opened up only through a reflection on this life-world and man as its subject--can be shown only when we are much further advanced in the elucidation of the historical development according to its innermost moving forces."[30]

A critical reflection in existential reasons takes shape gradually in the teleological consideration of history while serving to liberate us in terms of historical-critical inquiry and responsible critique.[31]

Different forms of life-world, into which we are thrown, find their truths as generally verified or verifiable, although they are by no means the same as one another (Chinese life-world in comparison to an African one). Despite all relativity, we make objects of the life-world common to all; they are identifiable and set up as the objective goal for them and for us.

This life-world stance enhances and reinvigorates Kantian history of teleology at the providential-evolutionary level through critical reflection and emancipation. The cosmopolitan vision can be advanced for human dignity, justice, and recognition in acknowledging other cultural and moral achievements. Such an aspect can relocate a Kantian individual notion of moral reason with the realm of life-world in intersubjective interaction with people of other cultures.

---

[30] *The Essential Husserl*, 356.
[31] Ibid., 363.

2. Cosmopolitan Constitution, Colonialism, and World Society

In the Stoic development the concept of two citizenships is articulated in terms of one's particular city, state, or nation as well as the cosmos (universe or world). Taking over the Stoic principle and citizen, Kant elaborates such a principle by combining his duty ethics with the philosophy of history, while relocating it in the republican democratic constitution in international affairs.

How would Kant universalize one's maxim, to the degree that one's maxim or moral rule should become a universal law without contradiction? Universalizing the maxim of one's action implies a test or a criterion, in which one's maxim is seen in accord with the categorical imperative.

Kant's *Groundwork for the Metaphysics of Morals* appeared after the American Revolution (1776) and just before the French Revolution (1789), in which the issues of human rights and independence of the State in an anticolonial sense become crucial. Kant was a liberal and critical thinker in positively assessing the idea of the French revolution, despite his distance from the violence.

Kant recurs to the positive side of the Enlightenment and its significance of public use of reason. However, he does not sidestep the development of the enlightenment with occasional nonsense and freakishness, viewing it as a great good in drawing humankind away from egoistic expansive tendencies.[32] The Enlightenment principle remains crucial in Kant's moral theory of freedom, autonomy, and maturity in terms of the public use of the reason in society without restriction. In fact, he is not merely interested in justifying the Prussian monarchy and its despotism.

---

[32] Kant, "Idea for a Universal History with Cosmopolitan Intent," in *Basic Writings of Kant*, 130.

Democratic Constitution, Civil Society, and Perpetual Peace

Kant is convinced of the democratic constitution and civil society in terms of moral progress and rationality, to the extent that he envisions the cosmopolitan state by enhancing moral theory in international relations; he seeks to establish perpetual peace through the law of hospitality. To be true, Kant regards a civil constitution as what all the natural predispositions of our species forced them to enter into; they compel our species to introduce a cosmopolitan state of public security and to discover a counterbalance to evils.

A completely just civil constitution is the highest task for humankind. Under such a constitution can be achieved the supreme objective of nature, that is, the development of all the faculties of human beings by their own effort. They should secure all these ends in a society, in which the greatest freedom is allowed, while it possesses the determination and enforcement of the limit of this freedom. In society, freedom under external laws is found to be combined with irresistible force, in other words, a perfectly just civil constitution that nature sets as the supreme task for humankind.[33]

This perspective finds its consonance with Rousseau's social contract theory and general will. Kant maintains that "*Rousseau* was not so very wrong when he preferred the condition of savages, provided one omits this last stage which our species will have to reach."[34]

Kant regards this civil society under a lawful constitution as the inevitable escape from the brutal freedom of the savages and also "from the destitution into which human beings plunge each other." A state, like a civil commonwealth, can be constructed

---

[33] Ibid., 124.
[34] Ibid., 128.

and maintained "partly through the best possible arrangement of the civil constitution internally, and partly through the common agreement and legislation externally."[35]

A rational being desires law, which would provide limits for the freedom of all. This demand requires sovereignty which compels humans to obey a general will, under which every individual could be free in reference to the public and common good.

Along with Rousseau, Kant envisions the great union of nations in a historical transition from the lawless state of savages to entrance into a union of nations; the latter is equipped with "united power and decisions according to the united will of them all."[36]

Relocating Rousseau's social contract theory within the evolutionary scale of history, Kant's philosophical history is culminated in elaborating the perpetual peace within the cosmopolitan framework underlying a new impulse to social contract reasoning. This cosmopolitan vision can be seen as enhancing Rousseau's principle of solidarity by relocating his general will and republican democracy in the international context; he challenges the reality of inhospitable colonialism and promotes hospitality as the universal law.

General will and popular sovereignty need to be discussed in reference to reason, autonomy, and freedom in the cosmopolitan context. We live in the realm of necessity under influence of nature, society, and history, while moral rationality guides and dictates human life in the realm of freedom; a gap or a conflict should be filled between what we do and what we ought to do in terms of a civil constitution based on liberty, justice, and maturity.

---

[35] Ibid., 126-7.
[36] Ibid., 126.

Kant's ethics of hospitality refers to ethics of responsibility and emancipation in his teleological consideration of history and moral progress against evil. It provides a constitutional-institutional model which is applicable to political reform and social policy while extending to the international community.

Practical reason grounded in the kingdom of God and its faith in moral progress is of personalistic character instilled with human dignity as the end, while public use of reason is undertaken in the social-political sphere through the republic, democratic constitution. Finally, it finds its climax at a historical-evolutionary scale, in which we as moral agents are in an endeavor to envision international constitutional democracy, cosmopolitan principle, and perpetual peace.

However, Hegel grounded on representative monarchy and ideal of the State rejects Kant's liberalism in the international sphere and peace on a permanent basis.[37] The State is conceptualized as the locus of a higher life in the sense of identification of patriotism (*Sittliche Gesinnung*; ethical conviction); it cannot extend more broadly to include the whole human race. He is suspicious of the liberal principle in which State is built upon individual liberty, equality, and responsibility of the government for the people; such society rather deserves to be leveled as a formless mass or crowd or a heap.[38]

Power over war and foreign affairs belongs to the Crown. Directed against 'liberty, equality, and popular sovereignty,'[39] the Prussian German State was endorsed as the fullest realization of the modern State underlying Hegel's German-centric position based on the German Reformation. Considered in this way, any world State or league of nations is deemed by Hegel to be a

---

[37] Hegel, *Philosophy of Rights*, para. 321-9.
[38] Ibid., para. 279; 303.
[39] Taylor, *Hegel*, 451.

chimera in international relations; "the norms of international law... cannot be made substantial, part of a self-maintaining common life."[40]

Against the Kantian international federation of states, Hegel argues that not peace, but war belongs to the task of the political society of the State. War in the moment of truth embodies the primacy of the universal in which death is the lot and destiny of the finite.

"In the ethical substance, the state, nature is robbed of this power, and the necessity is exalted to the work of freedom, to be something ethical. The transience of the finite becomes a willed passing away, and the negativity lying at the roots of the finite becomes the substantive individuality proper to the ethical substance."[41]

If power over war lies in the hands of the Crown, the destiny of the individual is at the disposal of the powerful in their arbitrary or totalitarian sense. Hegel's ethics of recognition fails to extend its pluralism in the world states because the league of nations is nothing but a chimera. His critique of Kant backfires upon himself in "sacrificing the individual on the altar of a state divinity."[42]

Colonialism and Slavery

Kant keeps the ethics of hospitality in mind, and takes issue with colonialism; there is no relation of superior and subordinate between states.[43] In the trading nations of the European continent, the civilized displayed the injustice simply identified

---

[40] Ibid., 449.
[41] Hegel, *Philosophy of Right*, para. 324 E.
[42] Taylor, *Hegel*, 449.
[43] "To Eternal Peace," in *Basic Writings of Kant*, 438.

with conquest, as seen in "America, the lands of the Negroes, the Spice Islands, the Cape of South Africa, etc."[44]

For example, in East India (Hindustan) foreign mercenaries were brought in under the pretense of establishing trading ports, but these troops suppressed the natives, inciting them to rage war against one another. They had "brought famine, sedition, treason, and the rest of evils which weigh down mankind."[45] The sugar islands, according to Kant, are denounced as the seat of the cruelest and systematic slavery, and they raised recruits only for navies. Although the European civilized considered themselves among the morally elect, in fact, they served the conduct of war, wars of powers, consuming "[the fruits of] injustice like water."[46]

As we have already seen, Rousseau reacts against the right of slavery as absurd and meaningless, as seen in the French practice of slavery (ended in 1794). This perspective implies a critique of the French slavery system for economic profit, which underlays the system of injustice in the French monarchy. It can continue to be articulated in Kant's critique of colonization.

Kant sharply acknowledges the dark side of the enlightenment, its blackmail of progress and development through a violation of war and right felt in all others. In contrast to this dialectic of the enlightenment or progress embedded with colonialism, Kant maintains that "the idea of a cosmopolitan or world law is...a necessary completion of the unwritten code of constitutional and international law to make it a public law of mankind."[47]

However, it can be argued that Kant relies on the teleological scheme with respect to the spread of European culture and civilization throughout the world. Kant condemns the violence

---

[44] Ibid., 449.
[45] Ibid., 450.
[46] Ibid.
[47] Ibid.

committed in the French Revolution from a normative standpoint of morality, whereas welcoming the political and legal advances from a functional standpoint of human progress. Should this stance retain a lack of fit between the normative morality and functionality of human progress, as McCarthy argues?[48]

Indeed, Kant had extensive knowledge of the African slave trade and denounced such practices and institutions: His ethics of hospitality runs counter to the inhospitable, colonial conduct of the "civilized" Europeans, which identify visitation of foreign countries with conquest. "For if the master is authorized to use the powers of his subjects as he pleases, he can also exhaust them until his subject dies or is driven into despair (as with the Negroes on the sugar islands); his subject will, in fact, have given himself away, as property, to his master, which is impossible."[49]

Kant combines moral theory with a critique of colonialism and proposes a cosmopolitan project for global sovereignty in international affairs through an anti-colonial aspect and global peace and justice. But his evolutionary perspective tends to be vulnerable to subordinating Africans to the European whites who alone are fitted for cultural and political progress.[50]

Kant does not undermine the significance of distributive justice in the renewal of the social system through the principle of respect for the rights of others. As he writes, "Although we may be entirely within our rights, according to the laws of the land and the rules of our social structure, we may nevertheless be participating in general injustice, and in giving to an unfortunate man we do not give him a gratuity but only help to return to him

---

[48] McCarthy, *Race, Empire, and the Idea of Human Development*, 62.
[49] Kant, *The Metaphysics of Morals* [1797], 104.
[50] Kant, "Of the Different Races of Human Beings," in R. Bernasconi and T. Lott (eds.), *The Idea of Race*, 8-22.

that of which the general injustice of our system has deprived him."[51]

A notion of redistribution of material resources is not entirely foreign to Kant, to the extent that it would alleviate the poverty of the society. Rousseau's solidarity principle still resonates with Kant's philosophy of the right.

Kant refines Rousseau's insight into civil society in his distinguished manner and emphasizes the significance of history and moral progress.

In Kant's position, the arrangement of God or divine providence plays an important role in the underlying moral progress of society from nature. "Thus, a *pathologically* enforced coordination of society finally transforms it into a *moral* whole."[52]

This perspective has no intention to justify the barbarism of past injustice in defending European supremacy or colonialism as a way of a legitimate, benign despotism, as seen in J. S. Mill. In the latter, the means are justified by the end. Kant has never justified slavery as a contributing factor to advancing the human race through European culture and its civilizing mission. In acknowledging the difference between the European savages and those in America, Kant is concerned with the evil nature of human beings and seeks to undertake a federation of free states for perpetual peace against war.[53]

What is at issue is for Kant to look at the concept of world citizenship in terms of a relationship of mutual influence, in other words, citizens of a universal state of all humankind.[54]

---

[51] Kant, "Duties toward Others," in *Lectures on Ethics* (1779). Cited in *Ethics for Life*, 331.
[52] "Idea for a Universal History with Cosmopolitan Intent," in *Basic Writings of Kant*, 123.
[53] "To Eternal Peace," Ibid., 445.
[54] Ibid., 441.

"Between states no war of punishment can be conceived, because between them there is no relation of superior and subordinate."⁵⁵

A Cosmopolitan Constitution and the World Society

Kant introduces the constitution in the threefold sense under law (1) *jus civitatis* is constitutional law which is in accordance with the law of national citizenship of all people; (2) *jus gentium* is international law, which is in accordance with international law; (3) *jus cosmopoliticum* is cosmopolitan or world law, which is in accordance to the law of world citizenship, citizens of a universal state of all humankind.⁵⁶

The republican constitution is the only one fully adequate to realize the rights of human beings. A good constitution should not be expected from morality, but good moral develops from a constitution. Reason employs the evolution of the world as a means to provide a field for the operation of legal rules by which to secure peace internally and externally.⁵⁷

In the republican constitution, the consent of the citizens is required regarding the decision-making of war or not; it can lead to eternal peace. The form of government, the constitution is "an act of the general will by which mass becomes a nation."⁵⁸ The constitutional principle in the republican form of government maintains that the executive power is separated from the legislative power.⁵⁹

As Kant writes about the civil constitution, "a republican constitution is a constitution which is founded upon three

---

[55] Ibid., 439.
[56] Ibid., 441 footnote 2.
[57] Ibid., 455.
[58] Ibid., 443.
[59] Ibid.

principles. First, the principle of the *freedom* of all members of a society as men. Second, the principle of the *dependence* of all upon a single common legislation as subjects, and third, the principle of the *equality* of all as citizens. This is the only constitution which is derived from the idea of an original contract upon which all rightful legislation of a nation must be based."[60]

Kant incorporates Rousseau's social contract theory and his republican constitution into three principles freedom, dependence, and equality, which should be based and guided by his moral theory. Duty ethics cannot be comprehended adequately without social justice ethics, especially cosmopolitan ethics of social justice and peace. The highest good, considered in itself good, is founded upon the goodwill under the rule of pure practical reason. Furthermore, it finds an indispensable expression in the rights and justice set forth within the social contract theory and finally extends to social justice cosmopolitanism with the significance of universal hospitality.

Kant advocates an ideal of federations of states rather than abolition of all states for a universal Republic. This implies a plurality of independent states, which is favored over the amalgamation under a single power of a universal monarchy. A cosmopolitan civil state cannot be achieved by conquest to create a universal monarchy or despotism achieved by conquest. A liberal world republic would be achieved through a peaceful merger or federation of republics of nation-states.

In the cosmopolitan conception of a world republic for perpetual peace, Kant argues, states in their relation to one another cannot be out of their lawless state (*statu iniusto*). Like individual human beings, they should give up their wild lawless freedom, adjusting themselves to public coercive laws; they

---

[60] Ibid., 441.

establish a continuously growing international state, state of all nations (*civitas gentium*), which includes all nations in the end.[61]

Kant replaces the positive idea of a world republic with the negative substitute of a union of nations, which implies a pacific union of nations through federalization rather than a state of nations. The federal union of other states in the republican form would gradually lead to eternal peace.[62]

Kant's Aftermath and Utopian Realism

Kant was aware that any world state would invariably lead to despotism or civil strife while envisioning a just world government as feasible. He is credited as being a utopian realist, whose impact continues to be found in further discussions of his cosmopolitan project in the present.

First of all, Kant's idea of universal Republic may find its impulse in the work of Hans Kelsen (1881-1973), an Austrian jurist and political philosopher, who remains central in the formation of the federalist systems of the United Nations. In the 1910s and 20s, Kelsen drew attention to the significance of the international juridical system to cut across limitations of the nation-states; he sought to bring to an end to the conflicts between states of unequal powers by grounding the domestic law of nation-states in part on the universality and objectivity of the international juridical formation and constitution.

In contrast to Carl Schmitt's political decision in the state of exception, Kelsen's constitutional position shared in the Kantian legacy of Enlightenment and organized a notion of human rights, equal ranks of nation-states, and peace among them in accordance with the supreme ethical idea. His appraisal of Kant's

---

[61] "To Eternal Peace," in *Basic Writings of Kant*, 448.
[62] Ibid., 447.

political philosophy and perpetual peace has much in common with John Rawls. A world and universal state could be organized as a universal community, which implies the foundational idea of the United Nations and its various institutions as superior to particular states.[63]

What is crucial in the cosmopolitan context is Rawls' cosmopolitan approach to social justice or social justice cosmopolitanism. He writes: "I follow Kant's lead in *Perpetual Peace* (1795) in thinking that a world government ... would either be a global despotism or else would rule over a fragile empire torn by frequent civil strife as various regions and peoples tried to gain their political freedom and autonomy."[64]

For global social justice, Rawls seeks to provide "a particular political conception of right and justice that applies to principles and norms of international law and practice."[65] Of special significance in this task are liberal principles of global justice. A decent people are moved to act on the law without necessary coercion. They would pursue the common aims, which are constrained by a common good idea of global justice. The liberal principles of global justice are tolerant of peoples with other moral and political traditions with a decent non-liberal background.[66]

In the original position between liberal peoples and decent non-liberal peoples, it is imperative to establish fair terms of cooperation. Two parties are situated equally behind a veil of ignorance. In Rawls' assumption, decent peoples are not unreasonable, since they do not engage in aggressive wars or pursue an expansionist policy. They do not fail to respect the civic order and integrity of other peoples.[67] They would accept

---

[63] Kelsen, *The Law of the United Nations*.
[64] Rawls, *The Law of Peoples*, 36.
[65] Ibid., 3.
[66] Ibid., 10.
[67] Ibid., 69.

principles, which respect and honor human rights while holding responsibility for social institutions and global institutional order. Social justice cosmopolitanism entails a strong ethical component.

In the liberal-democratic framework of the decent people, it would be a viable project to adopt the laws of peace through their interest in security, the benefits of trade, and their duties of contract and mutual assistance in times of need. This stance would allow for a possibility of war in the sense of self-defense.[68]

However, Michael Hardt and Antonio Negri, exponents of imperial sovereignty run counter to the Kantian-Kelsen legacy, while criticizing it as a fantastic utopia. Rather, they maintain that the juridical concept of Empire has taken shape through the United Nations' general framework in constitutionalizing a supranational world power. The idea of a single power in supranational sense overdetermines rivalry and imperialist dominion among nation-states, and its character "is decidedly postcolonial and post imperialist."[69]

On the contrary, in Habermas' account, Kant advocated the idea of a world republic and proposed the surrogate of a league of nations as the first stage in the transition to a world republic. In the legal and political networks of a pluralist, global society, the Kantian cosmopolitan condition needs to be reformulated and revised in a sufficient and qualified manner, in which it is kept from becoming utopian.

In fact, Kant under the tradition of Rousseau, Habermas continues, "neglected a different, competing constitutional tradition that rejects any such conceptual linkage of state and constitution. In the liberal tradition, the constitution does not have the function of constituting *authority* but only that of

---

[68] Ibid., 30-43.
[69] Hardt and Negri, *Empire*, 9.

constraining *power*...Liberalism develops this idea further in the modern sense of the constitutional division of powers."[70]

In the collaboration among different nation-states, the legal form of a constitution can be produced in multilateral networks or transnational negotiation, or in international organizations. The liberal type of republican democracy provides a conceptual model for constituting international law and constraining the power of the nation-states; this proposal suggests a form of a politically constituted world society alongside individual world citizens without presupposing a world government.

In a highly interdependent global society, the principle of popular sovereignty encounters difficulty, and the sovereign states are able to take part in collective efforts to address problems at the global and regional levels (international economics, environmental policies, securing peace and human rights); these are to be solved within the framework of international organizations.[71]

A question would be open to whether Kant's cosmopolitan view is constructed on the non-coercive league of states or the establishment of a stronger international federation with coercive powers.[72] If teleology of nature and history stands in for divine providence in his philosophy of universal history, a cosmopolitan order under a global rule of enforceable law would degenerate into self-interested politics, which could be achieved by a 'race of devils.'[73]

Nonetheless, nation-states with popular sovereignty remain intact, but are constituted under the law in accordance with the law of national citizenship of all people; such law is undertaken in

---

[70] Habermas, *Between Naturalism and Religion*, 316.
[71] Ibid., 319-20.
[72] Kleingeld, *Kant and Cosmopolitanism*, 6.
[73] McCarthy, *Race, Empire, and the Idea of Human Development*, 144.

accordance with international law. Then cosmopolitan or world law should be in league with the law of world citizenship, which emphasizes universal hospitality, while including enforcement for the state of peace.

For Kant, a good constitution is not supposed to come from inner morality, but people have good moral development from such a constitution. "Thus, reason's real purpose may be realized, namely, to provide a field for the operation of legal rules whereby to make secure internal and external peace, as far as the state is concerned."[74]

Kant's cosmopolitan vision can be renewed, revised, and reinterpreted for a realist utopian project in dealing with a reality of global civil society and the common good, which are plagued with conflict, disparity, and regional wars; the world society is stratified in hierarchical imbalance, and reified in terms of a system of structural violence driven by world political power, market economy between metropolis and periphery, and ideology of world communication.

The cosmopolitan principle should ameliorate international reality fraught with injustice, poverty, and inequality through social justice and equal opportunities for people with different backgrounds. In recognition of different life-worlds, it is imperative to take into account reparative justice for those on the margins of society.

3. Rejoinder of Kant from Critical Theory of Communication

Despite his leaning for the metanarrative of Protestant Christianity, Kant provides room for renewing his shortcoming by reconstructing multicultural universalism in the Stoic sense

---

[74] "To Eternal Peace," in *Basic Writings of Kant*, 455.

within the world republic of federated national republics, which is framed within the cosmopolitan vision and global peace.

However, a serious critique comes from a critical theory of racial justice and emancipation. On the politics of the memory of slavery, Thomas McCarthy presents a sharp critique of Kant's notion of universal history and his understanding of race and slave.

According to McCarthy, Kant develops a systematic theory of racial hierarchy in which non-European peoples would be incapable of realizing their full humanity as well as a just civil constitution in his theoretical rationale for global white supremacy—in other words, fraught with "the civilizing mission of the white race."[75]

However, this critical assessment must be seen against Kant's rejection of slavery and European colonialism. His critique of European colonialism cannot be seen in his way of justifying the spread of European culture and civilization, because Kant denounces any basis for the right to enslave people in the context of the African slave trade. His position has little to do with the standpoint of a disinterested observer, but with his sharp critique of one of the radical evils in this slave trade.[76]

Would Kant really sanction a slavery system as a contributing part to a civilizing mission from a historical-developmental perspective in the sense of social Darwinism? Should the end (European supremacy or kingdom of the ends) justify the means (civilizing mission) as a stepping stone assuming the role of benevolent despotism for this purpose in the Kantian categorical imperative? This question leads to an examination of Kant's idea of theodicy and chiliasm.

---

[75] Ibid., 26.
[76] Ibid., 449.

Kant, Theodicy, and Chiliasm

Kant's idea of theodicy in history is framed under the guidance of practical reason, which incorporates a Stoic scheme of reason in a more egalitarian manner. His theodicy is grounded in his faith in God of justice, while his teleology of nature is framed within the Stoic scheme of universal reason.

His notion of theodicy can be compared with Augustine's philosophy of history, in which the city of God enlivens and penetrates the city of the world in their intermingling for a better course. Unlike Augustine, Kant proposes a philosophical-ethical form of Christian chiliasm, by translating prophetic kingdom-theology into faith in the reason and morality given by God; the kingdom of God is coming through the growth of reason and morality, as historically manifested in the French Revolution as a historical-eschatological sign of humanity toward improvement.

A philosophical chiliasm in a Kantian sense is undertaken to construct the condition of world citizenship based on the complete civil unification of the human race in a league of nations. This embraces all humanity in promoting eternal peace as the goal of world history.[77]

Kant's philosophical chiliasm is rather based on *kairo*s, the time of the kingdom of God into the present history; all people are united with each other toward the universal religion of reason, representing the invisible kingdom of God on earth. This philosophical chiliasm, which is differentiated from theological chiliasm, affirms the universal dignity of humanity as a moral subject. It cannot necessarily be rejected as a Eurocentric model of justifying those victims during the time of colonialism and slavery toward development and progress in social Darwinian iteration.

---

[77] Moltmann, *The Coming of God*, 188.

However, in McCarthy's account, a teleological idea, which is central in the Greek notion of *physis*, is associated with the idea of a natural process of development in a directional, cumulative manner toward an end state. Such Greek teleological thinking is involved in shaping Christian thinking about history which comprehends history as a grand narrative of creation, fall, redemption, and the final judgment. Christian eschatology is blended with a Greek teleological way of thinking in terms of growth, development, and the end. Historical development is understood as a part of the divine plan of creation and divine governance of the world for the purpose of history.[78]

If Rousseau historicized the transition from the state of nature to the social contract in the tradition of Hobbes and Locke, a problem is left how to fill the gaps between the empirical accounts of natural history and the normative demands of natural law through reason; this task belongs to Kant's contribution of universal history. Over the course of human history, a legal-political unity should become a cosmopolitan federation of nation-states, which aims finally at establishing the kingdom of God on earth in a chiliastic sense.[79]

A moral politics is of special significance as a countervailing force to self-interest in the pursuit of transforming a civilization (based on self-love) into a kingdom of ends, since achievements of civilization in the absence of morality would be reduced to a "glittering misery."[80]

Given this, a sharp critique is raised regarding the way in which Kant has "the business of justifying the horrors of history by

---

[78] McCarthy, *Race, Empire, and the Idea of Human Development*, 137.
[79] "To Eternal Peace," in *Basic Writings of Kant*, 441; McCarthy, *Race, Empire, and the Idea of Human Development*, 53.
[80] McCarthy, *Race, Empire, and the Idea of Human Development*, 150.

unfolding of reason, the steady march of progress, or an anticipated happy ending"—such business remains implausible.[81]

Despite this critique, McCarthy is not hesitant to appraise Kant's insistence on the primacy of practical reason with a moral perspective on history in comparison with Hegel or Marx in their disdain for moral significance in society and history.[82]

McCarthy endorses a post-metaphysical epistemology in dealing with the task of universal history as a viable option, as seen in Habermas in reference to Weber. If Weber spells out inner logic (*Eigensetzlichkeit*) of rationalization and institutionalization with purpose, instrumental rationality in the cultural and economic spheres, Habermas seeks to articulate the developmental logics in distinguishing life-world (civil society) and system (political society plus economics, administrative power, and ideology of mass media) in order to salvage the life-world from its colonization by the system through the process of capital accumulation.[83]

Given this, McCarthy questions whether a Kantian notion of moral politics remains a real form of hope in its pursuit of cosmopolitan justice under an ideal of a federation of national republics imbued with cosmopolitan law and world citizenship. The idea of perpetual peace cannot be realized unless nation-states are unwilling to surrender their sovereignty to the international form of institution and organization. Even reasonable hope is left to be contingent upon empirical conditions, unpredictable events, and conflict of interests; a politics of hope in this regard is less than a politics of disappointment.[84]

McCarthy's option falls on Habermas' theory of discourse or communicative rationality in the global discourse of modernity

---

[81] Ibid., 137.
[82] Ibid., 140.
[83] Ibid., 148.
[84] Ibid., 154.

and intercultural discussion; all participants are in principle operative and effective at the same level of communication in terms of contest, disagreement, and consensus.

Eventually, McCarthy's vision deserves attention in his attempt to transcend Eurocentric modernity along with different paths to each modernity in specific different cultural contexts (a notion of multiple modernities). As he writes, "the 'dialectic' of the general and the particular would lead us to expect, rather, that different cultures, different circumstances, and different histories—including different histories of domination by, and resistance to, European imperialism—normally give rise to quite different modern cultures and societies, that is, to multiple modernities" [underlying] "plurality and hybridity—the coalescence of diverse patterns and forms arising from heterogeneous origins."[85]

McCarthy challenges a Eurocentric model in treating the non-Western world as a resource base for Western development; but his concern is not far removed from a Kantian critique of colonialism, as can be seen also in Rousseau's anti-Eurocentric position against slavery.

Public Theology: Cosmopolitan Justice and Recognition

Public theology is defined as a theological attempt to articulate its distinguished ethical position in coping with public affairs and social institutions. I take on the significance of coordination between public theology and global civil society to explore the incomplete project of modernity in reference to cosmopolitan justice.

A theological reading of the kingdom of God on earth does not necessarily discredit Kant into a utopian-chiliastic quarter.

---

[85] Ibid., 223-4.

Instead, it finds a theonomous implication in the Kantian moral philosophy in his prophetic critique of radical evil and his cosmopolitan vision of perpetual peace. Moral rationality imbued with human dignity and social justice can be enhanced to present a cosmopolitan vision and deliberate democracy in global civil society and its postcolonial condition.

In my theological reading of Kant, I focus on the democratic value of human dignity, citizen initiative, common good, and solidarity principle, which can be enhanced in an eschatological reading of cosmopolitan vision, hospitality, and recognition of pluralist cultures.

In the theological context, *theologia crucis* is the core locus where God's theodicy must be found in terms of forgiveness and reconciliation; it is in contrast to a providential theory of justifying the powerful on the march of history in the name of faith in progress. An anamnestic reading of the victims and cosmopolitan morality facilitates public theology in developing its ethical stance with a reparative justice.

Cosmopolitan Principle and Global Justice

Kant writes: "The Cosmopolitan or World Law shall be limited to conditions of universal hospitality."[86] He implies an original concept of hospitality in terms of the duty of hospitality, and also the right to universal hospitality. Hospitality itself is the moral law at the heart of cosmopolitan ethics for human rights and global justice. Hospitality as the right of a foreigner does not necessarily mean the right of becoming a permanent guest, a fellow inhabitant for a certain period for the foreigner to request. This shows that Kant's problem is seen in his exclusion of hospitality as a right of residence.

---

[86] "The Eternal Peace," in *Basic Writings of Kant*, 448.

Kant relates it only to the right of visitation. This refers to the right to visitation belonging to all people. But the right of hospitality refutes the inhospitable conduct of the civilized related to colonialism.[87] Kant extends the cosmopolitan law to encompass universal hospitality without limit. Such is the condition of perpetual peace between all people. He expressly determines it as a natural law. All human creatures, all finite beings endowed with reason, receive "common possession of the surface of the earth," because it is a globe, and they must tolerate mutually.[88]

Kant inspires us today to reformulate hospitality as the moral law or the law of the land for welcoming stay in international relations, especially stateless refuges or asylum.[89] In fact, Kant may be comprehended as the one who reinforces and relocates liberty, justice, and civil society within anti-colonial confines.

According to Kant, politics, which means an applied doctrine of right, says: "Be ye therefore wise as serpents," whereas morals supplements as a limiting condition: "and innocent as doves." Morals are in themselves binding law and practice in an objective sense. There would be a conflict between politics and morals unless these two coexist in one commandment. The collective unity of the united general will for civil society brings forth a common will which implies the execution of the idea of eternal peace in practice.[90]

In recent times, the idea of cosmopolitanism is in resurgence with a strong awareness of moral responsibility and global justice. In *Cosmopolitanism: Ethics in a World of Strangers*, Kwame Anthony Appiah states:

---

[87] Ibid., 449.
[88] Ibid.
[89] Derrida, *On Cosmopolitanism and Forgiveness*, 10-11.
[90] "To Eternal Peace," in *Basic Writings of Kant*, 459.

"Only in the past couple of hundred years has every human community been drawn into a single web of trade and a global network of information. Each of us can realistically imagine contacting any other of our fellow humans and sending them something worth having; a radio, an antibiotic, a good idea. Unfortunately, we could also send something that would do harm; a virus, a pollutant, a bad idea. Each person you know about and can affect is someone to whom you have responsibilities: to say this is to affirm the very idea of morality."[91]

Cosmopolitanism is equipped with a responsibility to all humankind, valuing life in welcoming the life of a stranger and his/her culture. It has universal concern and respect for other people through recognition and global justice.

Furthermore, cosmopolitan theory and ethics of hospitality need to be deepened in reference to the brutal reality of innocent victims in European colonialism during the enlightenment and modernity. When the cosmopolitan theory is dissociated from a critical analysis of past injustice, it would betray its related principle of justice, popular sovereignty, and solidarity.

If the sovereignty of the nation-state is the backbone of colonialism and imperialism in the modern era, the Empire in the phase of late capitalism is embedded with the process of globalization in political, economic, and cultural realms; it eliminates the territorial boundaries of a nation through no territorial center of power. "[A] *decentered* and *deterritorializing* apparatus of the rule" emerges and "manages hybrid identities, flexible hierarchies, and plural exchanges through modulating networks of command."[92]

---

[91] Appiah, *Cosmopolitanism*, XII-XIII.
[92] Hardt and Negri, *Empire*, XII.

The cosmopolitan moral and politics cope with the neocolonial reality of global sovereignty; such a perspective facilitates public theology in taking on the significance of global justice and the solidarity principle, as deepening and critically renewing some limitations of Kant. It draws attention to the neocolonial condition which is embedded with public spheres in the social stratification as well as in the global civil society.

An interpretation of cosmopolitan epistemology in light of the life-world deepens a critique of the true content of social contract reasoning and its justice and solidarity with the poor and innocent victim, which would be obscure in a Kantian project of global sovereignty.

Public Theology: Anamnestic Eschatology and *Theologia Crucis*

Anamnesis, a form of radical reflection, remains decisive in the theological understanding of eschatology in terms of *theologia crucis*. This perspective characterizes a biblical symbol of the kingdom of God which gives a new impulse to cosmopolitan justice as fairness and reparation while underlying the gospel of reconciliation.

Walter Benjamin deserves attention in this regard. He keeps his "undialectical" way of thinking by holding in check dialectics of enlightenment and progress, which underlines the violent reality of the underside in marching history; the "angel of history" (in the ninth of "Theses on the Philosophy of History")[93] does not dialectically move forward into the future. Rather, the angel's face "turned toward the past." "The angel

---

[93] Benjamin, *Illuminations*, 253-64.

would like to stay, awaken the dead, and join together what has been smashed to pieces."⁹⁴

Benjamin sees the angel of judgment in Klee's "Angelus Novus," who looks at nothing but the expanse of ruins of the past; it is blown backward into the future by the storm of progress. Such a way of thinking problematizes what is taken for granted as a history of modernity while slamming its faith in the progress of rationalization in a consistent, dialectically explainable manner. "Nothing that has ever happened should be regarded as lost for history." (Thesis III).

In the discussion of the rebirth of messianic thinking, Moltmann involves Benjamin's philosophy of history. He takes into account the assumption that history in a genuine sense comes into existence only when the chaos of events can be comprehended; it swims against the path of progress. A genealogy of the subjugated history can be galvanized in terms of messianic power in which the past is present at the moment of danger; the spark of hope is fanned for the past.⁹⁵

A theological symbol of eschatology alongside *theologia crucis* provides a creative warrant for public theology, which correlates an anti-colonial aspect of cosmopolitan principle with the anamnestic theory of the messianic history.

Dietrich Bonhoeffer provocatively writes during the time of his imprisonment: "We have, for once, learned to see the great events of world history from below, from the perspective of the outcast, the suspects, the maltreated, the powerless, the oppressed, the reviled—in short, from the perspective of those who suffer."⁹⁶

---

[94] Ibid., 257 (Thesis IX).
[95] Moltmann, *The Coming of God*, 39.
[96] Bonhoeffer, *Letters & Papers from Prison*, 17.

A messianic form of *theologia crucis* remains crucial in bringing public theology to the cosmopolitan principle through reparative justice and solidarity. A critique of its colonial under-modernity comes to terms with an appropriation of the prophetic tradition of religious socialism. Such combined articulation relocates the significance of public theology in the postcolonial condition. The meaning of history is found in its wreckages, fractures, discontinuity, and rupture in counter-memory to modernity and its triumphal progress.

Concluding Reflection: *Kairos* and Religious Socialism

Kant's idea of radical evil assumes the biblical dimension, emphasizing moral struggle for human dignity and social justice in accordance with the kingdom of God. According to Tillich, the Christian symbol of the kingdom of God entails diverse connotations: political rule of God on earth, social characteristics (including the ideas of peace and justice), personalistic significance (providing eternal meaning to the individual person in fulfillment of humanity in every human individual), and universality (God being all in all).[97]

A Christian understanding of the Kingdom of God is featured by the dialectical relationship between the immanent and the transcendent; the eschatological significance in the prophetic literature retains an inner-historical-political-social implication in coping with the problem and the meaning of history.

This perspective might uphold a "theological" side of Kant, which is associated with the concept of universal human dignity and the kingdom of God, and it implies Christian

---

[97] Tillich, *Systematic Theology* 3: 358-9.

ethics of discipleship in terms of philosophical theology. He synthesizes the Greek notion of universal *logos* with Christian commitments to morality, virtue, and the kingdom of God. It is classified as prophetic-ethical religion with messianic significance in resistance to the reality of radical evil.

This prophetic-ethical Kant can assume the theonomous horizon, and life-world approach to Kant's cosmopolitan principle may remain a resource and inspiration for public theology and project of incomplete modernity which retains postcolonial implication.

Tillich sees *kairos*, the fulfillment of time, as maturity in terms of the central manifestation of the kingdom of God in particular religious and cultural contexts; he was especially committed to the religious socialist movement in contrast to quasi-religious forces in Fascism, Nationalism, and laissez-faire capitalism.

As Tillich writes: "The experience of a *kairos* has occurred again and again in the history of the churches,…Whenever the prophetic Spirit arose in the churches, the "third stage" was spoken of, the stage of the "rule of Christ" in the "one thousand–year" period…The fact that *kairos*-experiences belong to the history of the churches and that the "great *kairos*," the appearance of the center of history, is again and again re-experienced through relative "*kairo*," in which the Kingdom of God manifests itself in a particular breakthrough, is decisive for our consideration."[98]

Tillich's religious socialist principle may find space in the Kantian principle of ethical socialism in the thought of a neo-Kantian philosopher, Hermann Cohen (1842-1919), and his democratic socialism on behalf of a cosmopolitan confederation of ideal states.

---

[98] Ibid., 370.

As Cohen writes, "Socialism is right, insofar as it is grounded in the idealism of ethics, and the idealism of ethics has grounded the socialism...Kant as an ideal politician explicitly based himself on Plato, and he for the republic...he is the true and actual originator of German socialism."[99]

Karl Vorländer (1860-1928) was an outstanding advocate of the neo-Kantian movement in which he sought to combine Marxism with Kant's moral philosophy. An epistemological-critical foundation and its ethical enlargement can critically renew Marxism, which has a lack of such ethical reasoning and significance. In his report on *Die neukantische Bewegung im Sozialismus* (*The Neo-Kantian Movement in Socialism*) we read: "I emphasize explicitly that the Königsberg philosopher has not played a role of 'originator of socialism' historically, and that the development of socialism, in contrast, has run 'under completely other philosophical auspices.' What is at stake is only the possibility of a methodical, systematical, logical connection."[100]

Neo-Kantian democratic socialism in Cohen and Vorländer was also considerably influential in the theological-socialist development of the young Barth in his commitment to religious socialism. According to the report of F. W. Marquardt, an outstanding scholar of Karl Barth and socialism, Barth underlined the following sentence from Vorländer's book: "The crucial issue is not whether Kant somehow already had socialist ideas, but whether his ethics can really be the starting point for a socialist ethics."[101]

---

[99] Cohen, "Kant," 1896, in *Marxismus und Ethik*, 70.
[100] Ibid., 17.
[101] "First Report on Karl Barth's Socialist Speeches," in *Theological Audacities*, 112.

This perspective further examines the prophetic tradition of public theology, as explicitly expressed in Christian political realism (Reinhold Niebuhr) and theological engagement with religious socialism (Paul Tillich and Karl Barth). These theological themes constitute my study of public theology and religious socialism in the next two chapters.

Chapter 6
Christian Realism

Reinhold Niebuhr (1892-1971), an older brother of H. R. Niebuhr (1894–1962), is one of the most important public ethicists, conceptualizing neo-orthodox realist theology with a strong sense of responsibility and critique of social injustice. He undertakes an analysis of the political, moral theory of liberal democracy in a broader context, which I have investigated in previous chapters in dealing with deontology, social contract theory, utilitarianism, and teleology. He also involves interrogating Marxist theory and its moral and political reasoning.

His reading strategy is undertaken through interrogation, critical renewal, and semantic retrieval of democracy, social justice, and common good through his creative interpretation of the biblical symbol of the City of God.

This chapter is a study of the Christian realism of Reinhold Niebuhr in his critical dialogue with modern political philosophy and socialist theory. First, his creative analysis of original sin and freedom is scrutinized, because it marks one of his significant contributions by renewing the limitation of Augustinian original sin.

Second, Niebuhr's realist approach to conflict is based on his religious analysis of the relation between will-to-live and will-to-power. This approach remains an undercurrent in his critical analysis of State power, capitalist economic power, and colonialism while supporting the anti-colonial struggle. It is important to review his critical and constructive reading of Marx's historical materialism as social scientific inquiry.

Third, I deal with Niebuhr's positive assessment of the relationship between the Reformation principle, the Renaissance, and the Enlightenment through his synthesis. Niebuhr's critical position about political liberalism and Fascism is to be explicated, while his option for democratic society and justice remains decisive in his public ethical stance. Finally, I review James Cone's critique of Niebuhr in terms of racial justice.

Christian Political Realism

For Niebuhr, "Christian life without a high sense of responsibility for the health of our communities, our nations, and our cultures degenerates into an intolerable other-worldliness."[1]

For Christian political responsibility, Niebuhr calls attention to Augustine's notion of original sin. Realism is defined as a position that takes into account the factors of self-interest and power in their resistance to the established moral norms; it critically deals with the idealist position in a social and political situation.[2]

Augustine (354-430), the Bishop of Hippo in North Africa, presented his masterpiece of *De Civitate Dei* (*The City of God* begun in 413 and completed in 426) in theological, historical response to the sack of Rome by the Visigoths in 410 C. E. His history of salvation provides Niebuhr with a realist approach to human life, society, and history. Augustine's position is also characterized by his biblical realism in the conception of evil and

---

[1] Niebuhr, "The Christian Witness in the Social and National Order," in *The Essential Reinhold Niebuhr*, 100.
[2] Niebuhr, "Augustine's Political Realism," Ibid., 123.

original sin. Niebuhr credits Augustine as "the first great 'realist' in Western history."[3]

Democracy and Morality

Niebuhr reemploys Augustine's realist insight for his typology of children of light and children of darkness. He affirms that "modern democracy requires a more realistic philosophical and religious basis" "for a more persuasive justification." We read his realist position: "Man's capacity for justice makes democracy possible, but man's inclination to injustice makes democracy necessary."[4]

Justice comes to terms with democracy, thus justice without democracy would be empty, while democracy without justice is vulnerable to blind populism. Morality, in the relation between justice and democracy, plays a major role in categorizing the type of children of light or darkness in a more dialectical manner than remaining binary opposition.

Niebuhr classifies the moral cynics with no law, beyond their own will and interest (in the case of Machiavelli's amoral Prince) into children of this world or children of darkness. On the contrary, he terms the children of light to designate those who seek to bring self-interest under the guidance of a higher law and a more universal law on behalf of a better universal good. What remains crucial in Niebuhr's political realism is a biblical stance expressed in the statement: "the children of this world are in their generation wiser than the children of light."[5]

---

[3] Ibid., 124.
[4] Niebuhr, "The Children of Light and the Children of Darkness," Ibid.,160.
[5] Cited in Ibid., 166.

The children of darkness are evil with no law except for their own self-interest and power, while they are wise to understand the power of self-interest in the shrewd assessment of it in mundane affairs. However, the children of light are virtuous with a higher and universal good, while they are foolish because of their incapability of recognizing the power of self-interest and even this reality among themselves. Christian children of light, Niebuhr holds, have been accountable and even guilty in this charge.[6]

In dealing with the dialectical relationship between the children of darkness and the children of light, Niebuhr utilizes the Augustinian conception of the city of the world and the city of God. Self-love, or to be exact, pride (*superbia*), is the source of evil, which is explained as the consequence of one's abandonment of God, that is egocentricity (making the ego its own end).

Christian realism is based on Augustine's interpretation of sin and biblical faith, and his definition of self-love or egocentricity is contained in his notion of the city of this world (*civitas terrena*) (to the point of contempt of charity). It is comingled with the city of God (*civitas dei*), which is actuated by the love of God (*amor dei* or charity) to the point of contempt of self.[7] Good and evil are not determined by some fixed structure of human nature or universal reason, as seen in the theory of the natural law (Thomas Aquinas).

Teleological Reasoning and Theological Realism

Thomas Aquinas (1225-1274) sought to synthesize Aristotle with Augustine. Thomas holds that all things proceed from God (*exitus*) and return to God (*reditus*). The pattern of *exitus* (God as origin) and *reditus* (God as the goal) has the significance

---

[6] Ibid., 166-7.
[7] "Augustine's Political Realism," Ibid., 126.

of ordering nature for theological ethics in the teleological framework.

In this pattern, the natural moral law (reason and conscience) takes part in the eternal law of God's governing of things in the universe. The principle of synderesis is a natural disposition of the human mind in which good is to be done, while evil is avoided. The reason is endowed with understanding (theoretical principle) and synderesis (practical principle), working together with human law and conscience. Natural law becomes a part of God's eternal law in creation.[8]

The Thomist meta-ethical position in an Aristotelian framework shows a structure of synthesis in the juxtaposition of the natural law of creation with the divine law of revelation (grace perfecting nature, not destroying it); however, a reality of radical evil disappears in the realm of creation, since human nature is not wholly corrupted.

The image of God in Aquinas refers primarily to intellectual nature as a natural endowment, which is to be found in the human creature in his/her resemblance of God; knowledge and understanding (human soul) have remained intact after Adam's sin. Thus, it could not be destroyed or lost by the Fall.[9]

In the Catholic tradition, the formal element of the original sin is the privation of original justice, whereas materially, through the efficacy of baptismal grace it is regarded as concupiscence, which is not sin in the strictest sense; it is a form deriving from sin with an inclination to sin.[10]

Against this, Niebuhr calls attention to Augustine's understanding of the image of the triune God, which is immortally implanted in the soul of human beings. Augustine's primary

---

[8] ST, Ia2ae. 91. 2.
[9] Niebuhr, *The Nature and Destiny of Man* 1: 153. Footnote 4.
[10] Ibid., 248.

concern is with the human capacity for self-transcendence in the human spirit through memory in religious search for God.[11] A human being transcends itself through mind or reason, and self-transcendence leads us to the search for God who transcends the world. The rational and intellectual soul cannot be properly understood apart from self-transcendence in its religious longing for God; it is differentiated from Aquinas' definition of the image of God as "primarily intellectual nature."[12]

Niebuhr brings Augustine's aspect of self-transcendence to be relevant to the biblical faith. In the biblical context, evil had come into the world through human responsibility. It is not naturally *necessary*, because God did not predestine human beings to sin, but historically *inevitable*, because they are responsible for it.[13]

Niebuhr further looks at the social and political dimension of "city" in the Augustinian sense, which includes the family, the commonwealth, and the world. In the description of the whole community, there are "fuller of dangers as the greater sea is more dangerous." It is exposed to "tensions, friction, and competitions of interest, and overt conflicts."[14]

In Augustine's account, without injustice or the imposition of power "the imperial city to which the republic belongs could not rule over provinces apart from recourse to injustice. For it is unjust for some men to rule over others"[15] To the extent that social peace and order are established by a dominant group, this group within the society is not exempt from the corruption of self-interest.

---

[11] Ibid., 154.
[12] Ibid., 153. Footnote 4.
[13] Ibid., 260.
[14] Niebuhr, "Augustinian Political Realism," in *The Essential Reinhold Niebuhr*, 127.
[15] Cited in Ibid., 128.

In Augustine's account, the *civitas terrena* (the earthly city) is corrupted by self-love, even to the contempt of God, destined to fail, while in divine providence it may contribute to the temporal well-being of humankind, despite its imperfect state. The heavenly city is formed by the love of God, even to the contempt of the self; it exists within the earthly city, becoming church as a foretaste of the eternal city, despite its imperfect form. These two cities are interacted and fused together until they are separated at the Last Judgment.[16]

Augustine's realism about the commingling implies the conflict between love (caritas) and self-love, as seen in Luther's phrase *simul justus et peccator*.[17] In the comingling of two types of love or two cities, charity is not purely spiritual as a flight from this world, but it has social and historical character. It accepts the ordinary responsibilities of home and state in performing these responsibilities for the ultimate.[18]

Original Sin and Freedom

Niebuhr takes issue with the Catholic distinction between original justice as a special supernatural gift (with the transcendental freedom in the communion with God through the sacrament) and a natural justice of the creature (with unspoiled reason).[19] The former is lost in the Fall until it is restored by sacramental grace and through theological virtues (faith, hope, and love). But natural justice (in the ability of an

---

[16] Augustine, *City of God* I: 35.
[17] Niebuhr, "Augustinian Political Realism," in *The Essential Reinhold Niebuhr*, 135.
[18] Ibid., 137.
[19] Niebuhr, *The Nature and Destiny of Man* I: 269.

unspoiled reason) remains uncorrupted by the Fall.[20] This position is regarded as Semi-Pelagian in which original sin is comprehended as the privation of something supernatural rather than as a corruption of it.[21]

Against the Catholic position, however, Niebuhr argues that the distinction has to be made in a tentative and provisional sense between the original justice and the natural law. The original righteousness is not completely lost in the Fall, but it remains as the knowledge in the life of sinful humans regarding what he/she ought to do. There is no completely lost original justice, just as there is no uncorrupted natural law.[22]

Niebuhr's notion of original sin in terms of the historical inevitability of sin and human responsibility affirms that the exercise of freedom is done in the transcendental human spirit; it recognizes the false use of freedom in action. "Man is most free in the discovery that he is not free."[23]

Thus, original sin, though in an inherited corruption, is committed by the human free will within the realm of responsibility; it is not free to do good, but free for the responsibility, while the sin is not naturally necessary. This paradox was obscured by many Augustinians as well as Pelagianism.

In the teaching of the latter, the good of God's creation is guarded along with the free will against the original sin. Based on natural grace in creation, a human being is capable of fulfilling the law through autonomy and freedom of will. Natural grace does not necessitate divine special grace for redemption, which only pardons sin rather than changing human life. The aspect

---

[20] Ibid., 282.
[21] Ibid., 248.
[22] Ibid., 281.
[23] Ibid., 260.

of sin is found not in the human will as such, but in the habitual custom of sinning or the inertia of nature.[24]

Against this direction, Niebuhr recognizes the significance of the distinction between the likeness of God and the image of God; the fall destroyed the likeness but not the image of God.[25] Adam was sinless before he acted, but became sinful in his first recorded action. Niebuhr considers this stance as "a symbol for the whole of human history."[26] Indeed, we are not significantly differentiated from Adam.

The Augustinian teaching of love as the final norm is connected with his realistic assessment of self-interest and power. Thus, it should be distinguished from modern sentimental versions of Christianity, which undermines the power of egotism at the individual and collective level as well.

In liberal Christianity, the Kantian axiom (I ought, therefore I can) is accepted as relevant to what the Gospel demands. It tends to conflate the Gospel of the kingdom of God with the Kantian kingdom of ends, as obviously seen in Albrecht Ritschl, who brands the transcendental side of the kingdom of God with German bourgeois culture.

Niebuhr shares his critique with Karl Barth.[27] the Kingdom of God tends to be conflated with completed reconciliation, which could be seen in German national culture.

Niebuhr senses in the tradition of Aquinas that there is a lack of realism in the tradition of natural law and its teleological thinking. The latter sidesteps radical forms of human freedom and sin, violating fixed forms of human behavior and social organization. It is also true of the Augustinian definition of

---

[24] Ibid., 245.
[25] Ibid., 270.
[26] Ibid., 280.
[27] Niebuhr, *An Interpretation of Christian Ethics*, 39.

evil as a privation of goodness (*privatio boni*), in which evils are accidents like disease and wounds.

Despite some of Augustine's errors, Niebuhr finds it more significant to appreciate Augustine's leavening self-love (in the city of this world) with the charity (in the city of God) than the classical and medieval school of thought within the natural law foundation.

Niebuhr concurs with Anders Nygren's critical view of Augustine's *amor dei* which misrepresents the agape form of love in the New Testament. God's grace of self-sacrifice on the cross must be the foundation for the human act of love, which is comingled with self-love and sin. God's grace in Christ justifies and dwells really within the faith, guiding, renewing, and restoring human life (including the human act of caritas). *Theologia crucis* is not the consistent principle in Augustine's theology of justification and sanctification in distinction from Luther.[28]

In every case of earthly peace, Augustine holds, the collective self-interest, unless guided in a qualification of love or loyalty, would expose the community to either an overt conflict among competing groups or to the injustice of a dominant group. "When it is victorious, it will become vice's slave."[29]

Augustine's formula of leavening the influence of the charity at a higher level upon self-love at a lower level becomes crucial and effective in preventing the latter from being involved in self-defeat.

---

[28] Ibid., 133. According to Luther, the essence of the original sin is found in a personal ethical act, unlike Augustine. Bonhoeffer follows in the footsteps of Luther, maintaining that the doctrine of original sin in transmission by procreation is a poor attempt in doing damage to humanity. Bonhoeffer, *Creation and Fall*, 150. 125.

[29] Niebuhr, "Augustinian Political Realism," in *The Essential Reinhold Niebuhr*, 133. 136.

In his critical retrieval of Augustine's political realism, Niebuhr takes into account Jesus' saying about the wisdom of the serpent and the harmlessness of the dove. "The children of light must be armed with the wisdom of the children of darkness but remain free from their malice. They must know the power of self-interest in human society without giving it moral justification. They must have this wisdom so that they may beguile, deflect, harness and restrain self-interest, individual and collective, for the sake of the community."[30]

Niebuhr considers human beings with responsible freedom in changing society through caritas, which does not downplay the power of self-interest: a human being as a leavening agent. A Christian realist seeks to leaven the society with Christian values such as love, forgiveness, and advocacy.

Conflict Model in Christian Realism

In a biblical imagery of children of light and the children of darkness, Niebuhr reinvigorates a conflict model in terms of the human being-the-leavening agent. The children of light can be termed those who bring self-interest under the principle "of a more universal law, seeking its problem "in harmony with a more universal good."[31] But the children of darkness are moral cynics, who acknowledge no law beyond the self or the strength of the nation. But they are wise because they understand the power of self-interest at the individual and collective level in modern society. However, the children of light, moral sentimentalists, underestimate the power of self-interest and self-will, ignoring

---

[30] Niebuhr, "The Children of Light and the Children of Darkness," Ibid., 181.
[31] Ibid., 166.

"the peril of anarchy in both the national and the international community."[32]

The democratic civilization has been built by children of light, but is under attack by moral cynics, since the former has a naive and superficial view of human beings and moral sentimentality; it leads them to underestimate the power of self-interest and class interest among themselves and in their societies.

Niebuhr's evaluation is applied to the secularized idealists, modern children of light. On the contrary, moral cynics, despite their moral protestations, have a provisional advantage over them, because they are based on the shrewd assessment of the power of self-interest among the children of light.[33]

Modern liberal Protestantism, which arose against medieval Catholicism, as Niebuhr writes, is driven by rationalization and individualism. But it is more sentimental or more blind in its appraisal of the moral realities and corruption of self-interest in the social, political life than secular idealism.[34]

Modern secularism, which is on the wave of boundless social progress and optimism of human nature, contradicts the Christian idea of original sin. But Niebuhr makes a creative retrieval of such doctrine for an adequate social and political theory. He challenges the confidence of modern secular idealism and its democratic culture as rooted in its too optimistic view of human nature and its individualism.[35]

---

[32] Ibid.
[33] Ibid., 167.
[34] Ibid.
[35] Ibid., 170.

Critical Appropriation: Augustine and the Image of God

Eventually, Niebuhr cuts through limitations of the Augustinian theology of original sin, in which the original sin has been made a doctrine of an inherited corruption through sexual propagation; it is transmitted with the sexual act and selfish or immoderate desires (concupiscence) resting on a perversion of the will, which is the basic form of sin in Adam's offspring. The concupiscence is connected with immoderate self-love (superbia or pride) as the core of the concupiscence, which implies a general or universal structure of human conduct underlying all sins.

According to Augustine, immoderate or unlimited desire, which is to draw the whole of life reality into one's self-interest, is called concupiscence; determining all aspects of the human relation to one's self, fellow person, and the world, concupiscence retains the all-embracing meaning of spiritual value and material wealth in dealing with physical hunger, sex, knowledge, and power, etc.[36]

Concupiscence is a basic form of human sin, which cannot be so found in an infant, who has no responsible decision of the free will. In Augustine's equation between concupiscence and sin, it is hard to identify concupiscence simply with sexuality, without further ado. A sexual desire can become an example in demonstrating the perverted nature of concupiscence; concupiscence is seen as a structural deformation or perversion of the human will or sinful desire in a general anthropological context.

Pride makes the self into the principle of all things in the place of God, and it refers to the core of perverted will. Pride (love of self) is seen in connection with concupiscence in anthropological implication. Such connection between self–love (*superbia* or

---

[36] Tillich, *Systematic Theology* 2: 52.

pride) and concupiscence in Augustine is undertaken in the philosophical analysis of the structure of sinful desire.[37]

Nonetheless, the all-embracing meaning of concupiscence has often been reduced to the specific striving for sexual pleasure, identifying it with sexual desire. It has been assumed that "hereditary" sin is rooted in sexual pleasure in the act of propagation.[38]

This position has been a tremendous influence on the Christian understanding of sexual desire and pleasure with negative consequences in its historical development. However, it completely dismisses God's original blessing on sexual life (Gen. 1:28) in reference to its community in the life of humankind in post-fall genealogy (Gen. 5: 1-2).

Apart from a concept of hereditary sin in sexual terms, however, Augustine still articulates the union between God and human beings with the mystical power of God's grace in sacraments. Although human will is not destroyed by the Fall, it is tainted with sin and incapable of spiritual ascent to God; it must be liberated by the grace of God, which establishes human will, far from abolishing it. Human free will as taken captive to sin requires God's grace for liberation, which is given to us and moves human freedom toward redemption.

Grace refers to the infusion of love, the power which can overcome human sin. God, in the infusion of love, cooperates with humans in the life of faith for the growth in sanctification and the spiritual life until the end of life. A supernatural fuel (*gratia infusa*) is in preparation for the grace of inspiration in collaboration with human will as a cooperative mode of grace to perform good works (in the process of justification); *amor Dei*

---

[37] Pannenberg, *Systematic Theology* 2: 243-5.
[38] Tillich, *Systematic Theology* 2: 52.

remains central because faith without love is of no value; faith works through love (Gal 5:6).

As concupiscence is the root of all evil, so caritas is the root of all good. Through caritas, God comes to inhabit the soul of the justified sinner, as the latter takes part in the divine life.[39] In the subsequent Catholic tradition, concupiscence is not defined as a sin in the strict sense, but the inclination to sin, when seen from the efficacy of baptismal grace; it is differentiated from the Reformation view in which the original sin remains even in those baptized, though no longer imputed.

Thomas continues in Augustine's tradition, arguing that original sin as the inheritance of Adam's guilt is no longer a matter of individual responsibility. Evil is seen in one's failing to actualize goodness or happiness as the ultimate end regarding teleological character; it is not the absence of good in the Augustinian sense. But it refers to a certain absence of a good as a privation of form. This position understands evil in Aristotelian terms of cause and effect, potency and act, and lack and perfection. Natural evil (unrealized potential) contributes to the goodness of creation, while moral evil ("evil done") is willed by agents; it is caused by a defect of the will, in other words, a lack of understanding of the good.[40]

Thomas makes a distinction between sanctifying grace (*gratia gratum faciens*) and freely bestowed grace (actual grace; *gratia gratis data*—gratuitous grace such as charismata, the priestly power of consecration, absolution, and ecclesial jurisdiction), which has no significant role in the grace of justification.[41]

---

[39] McGrath, *Iustitia Dei*, 32.
[40] However, the Thomist account of evil as lack or deprivation becomes questionable when faced with the Holocaust or genocide in the sense of radical evil. ST Ia. 48. I.
[41] Davies, *The Thought of Thomas Aquinas*, 270.

Furthermore, Aquinas introduces the habitual (or sanctifying) gifts of grace infused within the human soul; its operative side consists in the formal principle of justification, while its cooperative side interacts with human will, becoming the basis of human meritorious action.[42] Grace is understood even as a habit 'possessed' within the human soul, taking the form of an intermediate between the divine and human nature created by God. This habitual grace as *gratia creata*, by which a believer takes part in the divine life, is distinguished from the uncreated grace of the Holy Spirit, which acts continually on those in a state of habitual grace.[43]

Thomas' notion of habitual grace in the sense of created grace contrasts with Augustine, who is concerned with the operative grace of God as the primary source of exciting the human will to desire good deeds in the cooperative sense.

Taken all together, Niebuhr develops a critical but realist reorientation in exposing humanity's nature and destiny, appropriating Augustine who sees the image of God in terms of self-transcendence and freedom. Niebuhr reinforces Augustine's position that the evil of sin cannot completely destroy the essential character of human beings—what God has created in human beings. In the statement of Augustine: "And it was manifested unto me that those things be good, which yet are corrupted...But if they be deprived of all good, they would cease to be...So long therefore as they are, they are good: therefore, whatsoever is, is good."[44]

---

[42] McGrath, *Iustitia Dei*, 109.
[43] Ibid., 108.
[44] Cited in Niebuhr, *The Nature and Destiny of Man* I: 267.

Niebuhr Concerning Brunner and Barth

The Thomist structure can be seen in Emile Brunner's conception of the image of God; its formal side is indestructible, yet always obscured by sin. It does not stand in the way of the material side of *justitia originalis*, although the latter is completely lost and abolished. All ordinances or civil and secular office or historical and social arrangements of life become basic parts of all ethical problems such as family and state. This refers to the ontological capacity for divine revelation through the point of contact between God and a human being.[45]

Against this direction, Barth relocates terms such as "capacity for revelation" or "capacity for words" or "receptivity for words" within the sphere of "sovereign, freely electing grace of God."[46] Thus, Barth rejects Thomas' dictum in independence from Jesus Christ as an arch-heresy: *gratia non tollit naturam sed perficit* ("grace does not destroy nature but perfects it")[47]

Given the debate between Barth and Brunner, Niebuhr may concur with Brunner's ontological side, while reacting against his Thomist structure of distinction. Brunner's metaphysical distinction would become politically dangerous, even devastating with German Christians utilizing Brunner's natural theology and his point of contact with the divine saving grace through Nazi ideology.[48]

On the other hand, it is difficult for Niebuhr to affirm that Paul conceptualizes Adam's sin through historical inheritance through propagation in a sexual generation.[49] Niebuhr's position

---

[45] Barth, *Nature and Grace*, 24; 29.
[46] Ibid., 79.
[47] Ibid., 21.
[48] In the Deutsche *Pfarrerblatt* (German Pastor's Journal), a representative of National Socialism, Brunner's article of nature and grace was praised as "a mine of treasure, a veritable gold mine." *Nature and Grace*, 72.
[49] Ibid., 261.

shows an affinity with Barth who also rejects the Augustinian notion of original sin as sexually propagated through the mortal sickness. Barth rejects the original sin as a hereditary sin, taking such a concept to be unfortunate and mistaken. Barth holds, "has a hopelessly naturalistic, deterministic and fatalistic ring."[50]

We are known by God in Adam, who is not our fate. Rather God fuses all people into unity with Adam as *primus inter pares* (a first among equals), while at the same time condemning Adam's disobedience as ours. Jesus Christ is the first and true Adam, the representative of all others, but not like the *primus inter pares*.[51]

Likewise, Niebuhr does not regard the original sin as belonging to essential human nature, because it exists within the realm of human responsibility and freedom. Sin is "historically" universal or inevitable, but not "naturally" necessary. He finds that Augustine's idea of human self-transcendence (more than a rational creature like Aquinas) remains crucial in understanding human religious nature in searching for God who transcends the world. This capacity for self-transcendence looks beyond the human self, knowing that self-projection is not God.[52]

In Niebuhr's view, human self-love and egocentricity are inevitable within the realm of human freedom and will. Nonetheless, they do not fit in the category of natural necessity. "The final paradox is that the discovery of the inevitability of sin is man's highest assertion of freedom."[53]

Niebuhr's ontological position parts company from Barth's Christological position in which a human being is not created to be the image of God, but in correspondence with the image of

---

[50] Barth, CD IV. 1: 501.
[51] Ibid., 512-3.
[52] Ibid., 166.
[53] Ibid., 263.

God, God's own being.⁵⁴ The divine likeness in human beings is in correspondence to the relationship within God's triune life. The analogy of relation "does not entail likeness but the correspondence of the unlike."⁵⁵ We are created *in* the image of God only through Jesus Christ, the image of the invisible God in the full sense (Col. 1:15). *Analogia relationis* is given, the passive sense is not equated with an *analogia entis* underlying the ontological capacity of establishing its connection with God's saving grace in a positive sense.⁵⁶

In fact, this perspective does not discard Niebuhr's position of freedom and responsibility, although the latter grounds freedom and self-transcendence in an ontological sense.

For his realism, Niebuhr integrates Irenaeus' distinction between likeness (destroyed by the sin) and image of God (preserved despite the sin),⁵⁷ but Iranaeus related the image of God to Jesus Christ in whom a human being is made. Thus, Christological conception maintains that the image of God is not to be found in us, but pointing to the direction for us to grow in the sense of the continuing creation. Irenaeus can be shared in Niebuhr and Barth.

Niebuhr elaborates the continued relationship between *justitia originalis* and sinful human being through freedom and self-transcendence in the human spirit in reference to the law of love. Niebuhr relocates the place of original righteousness within the human capacity of self-transcendence, from the moment of which the consciousness and memory of original perfection emerge; but "it must not be regarded as the possession of perfection."⁵⁸

---

54 Barth, CD III/1: 197.
55 Ibid., 196.
56 Barth, CD III/2:195.
57 Niebuhr, *The Nature and Destiny of Man* 1: 270.
58 Ibid., 277.

If the *justitia originalis* is in reality present (rather than in possession) with a human being, it refers to the biblical law of love (love of God and of your neighbor) for the ultimate requirement of human freedom.[59] The fulfillment of love does not mean a simple possibility. Such freedom of the law of love is not completely free because of human corruption by sin. It requires the grace of God.[60]

This perspective cuts across the position of the Social Gospel (Walter Rauschenbusch), who argues that sin is transmitted through the social institution and the power of the social group against the biological transmission of evil.[61]

However, in Niebuhr's view, the injustice of social institutions and the power of social groups should be first exposed in the perversion of the unlimited desire (concupiscence) to power and domination (will to power) in the social-political context.

Niebuhr is convinced of Augustine's biblical realism in his rejection of metaphysical dualism between good and evil. Insofar as evil is nothing but a privation of good, it refers to a misdirected will. In the gospel, there is divine mercy of forgiveness by which to overcome a contradiction that we cannot transcend (Rom. 7:23). On the one hand, the grace of justification is conceived as pardon (forgiveness of sin), while the grace of God is taken as the power of righteousness healing the contraction within our souls and hearts.[62]

Niebuhr's paradoxical vision seeks to integrate political radicalism with a more classical and historical interpretation of Christianity through the experience of grace and sin because the experience of grace cannot be found in Marxist radical

---

[59] Ibid.
[60] Ibid., 296.
[61] Ibid., 246.
[62] Niebuhr, "Why the Christian Church Is Not Pacifist," Ibid, 103.

utopian vision as well as in liberal optimism in progress. Niebuhr's religious disinterestedness in the frame of grace does not discourage interest in the social commitment. Rather it contributes to politics, in challenging the myth of progress captive to the chaos of the Great Depression.[63]

The Conflict Model and Marxist Theory

Niebuhr's creative appropriation of Augustine's theology of two cities helps to articulate a form of religious piety, which does not eliminate its moral connotation. He recognizes Augustine's realistic interpretation of social life in the sense that the city of this world is "compact of injustice," and "it was built by Cain and its peace is secured by strife."[64]

Augustinian realism can be furthered and elaborated in Niebuhr's religious approach to the two types of will in dealing with religion and society. His appraisal of the transition is seen from the survival impulse and its egotistic drive to the two different and contradictory forms: the will-to-live and the will-to-power.

Will-to-Live and Will-to-Power

Schopenhauer comprehends religious asceticism in terms of the denial of will-to-live, which implies "a constant mortification of the will."[65] Niebuhr concurs with Schopenhauer since the religious person is reinforced for the moral will through the holiness of God while restraining the will-to-power. For Schopenhauer the inner essence of everything is the will which

---

[63] McCann, *Christian Realism and Liberation Theology*, 36.
[64] Niebuhr, *Moral Man and Immoral Society*, 70.
[65] Ibid., 55.

replaces the thing-in-itself (Kant), thus the world is represented as the objectification of the will. Servitude to the endless will is the root of suffering, thus true redemption from life derives from an ascetic negation of the will to live.

Against Schopenhauer's ascetic position, Niebuhr focuses on the paradoxical character of Christ (Matt. 10:39). Whoever seeks to find one's life shall lose it; anyone who loses his/her life for Christ's sake shall find it. The will-to-live without religious sublimation would be transmuted into the will-to-power (Nietzsche), or into the desire for power and glory. The will-to-power as the fundamental drive is the constructive principle of life, and it stands as the substance to other drives as an accident. Self-preservation, in a struggle for existence or survival of the fittest, could be understood as an indirect consequence of the will-to-power, which locates Nietzsche within the camp of social Darwinism. Struggle for power is wherever struggle is.[66]

If life is conceptualized as the will-to-power, it would be a social manifestation of concupiscence in the Augustinian sense. More than a struggle for existence in nature, individuals or groups in their conflicts seek to guard their power and prestige in encroachment upon the prestige and power of others. The will to live cannot be easily renounced by the ascetic ideal, but it would be transformed into the will-to-power in all corners of human life.

What strikes in Niebuhr's analysis of power is seen in the two types of military and economic power; the justifications of the disproportion of power in social systems "are usually dictated by the desire of the men of power to hide the nakedness of their greed, and by the inclination of society itself to veil the brutal facts of human life from itself."[67]

---

[66] Danto, *Nietzsche as Philosopher*. 223-4.
[67] Niebuhr, *Moral Man and Immoral Society*, 8.

This conflict of power is expressed more cruelly in collective terms in the struggles between classes, races, and other groups in human society rather than in individual terms that liberal democratic idealists assume. The conflict model between the will-to-live and the will-to-power is mixed and compounded, despite its contradiction. With this conflict model in mind, Niebuhr finds the simple distinction between good and evil, or selfishness and altruism to be invalid when such a solution is proposed in liberal democratic idealism.[68]

In Niebuhr's theory of power, the rise of modern democracy in the eighteenth century has never been dissociated from the special interests of the commercial middle classes. The concept and laws of human rights have been developed in accordance with the ideology of the liberal bourgeois interest. With the augmented centralization of economic power, economic power has become the significant coercive force of modern society. It challenges the authority of the State in the sense of laissez-faire capitalism while employing the institutions of the State for its own purpose.[69]

In this scheme of interpretation Niebuhr maintains that every social group together with every individual developed such expansive desire rooted in the instinct of survival that the will-to-live turns into the will-to-power. The will-to-power among competing national groups becomes the cause of the international anarchy, which was at times curtailed and prevented by effective imperialism. "Thus, society is in a perpetual state of war."[70]

---

[68] Niebuhr, "The Children of Light and The Children of Darkness," in *The Essential Reinhold Niebuhr*, 171.
[69] Niebuhr, *Moral Man and Immoral Society*, 15.
[70] Ibid., 19.

Niebuhr and Social Contract Theory

In the genealogical analysis of the Scylla of despotism or imperialism and the Charybdis of anarchy, it seems difficult to fully concur with Niebuhr's theory of conflict model. If the will to live is degenerated into the will-to-power, whether in Nietzsche or social Darwinism, it is significant to call into question the theory of social Darwinism and its social, political theory in the context of racism and colonialism.

Niebuhr certainly considers equal justice as "the most rational ultimate objective for society." If a social conflict strives for greater equality, it retains a moral justification in rejecting the perpetuation of privilege or imperial rule, or class dominance. "The oppressed, whether they be the Indians in the British Empire, or the Negros in our own country or the industrial workers in every nation, have a higher moral right to challenge their oppressors than these have to maintain their rule by force."[71]

Niebuhr recognizes moral impulse in resistance, but fails to acknowledge the aspect of social justice in the context of social contract theory; Locke calls attention to natural law of reason and human rights ethics based on the biblical idea of the image of God rather than original sin. Rousseau sought to prevent the transition from the will-to-live to the will-to-power through his general will and democratic legislation while safeguarding the rights and dignity of the poor in the critique of slavery and colonialism.

Although Niebuhr maintains that Rousseau resolved the conflict between the individual and the community by the concept of the general will,[72] unfortunately, he charges Rousseau's idea of general will with a sentimentalist totalitarian thought, which is relevant in Lenin's Russian revolution. In the end, Niebuhr

---

[71] Ibid., 234.
[72] Ibid., 178; 180.

recognizes Rousseau's general will in Bukharin's thought in which all relations among people will be the organization of all their wills in the fully developed communist one.

However, Bukharin's identification of the individual will with the general will refers to Marx's utopian idea of the realm of freedom overcoming the realm of necessity. This utopian state does not necessitate private property, constitutional democracy, and judiciary protection of the poor that becomes crucial in Rousseau's own idea of the general will.[73]

Niebuhr's analysis of democratic tradition remains limited and inadequate. Thus, it is significant to relocate the democratic ideal within the critical-emancipatory tradition of the social contract theory in order to renew Niebuhr's conflict model more appropriately. Here, his model of the human being–the-leavening agent can be more featured in supporting participatory democracy, its constitution in communal life and justice, and individual freedom, while taking issue with postcolonial reality.

Christian Realism: Marxist Theory and Dictatorship

Christian political realism takes Hegel-Marxist theory as a critical dialogue partner, whose political theory entails atheism in confronting public theology and its religious symbols. In dealing with Hegel, Niebuhr takes Hegel's position to be a theory that comprehends the necessity of social fulfillment for the individual. Hegel regards the demand of the State as final, while a more ultimate law stands over the nation. The State has its real content in *Weltgeschichte* which holds the supreme absolute truth in regard to absolute spirit (art, religion, and philosophy

---

[73] Ibid., 195.

of absolute knowledge). The world spirit "constitutes itself the absolute judge over states."[74]

In Niebuhr's account, Hegel has little to do with the doctrine of moral cynicism, but with a sentimental doctrine. The nation in Hegel's sense is not free of moral inhibitions, because he conceptualizes it in *Weltgeschichte* as the concrete universality. Rather Hegel's problem lies in laying excessive reliance upon the human capacity for transcending self-interest through the dialectical movement in the historical course of development.[75]

Niebuhr seems to locate Marx within the tradition of democracy. He acknowledges the optimistic creed of democratic thought within the Marxist idea, although the latter arises in revolt against to political idea of Hegel and liberal democracy. Marxism means the social creed, which represents the social cry of the proletariat, while their misery denounces the liberal creed as "a snare and a delusion."[76]

But Marxism is convinced that the harmony between all social forces would be established after the triumph of the revolution. It can be seen even in Adam Smith, who sees the social harmony between self-interest and the providence of the invisible hand. Niebuhr takes into account the significant "similarities between classical laissez-faire theory and the vision of an anarchistic millennium in Marxism." In the utopian hope, the revolution should lead to a period of history culminating in the Marxist millennium of anarchism (the State withering away).[77]

Niebuhr cites from Lenin: "All need for force will vanish since people will grow accustomed to observing the elementary

---

[74] Ibid., 180.
[75] Ibid., 181.
[76] Ibid., 176.
[77] Ibid., 177.

conditions of social existence without force and without subjection."[78]

Despite the element of provisional cynicism, as Niebuhr argues, the Marxists have a creed of moral sentimentality rather than the cynical creed. They belong to the category of children of light. Niebuhr takes into account the critical view according to which the Marxian idea of class struggle as a dogma creates the conflict experience of the worker itself. Although such critique has validity, Niebuhr maintains that Marxian socialism was an interpretation of the situation of the industrial workers in their feeling and attitude about society and culture.[79]

However, Marxist provisional cynicism is not capable of salvaging them from the usual stupidity and their fate, in which their creed has been made "the vehicle and instrument of the children of darkness."[80] In Niebuhr's account, Stalin is to the early dreamers of Marxism, what Napoleon is to the liberal dreamers in the eighteenth century.

Stalin was based on the Leninist principle in which morality is entirely subordinated to the interests of the class struggle of the proletariat. Soviet power must be maintained and strengthened and it becomes the sole criterion of morality and all cultural values as well. If dictatorship and violence serve the ends of the power as devoted to the liberation of the working class, the good of society can be maximized by sacrificing human rights. Soviet utilitarianism transforms the categorical imperative of Marx and his morality committed to the emancipation of the masses into its opposite by reinforcing the power of the Soviet State and its totalitarianism.[81]

---

[78] Ibid.
[79] Ibid., 144.
[80] Ibid.
[81] Kolakowski, *Main Currents of Marxism* 2: 516.

Taken together, Niebuhr appropriates Marxism as the critical theory of society to take issue with "the individualism and optimism of the old liberalism,"[82] which is built upon the enlightenment as well as such utopian moralism within the Social Gospel. Moral cynicism or totalitarianism in Marxism or Fascism should be held in check while doubting moral utopianism in the liberal democratic tradition.

His political realism becomes interested in undertaking reform politics with pragmatism, which can be seen in his appreciation of Roosevelt's New Deal imbued with its social democratic reform because of his dismay with Marxist socialism. Niebuhr credits the New Deal with significant achievements through economic recovery and improvement in the life of the American working class. But his ideological drift can be seen in his stance for Edmund Burke (1729-1797) in his critique of Rousseau.[83]

In his democratic reading of Marx, Niebuhr does not undercut his critical analysis of the proletarian class and its dictatorship which is only a transitory state. His moral charge against dictatorship is based on unveiling the romantic element inherent in the Marxist interpretation of human nature; it underwrites the mystical glorification of the communist society. Niebuhr argues that the symbol of this Marxist romanticism in its anticipation of automatic mutuality means the virtual anarchism crowning the structure of communist theory.[84]

---

[82] "Intellectual Autobiography," in *Reinhold Niebuhr: His Religious, Social, and Political Thought*, 8.

[83] Niebuhr, *An Interpretation of Christian Ethics*, 140. In the mid-1950s he found himself sympathetic even to Edmund Burke, the representative of political-modern conservatism in Britain. Niebuhr, *The Self and the Dramas of History*, 163-82.

[84] Niebuhr, *Moral Man and Immoral Society*, 194.

According to Niebuhr, the complete moral cynicism underlays the Marxian determinism and proletarianism, because Marx comprehends "all cultural, moral and religious forces as "ideologies," "which rationalize… the economic behavior of various classes."[85]

Niebuhr maintains that the moral cynicism of Marxism discredits all ethical pretensions and achievements in the field of politics in its evaluation of the democratic State. He cites the dictum of Lenin: "Freedom in capitalist society always remains more or less the same as it was in the ancient Greek republics, that is, freedom for the slave-owners."[86]

Lenin's uncompromising anti-patriotism found inspiration in the hearts of the Russian proletariat during World War 1, and he saw the attitude of social democrats in Europe for the war as apostasy in betrayal of socialist internationalism.[87]

In the Marxist-Leninist tradition, Niebuhr argues that Marx calls for the proletariat in terms of religious interpretation of proletarian destiny, in which the proletariat is ascribed to the harbinger of the final victory. This can be seen in parallel with prophetic critique and denunciation of idolatry in the Hebrew Bible. It presents a revolutionary "transvaluation of values."[88]

However, Marx's position of the proletarian dictatorship has detrimental consequences in Lenin's distorted version of the dictatorship into the party's dictatorship over the proletariat as a whole. For Lenin, the dictatorship of the proletariat means "the organization of the vanguard of the oppressed as the ruling class for the purpose of suppressing the oppressors,"[89] which entails anti-democratic violence and suppression by force.

---

[85] Ibid., 146.
[86] Cited in Ibid., 149.
[87] Ibid., 150-1.
[88] Ibid., 154.
[89] Lenin, *The State and Revolution*, 41.

In fact, Marx failed to clearly see a dangerous consequence of the transitional period embedded with the political dictatorship by the party and its suppression. The end (revolution) justifies the means. Now the means (apparatuses of the State, bureaucratic administration, and emergence of privileged class over against the working class) dominate the end in the communist society. The State does not wither away but resurges as a socialist despotic regime.

Religious Reading of Marxist Eschatology

According to Niebuhr, if Nietzsche regards Christianity as the revolt of slaves through spiritual forces of the poor and the meekness, Marxism is another kind of slave revolt through the historical, materialist forces with revolutionary violence robbing the strong of their strength. Marxist theory is instilled with an apocalyptic vision or millennial hope in which Marxist eschatology seeks to establish justice, but it is charged in exaltation or deification of proletarian class with immoral elements such as egotism and vindictiveness.[90]

In Marxian eschatology, justice is established to make the proletarian class strong through economic forces in human history. In a classless society, a vigorous ethical idealism is formulated: "From each according to his ability, to each according to his needs,"[91] though it is an impossible ideal, toward which a modern society must strive.

Niebuhr acknowledges that Marxist utopian thinking would be a secularized form of Jewish millennia hope. Jewish religious thought expresses the millennium in this-worldly terms, which finds the significance in the gospel conception of the kingdom

---

[90] Niebuhr, *Moral Man and Immoral Society*, 156.
[91] Cited in Ibid., 159.

of God; a highly spiritualized version in the sense of fulfillment of the prophecy is seen in facing up to the Jewish millennial hope. It is heavily indebted to the version of the Second Isaiah in dreaming of the Messiah, in which the wolf and the lamb shall graze together (Is. 11:1-6; 65:25).

A millennial hope was born with the social realities plagued by injustice and oppression, while it creates courage in an effort to redeem society of injustice. The Communist's dream of a classless society in a completely equalitarian sense implies a secularized, yet essentially religious iteration of the Jewish religious vision.[92]

Moreover, Niebuhr calls into question Lenin's position, in which Lenin's brutal idealism turns into sentimentalist in envisioning the future: "When people become have become accustomed to observing the fundamental principles of social life and their labor is so productive that they will voluntarily work according to their abilities...there will be no need of any exact calculation of the number of products to be distributed to each of its members; each will take freely 'according to his needs'"[93]

Beyond "according to his needs," human beings will always be concerned enough with enlarging their needs by more than the minimum requirements and more selfish enough than the needs of others. Although people "become accustomed to observing the fundamental principles of social life" in cooperative attitude and through education, Niebuhr regards such stance as sentimental and romantic. Any education does not completely destroy the inclination of human nature in seeking special advantages and individual self-interest at the expense of others.[94]

Niebuhr's realist view of Marxism is highly dialectical. He draws attention to Lenin who maintains that "Marx splendidly

---

[92] Ibid., 61.
[93] Cited in Ibid., 194.
[94] Ibid., 197.

grasped the essence of capitalist democracy, when, in his analysis of the experience of the commune, he said the oppressed are allowed, once every few years, to decide which particular representatives of the oppressing classes are to represent and repress them in politics."[95]

In contrast to the Marxist theory of religion, Niebuhr maintains that religion serves as an instrument and inspiration for social justice while confronting many perils to the right and to the left. Religion always leavens the idea of justice imbued with the idea of love, keeping the idea of justice in a purely political ethical ideal. Every genuine passion for social justice always contains a religious character and dimension within itself.[96]

Both the state and church are involved in each other to the end. The Kingdom of God is around the corner, yet it is impossible to realize it, except by God's grace. This Christian eschatology is differentiated from Marxist utopianism in the secularized Jewish iteration because the Christian eschatology affirms God as the final Lord; "The triumph would have to come through the intervention of God."[97]

Political Liberalism and Democracy

In the second volume of *The Nature and Destiny of Man*, we read: "There are no limits to be set in history for the achievement of more universal brotherhood, for the development of more perfect and more inclusive mutual relations. All the characteristic hopes and aspirations of Renaissance and Enlightenment, of both secular and Christian liberalism, are right at least in this,

---

[95] Cited in Ibid., 149.
[96] Ibid., 80.
[97] Ibid., 82.

that they understand that side of the Christian doctrine which regards the *agape* of the Kingdom of God as a resource for infinite development towards a more perfect brotherhood in history...The freedom of man makes it impossible to set any limits of race, sex, or social condition upon the brotherhood which may be achieved in history."[98]

This statement characterizes his model of the human being-the-leavening agent in transmuting the problem of social order into better order, in which the Christian ideal of love comes to terms with that which was brought by the Renaissance and the Enlightenment.

Niebuhr's synthesis of Renaissance and Enlightenment does not bypass the principle of Reformation in its doctrine of justification by faith, which "represents the final renunciation in the heart of Christianity of the human effort to complete life and history, whether with or without divine grace."[99] The principle of Reformation helps to thwart the logic of Renaissance and Enlightenment toward the modern idea of progress.

Niebuhr does not sidestep his critical analysis of the political theory of liberalism. But he has confidence in the identity of particular and universal interests to transmute egotism into a concern for the general welfare through the intervention of the government. In Niebuhr's account, John Locke thinks of the government as necessary in order to transcend the "inconvenience of the state of nature" in the sense of moral obligation. Such moral reasoning takes place to the point where self-preservation contrasts with the interests of others.[100]

---

[98] Niebuhr, *The Nature and Destiny of Man* II: 85.
[99] Ibid., 148.
[100] Niebuhr, "The Children of Light and The Children of Darkness," in *The Essential Reinhold Niebuhr*, 174.

"Everyone," according to Locke, "as he is bound to preserve himself and not to quit his station willfully, so by the like reason, when his own preservation comes not into competition, ought as much as he can preserve the rest of mankind."[101]

For Niebuhr, Locke's position is no creed of a moral cynic, nor a profound expression of the sense of universal obligation. Locke requires the government to overcome the inconvenience of the state of nature and sees self-interest in conflict with the general interest to the point where self-preservation contrasts with the interest of others.

Given this, it is unfortunate that Niebuhr argues for a real universalism in intent within the laissez-faire capitalism, which "was intended to establish a world community as well as a natural harmony of interests with each nation."[102]

Niebuhr relates Adam Smith to laissez-faire capitalism and charges Locke, not with a profound expression of the universal obligation. Unlike Niebuhr's assumption, however, Locke's moral principle is grounded in securing individual freedom and rights of property and requiring civil society through a social contract for protection and justice. Locke's universal obligation is based on the constitution because the state of nature is bounded by a law of nature, that is, God's law written in the hearts of all humankind. God's law does not cease in the civil constitution.

Although Locke's problem can be seen in his failure to extend universal consent of the people and God's workmanship to the situation in the American colony and slavery, he was concerned with legitimate civil society with good laws, which enhance

---

[101] Ibid.
[102] Ibid.

freedom and morality. Locke's idea of God's workmanship protects the impoverished for the public good of the society.[103]

Liberal Democracy, Fascism, and Religion

Niebuhr judges that a liberal democratic position of the common good cannot be accepted as absolutely true on the part of opponents of proponents of particular interests. In fact, he does not discard the potential of liberal democracy in its protest against fascistic politics, in which the will-to-power turns its collective form into boundless ambitions and imperial desires. The technical civilization has become an instrument to arm the will-to-power in its nihilistic sense with destructive power. The political phenomenon of Fascism represents a historical refutation of the liberal democratic or philosophical concept of individual human life in the eighteenth and nineteenth century.[104]

Niebuhr defends his political realism against the Roman Catholic argument, in which Nazism is the final fruit of a moral cynicism arising from the Renaissance and Reformation. For Niebuhr, Nazi diplomacy and propaganda succeeded in claiming the poor in democratic civilization as their allies against the plutocrats. Nazi politics sought to be allied with the privileged classes in its fight against communism. In this tactic of combination, Nazi barbarism came to a triumph over civilization.[105]

Eventually, Niebuhr refutes the Catholic thesis of alliance between Nazi collectivism and Renaissance and Reformation.

---

[103] Locke, *First Treatise*, art. 42.
[104] Niebuhr, "The Children of Light and The Children of Darkness," in *The Essential Reinhold Niebuhr*, 172.
[105] Ibid., 164, Footnote, 1.

Renaissance and Reformation must not be taken as the watershed to National Socialism in Germany, but its totalitarian State with anti-Semitism was partly buttressed by Catholic political compromise with it.

The religious sublimation of the will-to-live in historical and social terms runs counter to Fascist will-to-power.

Niebuhr would be convinced that "the religious sublimation of the will-to-live mitigates the sharpness of the conflict between the will-to-power," while "lifting the energy of life to a higher level." It could enchant "the soul to seek ultimate satisfaction in a transhistorical and supramundane world," in other words, the soaring of the soul beyond history.[106]

Niebuhr goes on to look at the early victory of fascism in Italy in which the socialist leaders adopted pacifist principles. In the context of socialist pacifist policy, the working class was advised to meet and endure the terror of fascism without any provocation. "Listen to the mind and to the heart which advises you that the working people should be nearer to sacrifice than to vengeance."[107]

In the end, the Italian socialists instilled with pure moral principles were eliminated by the brutal will-to-power of fascists, while workers were subordinated to the State power. The selfishness of human collectives becomes inevitable, rendering a morality of pure disinterestedness to be impossible.[108]

His realist position can be seen in his critical analysis of the Black community and the American labor movement. Niebuhr asserts that there is a social reason for the failure to develop the human rights of Black people because many capable and educated Black people have an inclination to strive

---

[106] Niebuhr, *Moral Man and Immoral Society*, 65; 82.
[107] Ibid., 269.
[108] Ibid., 272.

for identification and assimilation with the more privileged white race. However, Niebuhr has not managed to analyze the extent to which a reality of social stratification in white privilege becomes an obstacle to the Black people's capacity to fulfill their dignity and cultural integrity. There is a definite aspect of the Black agency in the prophetic contribution to human rights, cultural creativity, and social justice in civil society beyond identification or assimilation.

Likewise, the working-class movement was not capable of fulfilling their cause, because the able working people are socially integrated into the system of American individualism.[109] "No political realism which emphasizes the inevitability and necessity of a social struggle, can absolve individuals of the obligation to check their own egoism, to comprehend the interests of others and this to enlarge the areas of co-operation."[110]

To promote his Christian realist position, Niebuhr advocates that a democratic civilization should be preserved with individual freedom, morality, and social justice against totalitarian propaganda, secular utopianism, or blind accommodation to the social system of privilege. "We cannot build our individual ladders to heaven and leave the total human enterprise unredeemed of its excess and corruptions."[111]

What is decisive is for Niebuhr to take into account "the political necessities in the struggle for justice in human society," while acknowledging those elements in human collective behavior embedded with the order of human nature; these elements can be brought to light through Christian realist

---

[109] Ibid., 274.
[110] Ibid., 276.
[111] Ibid., 277.

stance rather than under the dominion of reason, natural moral law, or conscience.[112]

Christian Realism and Democratic Society

Niebuhr's realist model of conflict within the democratic tradition is grounded in Augustine's theory of original sin and history of philosophy in which he seeks to overcome what is false in democratic theory through what is true in democratic life. It implies the significance of immanent critique in undergirding the democratic principle (liberty, popular sovereignty, justice, and solidarity) against the false direction of liberal democracy and modernity in the historical course of time, as expressed in Fascism, militarism, and imperialism.

Thus, Christian eschatology entails greater political relevance to the degree that it finds "the inspiration of high morality and a consolation for the frustrations which moral purpose faces in history."[113]

Eschatological thinking entails political and moral significance in leavening and permeating the secular society through the city of God, which is active in our midst. Modern secular civilization or moralist version of Christianity does not find meaning and significance in the doctrine of forgiveness and grace of justification. However, of special significance in Niebuhr's realist eschatology is the forgiveness of sin. Niebuhr emphasizes love as the highest virtue, while a rational ethic strives for justice.

The religious ethic of love is purer than a rational ethic of a justice imbued with reason. Religious emphasis upon love is expressed in another fruit of the religious sense of the absolute,

---

[112] Ibid., XII.
[113] Niebuhr, *Reflections on the End of an Era*, 280.

which elevates the sentiment of benevolence to a higher level by making it into the norm and ideal of the moral life.[114] In the doctrine of forgiveness and justification the reality of sin is taken in full seriousness as a permanent factor in human history. This theological perspective disavows the very utopian illusion rigorously.[115]

Niebuhr's realist position confronts any political philosophy, which would pretend to completely control or sublimate natural impulses such as greed, the will-to-power, or other forms of coercion only through reason and conscience. He takes issue with a form of secular political realism in the tradition of Machiavelli and Otto von Bismarck's *Realpolitik*, which assumes that power is required to destroy power in international relations, pursuing power for power's sake.

The coercion may be used as means to perpetuate injustice and violence to eliminate these. The nation in fighting against the principle of militarism increases its military power for the balance of the power. In the context of secular political realism, power would appear to become the highest goal toward that society should aspire; a tragic logic of resolving conflict by conflict.[116]

Niebuhr defines conflict as that between ethics and politics. The highest moral ideal is justice from the standpoint of society, while it is unselfishness from the standpoint of the individual; these two moral principles are not mutually exclusive, while their contradiction is not absolute nor easily harmonized. Niebuhr reacts against the illusion according to which the collective life can achieve perfect justice. Yet he affirms that "We

---

[114] Niebuhr, *Moral Man and Immoral Society*, 57.
[115] "Why the Christian Church Is Not Pacifist," in *The Essential Reinhold Niebuhr*, 103.
[116] Niebuhr, *Moral Man and Immoral Society*, 232.

can no longer buy the highest satisfactions of the individual life at the expense of social injustice."[117]

Given this, he justifies democracy with a more realistic vindication than presented by the liberal democratic theory. Rather, his suspicion is cast upon the democratic credo in its excessive optimism of human nature and history underlying a source of peril to democratic society and life. However, a consistent pessimism (for example, a war of all against all) ushers to the political theory of absolutist sovereignty in Hobbes, which would cause a totalitarian state. Here, the irresponsible and uncontrolled power of the State becomes the greatest source of injustice and corruption, which attains its highest peril in National Socialism.

Niebuhr's position of Christian political realism in the tradition of Augustine contradicts a secular form of political realism in the sense of *Realpolitik*, whereas clearly discerning the power of self-interest and collective egoism in the children of darkness imbued with the will-to-power.

For Niebuhr, a democratic society is exposed to too much optimism as well as too much pessimism. To cut through this dilemma, Niebuhr requires a more realistic philosophical and religious basis for renewing modern democracy. An ideal democratic order seeks unity within the conditions of freedom through property, judiciary voting system, and human rights, thus it maintains freedom within the communal framework of social order. Niebuhr's view of democracy is not allied with the excessive, possessive individualism or with libertarianism in the bourgeoisie worldview. In the latter, Niebuhr acknowledges that the proletarian pitted excessive collectivism in contrast to the false individualism.[118]

---

[117] Ibid., 277.
[118] "The Children of Light and the Children of Darkness," Ibid., 163-4.

Concluding Reflection

Niebuhr's political realism becomes helpful in developing public theology in reference to the critical assessment of the incomplete legacy of modernity. He facilitates public theology to be located between the moral-political tradition of liberal democracy and socialist theory. Niebuhr's realist position reinforces public theology in bridging Christian classic theology (Augustine and Protestant Reformation) with social, political issues. It retains the significance of immanent critique, which explores theological insight into grace, sin, and freedom, as it deals with the potential of the source (liberty, democracy, and solidarity) as critical leverage to break through the gaps taking place in the historical course of time.

Niebuhr remains a crucial figure in promoting love, justice, and democracy in the Christian realist framework, but his position is sharply noticed in its insufficient deliberation of racial problems.

In James Cone's account, Christian political realism takes the point of departure based on self-interest and power, which runs counter to Barth's position of the Word of God, revelation, and Trinity. What characterizes Niebuhr is seen in his approach to the cross as "transvaluation of values" (Nietzsche), in which God's love and mercy is sought in the cross of Jesus Christ as "the very key to history itself."[119]

However, Cone argues that Niebuhr retains a complex position on racial issues, but the problem of race never becomes one of his central concerns. It was Dietrich Bonhoeffer that took an interest in blacks during his stay at Union (1930-31).[120]

---

[119] Cone, *The Cross and the Lynching Tree*, 35.
[120] Ibid., 41-2.

For Niebuhr, "Love is the motive, but justice is the instrument"[121] –this basic thesis occurs in his dialogue with James Baldwin, a radical black intellectual.

Cone is critical of this position, but he does not sidestep the significance of Niebuhr's political realism expressed in *Moral Man and Immoral Society* for racial justice. A relation between class and race does not constitute one of the major problems in Niebuhr's Christian realism, but Cone concurs with Niebuhr: "...the white race in America will not admit the Negros to equal rights if it is not forced to do so. Upon that point, one may speak with a dogmatism which all history justifies."[122]

It is necessary to expose Niebuhr's critical reflection of colonialism, slavery, and racial justice. His realist position regarding this problem is of paradoxical and dialectical character, in which Niebuhr focuses on the brutal side of all human collective behaviors in reference to the power of self-interest and collective egoism.[123]

Oppressed nationalities in the colonial context have acquired a special measure of sympathy and moral approbation from the neutral nations. Such sympathy was denied to the working classes, which had no neutral communities. For example, European societies demonstrated sympathy for the disinherited Negros in the US, while Americans showed a special measure of interest in India's struggle for emancipation from the British Empire. There is a hidden reality of the balance of power in such partiality and prejudice.[124]

In his analysis of Gandhi's non-violent struggle, Niebuhr is concerned with Gandhi's deliberate distinction between an

---

[121] Ibid., 53.
[122] Cited in Ibid., 58; Niebuhr, *Moral Man and Immoral Society*, 253.
[123] Ibid., XX.
[124] Ibid., 236.

individual English person and the British system of colonialism. It is possible to condemn the British system of imperialism which is vile beyond description; it does not necessarily mean attributing bad motives to every English citizen. Although an evil social system cannot be dissociated from the personal moral responsibility for it, it is morally and politically wise and compelling to insist on the principle of personal responsibility for such a social system.[125]

In dealing with racial injustice against the Black Americans, Black resentment would make a larger contribution to their emancipation than those inflicted without emotional action or resistance. However, the egoistic element in resentment should be rid of to become a vehicle of justice. As he writes: "It is hopeless for the Negro to expect complete emancipation from the menial social and economic position into which the white man has forced him, merely by trusting in the moral sense of the white race. It is equally hopeless to attempt emancipation through violent rebellion."[126]

Niebuhr focuses on the significance of religious imagination in its contribution to non-violent resistance. But his assessment of Western civilization remains negative: "The occident may be incapable of this kind of non-violent social conflict because the white man is a fiercer beast of prey than the oriental. What is even more tragic, his religious inheritance has been dissipated by the mechanical character of his civilization."[127]

Religious moral meaning and spiritual power are needed to contribute to western civilization to avoid its cruelties and animosities. Niebuhr's Christian realism seeks to transcend the pitfall of excessive individualism, or unlimited confidence in

---

[125] Ibid., 249.
[126] Ibid., 252.
[127] Ibid., 255.

practical reason, conscience, and natural law; it reacts against Marxist utopian collectivism in its romantic orientation. In so doing, his realist stance of democracy is well expressed: "Man's capacity for justice makes democracy possible, but man's inclination to injustice makes democracy necessary."[128]

He appears to be an optimist with a pessimistic attitude toward the brutal character of all human collective behaviors in liberal democracy, Fascism, and Marxist socialism while confronting the power of self-interest and collective egoism in unfettered capitalism and excessive individualism.

Despite his critique of socialist dictatorship, Niebuhr's realist position retains a democratic reading of Marx in light of children of light; his realist public theology can be expounded in connection with political theology in the tradition of religious socialism (Karl Barth and Paul Tillich) in the next chapter.

---

[128] Ibid.

Chapter 7
Religious Socialism

In this chapter, I discuss public theology and religious socialism according to Tillich and Barth by way of a social scientific approach to religion, society, and political ethics.

First, I examine the historical background for theology and religious socialism and Tillich's contribution to improving the relationship between theology and religious socialism. Then, I seek to explicate the common ground of church and political responsibility between Tillich and Barth. For intermediary reflection, I draw attention to Bonhoeffer's critical analysis of modernity.

To conceptualize prophetic reasoning of religious socialism in a social scientific frame of reference, I deal with a sociological theory of division of labor, moral solidarity, and religion according to Emile Durkheim as well as the legitimacy of late capitalism (Habermas). Then, I further appraise the significance of public theology and religious socialism, taking on bureaucracy, reification, and resistance. An analysis of Barth's critique of lordless powers brings a closer look at Tillich's socialist principle.

This perspective brings a sociological relation between civil society and public spheres to a critical theory of social stratification, in which Christian eschatology in its theonomous framework is reinforced in terms of prophetic reasoning of reconciliation and *theologia crucis*.

1. Historical Background: Theology and Religious Socialism

Niebuhr argues that the German socialists in the Revolution of 1918 were an exception through the reform policy. They helped to establish a democratic republic through collaboration with non-proletarian parties in the government.[1] Niebuhr laments that the assassination of Jean Jaures on the eve of World War I was one of the great tragedies. Such tragedy blocked a possibility of international socialism to fight against the war tainted with nationalist hysteria.[2]

Philip Scheidemann (1865-1939), the German socialist leader, succumbed to German imperial ambitions with his support of imperialist World War I. As Niebuhr writes, "The impulse of nationalism grips the soul of every statesman whose hands are on the helm of the state."[3]

The Social Democratic Party of Germany (SPD) in 1907 became the largest party in Germany's parliament in 1912. Friedrich Ebert (1871–1925), the representative in the right wing of the SPD, was in league with the evolutionary, reformist socialism of Edward Bernstein (1850-1932). The SPD's right-wing (led by Gustav Noske, Philip Scheidemann, and Friedrich Ebert) supported the war and went on the offensive against Luxemburg with anti-war politics and imperialism.[4]

Throughout 1918, German workers suffered the predicament of war and were instigated by the example of the Russian revolution (1917). Around the same time, the USPD (Independent Social Democratic Party of Germany)

---
[1] Niebuhr, *Moral Man and Immoral Society*, 204.
[2] Ibid., 226.
[3] Ibid., 229.
[4] The Spartacus League (1916) was formed in Luxemburg's allies with radical socialists (Franz Mehring, Clara Zetkin, Leo Jogiches, and Paul Levi).

was separated from the majority of political conservatism of German social democracy (SPD). In November of 1918 sailors mutinied in Kiel and sparked a revolution in October 1918, spreading throughout Germany. When Kaiser Wilhelm II abdicated, the Weimar Republic was proclaimed in Munich in November 1918 by Philip Scheidemann.

The socialist opportunist group crushed a radical wing of socialism (which newly formed the German Communist Party). In its premature uprising (1919) a right-wing militia (*Freikorps*) assassinated Liebknecht and Luxemburg.[5]

Luxemburg's thesis "socialism or barbarism" was to be subsequently seen in the incapability of the Weimar republic to initiate social transformation and its extinction (1933). Luxemburg's essay on "Socialism and Christianity" (1905) was later developed in Karl Kautsky's *The Foundations of Christianity* (1911). This socialist appraisal of Christianity could be later met with a theological interpretation of religious socialism, which was associated with such theologians as Leonhard Ragaz in Switzerland, Walter Rauschenbusch in the U. S., Karl Barth, and Paul Tillich.

Niebuhr's appraisal of the revolution of 1918 finds an affinity with Barth's political position during his writing of the first edition of Romans as well as his political activity in the socialist party in Safenwil, Switzerland. The First World War, which his teachers in Germany supported, came upon Barth as disillusionment. During his pastoral work in the congregation, Barth was embedded in the social-political situation of the general strike of 1918 in Switzerland. As a member of the Swiss Socialist Party, he took issue with Lenin's theory of state and revolution, which was making inroads to the leftist group in the Swiss Socialist Party.

---

[5] *Socialism or Barbarism: Selected Writings Rosa Luxemburg*, 27-29.

In expounding the Romans, Barth characterizes his own position of just revolution of God in favor of establishing an ever-increasing social justice and democracy. His model of revolution of God, which was prevailing in the circle of religious socialism, acquires an ethical criterion and critical significance for Barth to break through the political absolutism and dissolve every form of class dictatorship.[6]

Like Barth, Tillich turned to the movement of religious socialism after the First World War and the German revolution in 1919. Tillich began to contact with those in plight and bitterness while coping with militarism, nationalism, and capitalism. The turning of the world was brought on by the world war and the revolution, such that that situation became one of the important moments (a kairos) for a breakthrough to the new beginning of synthesis between Christianity and economic justice. Tillich was allied with other Christians who supported the revolution and socialism.

Tillich and Socialist Principle

Faced with the crisis of war and revolution, Tillich wrote in a pamphlet: "representatives of Christianity and the church who stand on socialist soil to enter into the socialist movement in order to pave the way for a future union of Christianity and the socialist social order."[7]

In Tillich's take on socialism, Christianity has the task to provide socialist development with its moral and religious powers; thereby Tillich's position is to initiate a great new synthesis of religion and social structure.[8] Out of his reflection has emerged

---

[6] Chung, *Karl Barth*, 143.
[7] Tillich, *The Socialist Decision*, XII.
[8] Ibid., XIII. XIX.

something of a consensus between Christian prophetic ethics and socialist economic justice.

After Tillich had become a professor of theology and philosophy at Frankfurt (1929-1933), he played a major role in having Max Horkheimer as a new chair of social philosophy, a director of the Institute of Social Research. Tillich shared a return to the Hegelian-Marxist dialectics and its related social theory with the proponents of critical theory at the Frankfurt School. His religious socialism complements critical theory in terms of analysis of instrumental reason, social change, and emancipation.[9]

Marx's writing the *Economic and Philosophical Manuscript of 1844*, which was unknown so far, had been published in 1932. The young Marx attracts Tillich in his *Socialist Decision*. Tillich appeals to the real Marx and his concept of dialectics, alienated labor, and humanitarian praxis, which conjoins necessity with freedom. Tillich characterizes Marx as a secular prophet and an existentialist.[10]

In Tillich's socialist take, a concept of principle refers to *dynamis*, the power of historical reality, and it stands in a critical relation to judging its social reality by containing the real possibility. Socialism is comprehended in terms of a socialist principle only through a socialist decision. His standpoint interprets socialist reality or the proletarian situation, while critically judging it.[11]

According to Tillich, a Protestant principle entails creative and formative power by which to distinguish prophetic criticism from rational criticism; the latter measures and appraises the particular according to the ideal.[12]

---

[9] Wagoner, *Prophetic Interruptions*.
[10] Tillich, *The Socialist Decision*, XXXIV.
[11] Ibid., 10.
[12] Tillich, "Protestantism as a Critical and Creative Principle," in *Political Expectation*.

Tillich's notion of rational criticism finds an affinity with Horkheimer's concept of immanent critique in the dialectical frame. There is a rational potential or ideals residing within Western capitalist society imbued with freedom, justice, and equality. The normative rationale ideals function as standards for critically assessing and judging the society for change, solidarity, and emancipation.

As Horkheimer holds, "It opposes the breach between ideas and reality. Philosophy confronts the existent, in its historical context, with the claim of its conceptual principles, in order to criticize the relation between the two and thus transcend them."[13]

An immanent critique makes inroads in buttressing prophetic critique in a religious sense. In the treatment of Marxist humanism, Tillich strives to articulate Christian faith in connection with the prophetic-eschatological symbol of the kingdom of God. His theology of hope in prophetic expectation gives rise to political significance in the socialist movement:

"In the struggle *against* a demonized society and *for* a meaningful society, religious socialism discerns a necessary expression for the expectation of the kingdom of God…It regards this unity of the socialist dialectic, a unity of expectation and demand of that which is to come, as a conceptual unity and at the same time as a concrete and contemporary transformation of the Christian eschatological tension."[14]

Tillich's view on religious socialism is rooted in the Christian symbol of the kingdom of God, which helps socialists to strive for a meaningful society. He features Christian eschatological tension between the present and the future in contrast to socialist utopian reality. This perspective characterizes prophetic criticism in a dialectical fashion, which "combines an unconditional

---

[13] Horkheimer, *Eclipse of Reason*, 129.
[14] Tillich, *The Socialist Decision*, 50.

No with an unconditional Yes."[15] The Christian symbol of the kingdom of God remains a reservoir in functioning as the source of the immanent critique of the Christian religion as well as insufficiency of Marxist socialism.

Tillich's Critique of Dictatorship

Christian eschatological vision leads Tillich to confront Marx's notion of the dictatorship of the proletariat. In dealing with class struggle and the dictatorship of the proletariat, Marx in his letter to Weydemeyer, (5 March 1852) wrote that the class struggle necessarily leads to the dictatorship of the proletariat. It only constitutes the transition to the abolition of all classes and to a classless society.[16]

Dictatorship, according to Tillich, refers to a revolutionary elevation of the proletariat over against the existing power structure and class rule. If it takes place only in a democratic setting, submission occurs as a free choice, prevailing only for a limited time.

In reality, however, after the victory, Tillich argues, the proletariat or its government is not subordinated to democracy, but in fact, the democracy is subordinated to the dictatorial government. Another ambiguity implies that the proletariat as a whole cannot exercise the dictatorship, because power can be maintained only through its power elite, or political representatives, or party. It should amount to the consequence of bureaucracy. The conceptual ambiguity of socialist dictatorship or despotic socialism leads to renouncing the democratic principle in the class struggle for the sake of securing dominion. Tillich's question reads: "*Can socialism be the*

---

[15] Tillich, "Protestantism as a Critical and Creative Principle," in *Political Expectation*, 10.

[16] Marx, "Letters 1848-1857," in *Karl Marx Selected Writings*, 341.

fulfillment of the bourgeois principle when at the same time it is the expression of its destruction?"[17]

The bourgeois principle such as liberty, democracy, and individual rights must be kept intact against the despotic form of socialism, which was infamously embodied in the ex-Soviet Union. To cut across Marx's ambiguity, Tillich asserts that socialism entails a particular aspect as well as a universal aspect, both of which belong together. The universal aspect makes socialism into a general ethical and political idea, while socialism in its particularity is reduced to the resentment of a suppressed class. In this way, Tillich comprehends socialism in its dialectical interaction between the universal aspect and its particular one.[18]

The proletariat is not strictly based on an empirical concept, rather it is categorized as an ideal type which is characterized as an existential concept conscious of itself as a class. Every laborer does not necessarily become the proletariat with revolutionary significance, but the worker is idealized by Marx into the picture of the proletariat. It is a polemical concept stamped within the proletarian struggle or the socialist struggle. But the universal aspect in the sense of classless society facilitates the proletariat in transcending its particular form and interest. Weber's ideal type is utilized in Tillich's description of the proletariat in Marx's thought.

In fact, the dictatorship of the proletariat, which is based on unlimited power, coercion, and authority, is represented by power elitists in political organizations. In the dictatorship of one party, the proletariat needs a total state like Leviathan, which should not wither away.

At this point, Tillich's critical analysis of Marxist despotic socialism finds a parallel with Weber's sociological analysis of bureaucracy. Indeed, it is not surprising that Georg Lukacs, an

---

[17] Tillich, *The Socialist Decision*, 61.
[18] Ibid.

influential socialist philosopher, reemploys Weber's theory of rationalization to account for the reality of reification in social systems. Weber's stance becomes significant, even influential in underlying Lukacs' standpoint of totality between the superstructure and economic base.[19]

According to Weber, the Marxist scientific law of the collapse of the capitalist system has proven to be wrong, because the capitalist society has evolved in a different direction from the thesis of *Communist Manifesto*. As Weber argues, "the elimination of those who are weak in the capital takes the form of their subjection to finance capital, cartels or trusts. These very complex processes are accompanied, first, by a rapid increase in the numbers of office workers, the bureaucrats of the private enterprise system: their members increase at a much faster rate than those of the manual workers, and their interests clearly do not by any means lie in the direction of proletarian dictatorship."[20]

Weber's analysis of the limitation of Marx's theory resonates with Tillich's position, in which Marx requires more deliberation of democracy and human freedom in the Christian symbol of the kingdom of God. A concept of dictatorship threatens to shake the democratic element of Marx to the core.

Historical Materialism and Critique of Ideology

Tillich conceptualizes a historical materialist method in the critical examination of the Marxist context. The materialist interpretation of history is placed in the dialectical framework bound to a given social and economic context.

For Marx, a capitalist economy develops contrary to the knowledge and intention of its carriers, while industry, technical

---

[19] Lukacs, *History and Class Consciousness*, 95-6.
[20] "Socialism," in *Weber Selections in Translation*, 258.

progress, and concentration of finance serve the capitalist system of competition and accumulation. But it leads to crisis and catastrophe; and finally, it results indirectly in the abrogation of capitalism through the proletariat as the gravedigger of that system, thus to a classless society. It occurs in a historical shift from the realm of necessity to that of freedom. Freedom replaces necessity.[21]

For Tillich, the historical dialectic provides such assurance of utopianism for the proletarian struggle by turning the historical dialectic into a method of calculation and catastrophe. But it remains a source of disappointment. The dialectical necessity constitutes the point of departure for socialist proof of the historical dialectic in connection with the proletariat.[22]

However, in Tillich's account, history cannot be calculated, because it cannot be seen as an objective reality to be deciphered in terms of analysis of economic law. *"There is no universal history as a theodicy, demonstrating the successful transmutation of the 'ought' into the 'is.'"*[23]

The theodicy problem would be able to be resolved in the final consummation, which is symbolized in the new heaven and a new earth. The materialist inquiry built on the substructure-superstructure relation affirms the primacy of the economic sphere over other human functions, crediting the economic process into the fundamental factor in guiding the historical course of time. It threatens the system of all cultures and religions as forms of ideology.

Against this economic reductionism, Tillich retrieves the position of the young Marx, which contrasts with the cause-effect relation. Economic activity is examined in connection

---

[21] Tillich, *The Socialist Decision*, 119-20.
[22] Ibid., 124.
[23] Ibid., 122.

with all aspects of human beings and his/her praxis. There is an emphasis on the dialectical connection between the social being and human consciousness, which runs counter to a motion of reflection in a mirror.

Tillich takes into account Marx's dialectical position on the relationship between theory and practice by opposing it to Engel's and Lenin's successive theory of reflection or images.

According to the latter, sensation, perception, and other aspects of human cognition are reflected, copied, and even photographed in our minds through the influence of the material world. The mirror-reflections of external things in the human mind have taken inroads into Lenin through Engels.[24]

On the contrary, for Tillich social being, when apart from social consciousness, is a meaningless and empty concept, since the social being is bound to consciousness. Social consciousness and social being stand in mutual relationship and influence.

A materialist inquiry seeks to unveil the extent to which a specific false consciousness or ideological factor would emerge in particular social situations. A discrepancy arises in a certain relation of inherited concepts and symbols to a new historical reality. False consciousness is grounded in old social structures and should be destroyed by new ones. The underlying structure of a social order plays a normative role in determining whether it is true or false consciousness. New wine is put into new bottles rather than into old bottles (Matt 9: 17).

A symbolic world becomes ideological when the concepts and symbols are employed in the serving system of bourgeois society. It provides an ideological function in obscuring the actual situation of the proletariat in that society. As Tillich states, "*the exposure of the class situation was the most significant*

---

[24]   Kolakowski, *Main Currents of Marxism* 2: 454.

and most effective accomplishment of the Marxist theory of ideology."[25]

Tillich provides a theoretical acumen in synthesizing the significance of historical materialist inquiry with a critique of ideology, as seen from the dialectical standpoint between theory and praxis.

2. Barth and Tillich: Religious Socialist Principle

Epistemologically, Barth takes his point of departure from the living word of God in divine self-revelation in Jesus Christ through the power of the Holy Spirit. His theological epistemology is differentiated from Tillich's theology of correlation in a phenomenological, existential framework.

However, Helmut Gollwitzer, one of the most distinguished pupils of Barth, maintains that Barth is not necessarily separated from Tillich. In Gollwitzer's account, no one except for Tillich was passionately engaged in the whole philosophical, theological thought of connection by serving to explicate such a problem through his method of correlation. Gollwitzer relocates the method of correlation within hermeneutical principle for the understanding of the Scripture, which resonates with the Reformation principle of sin and forgiveness.[26]

Politically, Barth has much in common with Tillich's religious socialist principle. He shares in Tillich's interpretation of historical materialism since the latter is not in essentials the scientific law of calculating the necessity in history and society.

Barth comprehends a historical materialist theory as a scientific inquiry in delving into accidentals in the political, cultural, intellectual spheres; it does so by way of investigating

---

[25] Tillich, *Socialist Decision*, 118.
[26] Gollwitzer, *Krummes Holz-aufrechter Gang*, 34. Footnote 12.

the social-economic realm of the oppressed for liberation in history and society.

Historical materialist theory calls out for the proletariat to comprehend the significance of the critique of economic reality in the dominating class war. It does so by way of the economic and political solidarity of the working class toward the new classless society. The proletariat is to seize political power to establish its dictatorship in transition to the classless society. The socialist hope or eschatology that Marx inspires as the supreme good is to establish the socialist "State" with no more exploiters nor exploited.[27]

In Barth's account, the church has sided with the ruling class, thus its faith is denounced as "a relic of capitalism."[28] Nevertheless, Barth does not sidestep the limitation of Marxist theory embedded in its tyranny, injustice, and calamities. To break through Marxist theory, Barth is concerned with the political theory of Rousseau.

Barth: State and Civil Society

In his article "The Christian Community and the Civil Community" (1946), Barth elaborates on the public relevance of the Christian church for civil society. He expresses his affinity to Rousseau's idea of grounding democracy and social justice in terms of the social contract, which protects the life of the poor. This parallel can be seen in thesis 28, which states: "We bear no grudge against anyone who may have been reminded of Rousseau...We need not be ashamed of the affinity."[29]

---

[27] Barth, CD III/2: 387-8.
[28] Ibid., 389.
[29] Barth, "The Christian Community and the Civil Community," in *Karl Barth: Theologian of Freedom*, 290.

Barth's concern is to emphasize the political co-responsibility of the church with the state for the kingdom of God. It does not imply a model of idealizing the church, but its co-responsibility in discipleship for social justice. The politics of God or the active grace of God should be reflected in the earthly, relative, and provisional actions of the State.[30]

Barth does not seek to propose the Christian doctrine of the just State, but his concern is to articulate external, relative, and provisional embodiment of the kingdom of God "in the world that is not yet redeemed" (Barmen Declaration thesis 5).[31]

Barth's Christocentric position in the Barmen Declaration (May 1934) confronts the totalitarian concept of a political leader (*Führer*). He rejects the single and total order of the State over human life as false teaching while accusing the accommodation of the church of becoming an organ of the State (thesis 4 and 5).

In Barth's Christocentric distinction between theology and politics, he was concerned with defending the integrity and independence of the church in confrontation with National Socialism and its totalitarian politics. However, his expression—"As if nothing had happened" in *Theological Existence Today* (1933)—was not without blame.[32]

Nonetheless, Barth's Christological realism, which conceptualizes Jesus Christ as a power of resistance, finds its affinity with Tillich's notion of kairos. In *Church Dogmatics* in its doctrine of Word of God (1932), Barth already conceptualized his theology of God's speech-act in which God's speech as God's act is God's mystery.

---

[30] Ibid., Thesis 14.
[31] Ibid., Thesis 5.
[32] "Theological and Political Motivations of Karl Barth in the Church Struggle," in *Theological Audacities*, 192.

This perspective characterizes Barth's Christological realism in accordance with his experience of religious socialism in terms of kairos and theonomy. God's mystery does not repudiate a symbolic-prophetic horizon of God's living word. As Barth writes: "God may speak to us through a pagan or an atheist, and thus give us to understand that the boundary between the Church and the secular world can still take at any time a different course from that which we think we discern."[33]

God's speech-act in the Christological-universal framework does not necessarily counter Tillich's position that "*Verbum*, the Word of revelation, may (!) be in everything in which spirit expresses itself...even in the works of society and law."[34]

If Tillich comprehends the whole life of society to be ordained as symbolically powerful for God, Barth incorporates the whole life of society, culture, and the world into the mystery of God. Secular realms are comprehended as extraordinary ways of communication for God. A kairos would occur in prophetic awareness of signs of times against quasi-religious forces of demonic power, or reality of lordless power which contradicts the gospel of reconciliation.

According to F. W. Marquardt, a most distinguished Barth scholar, Barth in April 1937 said: "I remember as if I were today that when I gave an address in Berlin and came to its climax, I uttered—unintentionally I presume—this single word: resistance! I could not have anticipated the huge response to that word; I even had to interrupt my address for a few minutes. Resistance!"[35]

---

[33] Barth, CD 1/1: 55.
[34] Ibid., 63.
[35] "Theological and Political Motivations of Karl Barth in the Church Struggle," in *Theological Audacities*, 197-8.

It is part of his address text, entitled "Reformation as Decision," in which we read: "resistance is to be offered *joyfully* because the opponents' spears are hollow! —citing the famous words of the battle of Sempach...And Romans 13 cannot be used without reference to Revelation 13. A decision is called for now. "Confessing Church means to be a church in the act of decision."[36] Reformation as decision implies Protestant principle as prophetic critique, which underlies Barth and religious socialism.

Further, Barth initiates to make a conceptual clarity of the relation between church and the state in his article "The Christian Community and the Civil Community" (1946). He continues to distinguish the just state (in Rom. 13) from the unjust state (in Rev. 13). He formulates the "subordination" of the church to the state in ways that the church should carry out its responsibility as required for the establishment, preservation, and maintenance of the state. It means accruing to the good of the state. But this co-responsibility does not endorse Christian blind subjection or and even dangerous obedience to the State, as seen in Luther's translation of Rom. 13. 1.[37]

Given the co-responsibility before God, Barth justifies the State to be capable of becoming the parable and desirable of the parable. He identifies it as correspondence and analogy in accordance with the coming of God. Barth takes into account democracy and the greatest measure of social justice as an analogy or a parable in the service of the kingdom of God. The politics of God comes to terms with human politics, in which all citizens have equal freedom in the legal constitution without restricting

---

[36] Ibid., 198. The battle of Sempach (July 8, 1386) occurred between Leopold III, Duke of Austria and the Old Swiss Confederacy, resulting in the Swiss victory.

[37] Barth, "The Christian Community and Civil Community," Thesis 8.

religion, class, sex, and race. The church must stand especially in solidarity with "the poor, the socially and economically weak and threatened."[38]

As Barth states, "the Christian community both can and should espouse the cause of this or that branch of social progress or even socialism in the form most helpful at a specific time and place and in a specific situation...It can consist only in the proclamation of the revolution of God against "all ungodliness and unrighteousness of man" (Rom 1:18), i. e., in the proclamation of His kingdom as it has already come and comes."[39]

Proleptic Discipleship and Social Justice

Barth's conception of eschatology entails a proleptic character with strong ethical significance. We are called to take part in the prophetic struggle of living Christ in our midst, which is the second form of eschatology (resurrection) in expectation of the final consummation.

In the analysis of lordless, impersonal forces, Barth's special ethics of reconciliation acquires a strong political dimension in revolt against disorder in light of the kingdom of God. "Lordless indwelling forces" (Goethe) unleashes the rebellion against the gospel of reconciliation, having a certain autonomy, independence, and superiority over against humanity.[40]

The impersonal forces can be seen in political absolutism, economics, scholarship, technology, art, and ecologically destructive power. The reality of impersonal forces or powers implies unreconciled regimes in opposing the Gospel of reconciliation.

---

[38] Ibid., Thesis 17.
[39] Barth, CD III/4: 545.
[40] Barth, *Christian Life*, 215-6.

Fiat justitia (let justice be done)—Christians are claimed for action in the effort and struggle for human righteousness in resistance to the reality of lordless indwelling forces. These are real factors and agents of human progress, regress, and stagnation in politics, economy, culture, technology, art, scholarship, and ecology. There is a reality of lordless power and its impersonal force affecting life in the diverse fields of social stratification. Against this reality, Barth undergirds the *kingdom-like* character of human effort and struggle for justice and peace with respect to "Thy kingdom come."[41]

In a sign of the millennium of Christ, Barth allows for intimations of the eschatological ultimate breaking into the penultimate events of history. This characterizes his proleptic stance regarding the relation between ethics of discipleship and the kingdom of God. God's kingdom has broken into the life of Jesus Christ, while the resurrected Christ continues to involve his prophetic struggle against the reality of impersonal forces. The church is called and awakened to join the prophetic history of Jesus Christ in our secular realm.

This characterizes proleptic discipleship in joining the kingdom of God in our midst because God's prolepsis took place in the Gospel of reconciliation as a gift. A future act is assumed and developed as we construct and realize kingdom-like reality as existing in society and history. This position comes to terms with Tillich's idea of theonomy in society, culture, and morality, which is demanded by God's proleptic moment of kairos.

In Tillich's account, at the moment of *kairos*, history has reached maturity "to the point of being able to receive the breakthrough of the central manifestation of the Kingdom of God." This qualitative moment is called the "fulfillment of time" in the New Testament, in other words, *kairos* in Greek terms. "Its

---

[41] Ibid., 263; 266.

original meaning—the right time, the time in which something can be done—must be contrasted with *chronos*, measured time or clock time." God's qualitative timing in the providential activity is taken to be closer to the meaning of *kairos*.[42]

Eschatology awakes and inspires us to proleptic discipleship in commitment to the kingdom-like reality through common good, social justice, solidarity, and peace in civil society and the State.

According to Barth, political society (the State) must be shaped following the principle of civil society based on participatory democracy and social justice. Public theology in this regard is involved in examining the public sphere dominated and reified under the spell of impersonal forces. It challenges the political society to commit itself to democracy, economic justice, and recognition of those disadvantaged in sexuality, class, and race.

What strikes in Barth's religious socialist project is the integration of the political tradition of civil society and participatory democracy (Rousseau) into his parabolic approach to the kingdom of God. Its proleptic character can be reflected in the just state which is in line and orientation to freedom, democracy, and a safety net of economic justice.

Natural law in the tradition of political democracy and civil society in Kant and Rousseau may find its significance in the theological, ethical elaboration of politics of God, or the kingdom of God in shaping the state and society.

What becomes crucial is for Barth to make the eschatology through the kingdom-like endeavor into the normative criterion for his special ethics, in which Jesus died in extreme poverty as the companion of the poor of this world. The kingdom of God has come in the poverty of Jesus. In Jesus' table fellowship with publicans and sinners, Barth articulates Jesus Christ as "partisan

---

[42] Tillich, *Systematic Theology* 3: 369.

of the poor" standing in solidarity with *massa perditionis* (the mass and multitude lost; the public sinners and tax collectors). Does not Jesus Christ as "the saving coup d'etat of God," Barth asks, call people out of the *massa perditionis* to bring them at God's side?[43]

Barth incorporates a discourse of *parrhesia* into special ethics in challenging the threat of inhumanity and exploitation of fellow people. A political dimension of the Gospel resists ideologically distorted forms of injustice and oppression, thus Christian discourse becomes the momentum of *parrhesia* in the veracity of God's truth.[44]

2. 1. Bonhoeffer and Under-Modernity

Thus far, we have dealt with theology and religious socialism in the examination of Barth's and Tillich's contribution to prophetic public theology. At the moment, I undertake an intermediary reflection of Bonhoeffer, because his analysis of modernity may become a background for conceptualizing public theology in conversation with liberation theology.

We live in cultural heritage, and no one escapes such historical givenness (history of effect) and socially constructed life-world. But with freedom, autonomy, and moral responsibility, we can reinterpret cultural values and moral norms in critical distance from the limitations of the tradition.

In doing so, public theology is differentiated from a wholesale attack on modernity in terms of the under-modernity, which can be seen in the camp of liberation theology. Like Marx, Gutierrez perceives pathologies of "unsatisfied modernity" (Hegel)[45]

---

[43]　CD 4/3. 2: 587; 620.
[44]　CD 2/1: 231-32. CD IV/2: 442.
[45]　Gutierrez, *The Power of the Poor in History*, 176.

in its consequence of individual freedom, private ownership, colonialism, and domination.

In his critical analysis of the limitations of modern theology, Gutierrez seeks to reread the history of the Other, from the side of the poor. He draws attention to the religious socialist dimension in Barth, who "is sensitive to the situation of exploitation in which these broad segments of humanity live."[46]

However, Gutierrez takes issue with Bonhoeffer, because he does not find the protest movement of the poor or the labor movement underlying Bonhoeffer's writings. Bonhoeffer's protest to National Socialism, as Gutierrez argues, did not move him "to a deeper analysis of the 'crisis in today's society.'" Thus, "Bonhoeffer was less sensitive to the world of injustice upon which the society was built."[47]

Gutierrez's critique of Bonhoeffer becomes enigmatic, and it marks a major interlocutor with public theology, which stands in its modern tradition of political democracy and its critical engagement with colonialism for the sake of postcolonial stance.

Enter Bonhoeffer. In his critical assessment of modernity and its blackmail, Bonhoeffer holds, a human being is emancipated in his/her tremendous power from all repressive authority and coercion, as well as the most terrible perversity in terms of emancipated reason, class, and people. "Reason became a working hypothesis," ushering into the unparalleled rise of technology, which turns into master over nature. "It became an end itself."[48]

Along with the discovery of human rights, all these are overthrown by the emancipation of reason, the project of Enlightenment: "Centralist and absolutist despotism, intellectual

---

[46] Ibid., 203.
[47] Ibid., 229.
[48] Bonhoeffer, *Ethics*, 99.

and social tyranny, class prejudice and class privilege, and the claims to power advanced by the Church."[49]

Bourgeoisie and reason were inseparable, but the underprivileged classes began to stir. The dark menace of the masses, the fourth estate has loomed behind the bourgeoisie as the masses and their misery. The millions of the undeserved wretchedness now raised their accusation and claim against the bourgeoisie. Their own law is that of misery rather than the law of emancipated reason. Technology, mass movement, and nationalism are the historical inheritance which the French Revolution has bequeathed to western modernity and "created a new unity." It lies "in the emancipation of man as reason, as the mass, as the nation."[50]

But this unity entails the seeds of decay within itself. The demands for absolute liberty have brought people to the depths of slavery. Nationalism went inevitably to war.[51] The dark side of the come of age transpires in the liberation of human beings as an absolute ideal, while it paradoxically results in human self-destruction. At the end of modernity initiated by the French Revolution, there is nihilism, a reality of western godlessness, which is a religion of hostility to God. This is the deification of human beings in the proclamation of nihilism, as seen in the religion of Bolshevism as well as amid the Christian churches.

What characterized Bonhoeffer's time was National Socialism, religious nationalism, and Socialist Bolshevism. Social democracy and the labor movement did not find their voice. The major issue was Jewish pogrom, which occupies Bonhoeffer's concern.

"Western history is, by God's will, indissolubly linked with the people of Israel, not only genetically but also in a genuine

---

[49] Ibid., 100.
[50] Ibid., 102.
[51] Ibid., 102-3.

uninterrupted encounter. The Jew keeps the question of Christ open…The expulsion of the Jews from the West must necessarily bring with it the expulsion of Christ. For Jesus Christ was a Jew."[52]

With this provocative stance, Bonhoeffer characterizes godlessness as full of promise, which is against pious godlessness corrupting the church.[53] The poor belong to an essential part of the church's confession in recognition of its guilt, "because the blood of the innocent was crying aloud to heaven."[54] The church witnessed in silence the spoliation and exploitation of the poor and the enrichment and corruption of the strong.[55]

Bonhoeffer championed the Gospel in solidarity with the poor and innocent victim against "bourgeois self-satisfaction… by a convenient reversal of the gospel."[56] His public theology is engaged in his critical analysis of modernity and its underside in history and society. It breaks with the dominant ideology, which is marked by the modern bourgeois spirit.

Already in his study of ecclesiology (*Sanctorum Communio*), Bonhoeffer articulated the significance of the sociological category, in which his position of the Gospel is not value-neutral. Rather he takes into account the deliberation of the Church and Proletariat. "It [social problem] includes the problem of the capitalist economic period and the industrial proletariat created by it; and of the growth of militaristic and bureaucratic giant states; of the enormous increase in population, which affects colonial and world policy; of the mechanical technique… that mobilizes the whole world for purposes of trade, but also that treats people and labor like machines."[57]

---

[52] Ibid., 90-1.
[53] Ibid., 103.
[54] Ibid., 113.
[55] Ibid., 115.
[56] Ibid., 64.
[57] Bonhoeffer, *Santorum Communio*, 236.

Hence, Bonhoeffer emphasizes his Christology in dealing with the working class in his Christology lectures. "The church is an institution for promoting stupidity and the sanctioning of the capitalist system...Jesus the worker is present in the shops of the factories...He is in the midst of the working class, a fighter in the ranks of the working class struggling against the enemy, capitalism."[58]

In Bonhoeffer's view, modernity has a Janus face in bringing out the profound change in human life and emancipation from religious superstition and dominion. But it causes a reality of iron cage or social pathology of reification in the colonization of life-world in justifying the neocolonial condition. The reality of modernity is unsatisfied, yet incomplete while requiring a meticulous exploration between reason, emancipation, and religion.

Nonetheless, Bonhoeffer does not reject the world coming of age while bringing the Gospel of solidarity to the incomplete legacy of modernity. A dialectic of modernity is so complicated that it cannot easily be reduced to a wholesale critique of under-modernity.

Gutierrez is aware of the significance of Bonhoeffer's theology of secularization in its original impulse. But he argues that Bonhoeffer "fails to do justice to the depth and richness of the Lutheran theologian's thought."[59]

What does Gutierrez mean by this critique? He acknowledges that Bonhoeffer's irreligious interpretation implies Christian faith in the suffering God in Jesus Christ. He cites Bonhoeffer in his prison letter: "God lets himself be pushed out of the world and on to the cross. He is weak and powerless in the world, and that is precisely the way, the only way, in which he is with us and

---

[58] *Who Is Christ for Us?* eds. and trans. Nessan and Wind, 36.
[59] Gutierrez, *The Power of the Poor in History*, 180.

helps us.... Christ helps us, not by virtue of his omnipotence, but by virtue of his weakness and suffering."[60]

Given this, shouldn't Bonhoeffer's *theologia crucis* enrich and radicalize Luther's profound insight rather than betraying its depth and richness?

Despite the critique of Bonhoeffer's coming of age, Gutierrez appreciates Bonhoeffer's statement in his prison letter: "We have learned to see the great events of the history of the world from beneath—from the viewpoint of the useless, the suspect, the abused, the powerless, the oppressed, the despised. In a word, from the viewpoint of the suffering."[61]

Bonhoeffer's *therologia crucis*, which underlays a theology of secularization, is to be understood in light of God's reconciliation with the world. In this, Bonhoeffer is convinced of Luther's insight into God's grace of embracing the ungodly. "No abyss of evil can remain hidden from Him through whom the world is reconciled with God. But the abyss of the love of God encompasses even the most abysmal godlessness of the world."[62] "To be confirmed with the risen One—that is to be a new man before God. In the midst of death, he is in life."[63]

Bonhoeffer's position comes to terms with Luther's saying: "perhaps God would rather hear the curses of the ungodly than the alleluia of the pious."[64]

A preferential option for the poor does not occupy the central tenet of Bonhoeffer's theology, But in Bonhoeffer's concern with the Jewish pogrom, the "poor" in Bonhoeffer's context is bound to the preferential option for Jesus Christ who suffers in solidarity is the preferential option for the poor.

---

[60] Cited in Ibid.
[61] Cited in Ibid., 203.
[62] Bonhoeffer, *Ethics*, 72.
[63] Ibid., 83.
[64] Ibid., 104.

Bonhoeffer may be allied with the critique of colonialism and the prophetic tradition of religious socialism. His *theologia crucis* is recast in anamnestic reasoning, and his theology of reconciliation aims at those on the margins.

Unlike Gutierrez, Cone is more convinced of Bonhoeffer than Reinhold Niebuhr, who takes the point of departure based on self-interest and power. What characterizes Niebuhr is seen in his approach to the cross as "transvaluation of values" (Nietzsche), in which God's love and mercy is sought in the cross of Jesus Christ as "the very key to history itself."[65]

However, Cone argues that Niebuhr retains a complex position on racial issues, but the problem of race never becomes one of his central concerns. "Niebuhr has "eyes to see" black suffering, but I believe he lacked the "heart to feel" it as his own." Cone continues ".... the problem of race was never one of his central theological or political concerns."[66]

In Cone's view, however, Bonhoeffer during his study at Union Seminary (1930-1931) took an existential interest in engaging with African American history and literature, while even preaching at Abyssinian Baptist Church in Harlem.[67] This perspective affirms Bonhoeffer's conversion to Black Jesus and his emersion experience with the poor and oppressed within the black American narrative in the Harlem Renaissance.[68]

A genealogical-anamnestic analysis of Bonhoeffer's *theologia crucis* gives a new impulse to reparative justice and postcolonial emancipation by involving those subjugated in history and society.

---

[65] Cone, *The Cross and the Lynching Tree*, 35.
[66] Ibid., 41.
[67] Ibid., 42.
[68] Reggie L. Williams, *Bonhoeffer's Black Jesus*.

Shouldn't the reality of late modernity be taken seriously in the post-Enlightenment context in the aftermath of the collapse of socialism? This changed situation requires a theological task of clarifying the reality of late capitalism, its legitimacy, and the significance of public morals.

3. Division of Labor, Late Capitalism, and Moral Solidarity

In a religious socialist reading of Marx's theory, I draw attention to a regime dysfunctional in Marx's theory of division of labor and alienation. A philosophical and sociological analysis of the division of labor and moral significance cuts through the limitations of Marx while reinforcing theological insights of religious socialism in the context of late capitalism.

In Marx's view, the division of labor makes humans an extremely abstract being, leading to an abortion of the intellectual and physical faculties. Alienation is a consequence of the social division of labor under capitalism, in which compulsory, forced labor mortifies one's body and ruins one's mind. Machines replace the labor, and "throw a part of the workers back to a barbaric labor." Thus "[the labor] produces culture, but also imbecility and cretinism for the worker."[69]

The commodity, the objectification of labor, confronts the worker as an alien being, placing him/her under its domination, capital. The dominion of the thing, reification is expressed: "What was a domination of a person over a person is now the general domination of the thing over the person."[70]

This refers to the twofold side of alienation underlying the technological rationality; from a product by alienated labor (the

---

[69] "On James Mill," in *Karl Marx Selected Writings*, 118.
[70] Ibid.

machine included) and from social reification qua commodities. This assumes the fantastic, even religious form of a relation between things in the act of exchange, stamping fetishism upon the commodity.

However, unlike Marx, division of labor advances along with the rationalization process in the intellectual, social-political, and material spheres, transforming human social existence and consciousness in particular through natural science and its technological rationality and progress.

If the relation between social existence and human consciousness is seen in dialectical reciprocity, it needs to be reformulated in a way that human consciousness and its rational thinking are involved in shaping and organizing the social existence of human beings. Scientific advances and technology have tremendously changed society and culture in the phase of late capitalism.

In the process of rational organization, specialization, and differentiation, the role of the State retains its remarkable performance and function with its ideological apparatuses and bureaucracy. This complex relation in the legitimacy of late capitalism is missing in Marx's reductionist thesis in prioritizing existence over consciousness.

Late Capitalism and Rationalization

According to Habermas, a reality of late capitalism cuts through the limitations of Marx, because the state-regulated system of capitalism includes the administrative system, and social-cultural integration, legitimation system, and fragmented class structure.[71] The State at the administration level performs

---

[71] Habermas, *Legitimation Crisis*, 34-40.

numerous imperatives of the economic system, which improves opportunities in investing capital in the international market between metropolis and periphery. This perspective requires a claim for legitimation in re-coupling the economic system to the political regulation, which is transferred into the socio-cultural system.[72]

The legitimacy of late capitalism brings us back to re-examine an idea of division of labor in a different manner from Smith, Marx, and Weber. For this task, Durkheim deserves special attention. His sociology of division of labor in the advanced society has brought rational organization and facilitated social solidarity.

In Durkheim's analysis, there is a detrimental consequence of the division of labor, when organized in an unqualified, mechanistic manner; yet there is still a positive aspect of the division of labor when effectively rationalized and specialized. This qualified distinction remains an undercurrent in comprehending the moral progress of organic solidarity in the judiciary system and economic system of cooperation within civil society.

This sociological inquiry helps to cut through limitations and setbacks of the pathology inherent in late capitalism. The legitimacy of the state and moral significance within civil society become important regimes for public theology to test with it in terms of ethical reasoning and the common good.

Durkheim, Division of Labor, and Moral Solidarity

Like Marx, Durkheim does not avoid the pathological consequence of modern society and its abnormal conditions, which are caused by the contemporary division of labor. It is

---

[72] Ibid., 39-40.

beset by hostility and struggle between labor and capital and unrestricted play of self-interest and anomie. He observes a variety of disorders, abnormal conditions, and human suffering which emerge in the critical period of transition from mechanical solidarity to organic solidarity.

What matters, Durkheim holds, is that "the division of labor does not produce these [deleterious] consequences through some imperative of its own nature, but only in exceptional and abnormal circumstances."[73]

It would imply Durkheim's ideal type of division of labor. Remarkably, Durkheim does not presuppose that alienation is not inherent in modern modes of production as such by flying in the face of Marx. The reason for the alienation can be seen in the lack of workers in losing the sense of cooperation with their fellows and superiors.

They feel like cogs in a vast machine, because an abnormal division of labor in the modern industry does not spring from spontaneity, but from forceful imposition through the industrial revolution and social-economic upheavals. These weakened and deteriorated industrial enterprises through coerced discipline and regulation of the human body under authority and control. If coercion in the division of labor has primacy over against human spontaneity and enterprise, such condition yields a low degree of social cohesion and solidarity.

Durkheim's strategy is to create new institutionalized moral bonds which safeguard the society against the malady and decay beset by strife and disorder which is bound to biopolitical discipline, regulation, and control. He understands morality to start with membership in a group or a community. The moral rules invested with special authority and rational organization

---

[73]   Durkheim, *Division of Labor in Society*, 307.

have little to do with authority, which is imposed by State power and administered by bureaucratic rule in the economic system.

In Habermas' account, Durkheim deals with the Kantian dualism between duty and inclination by relating moral precepts to the interests of the individual, while relativizing the dualism. The morally good is worth pursuing by satisfying real needs and desires. For Durkheim, "Morality must then not only be obligatory but also desirable and desired. The *desirability* is the second characteristic of every moral act."[74]

Durkheim is concerned with exploring the relationship between the autonomy of the individual and organic solidarity in modern differentiated types of societies. In other words, the connection between the individual personality ("cult of the individual") and social solidarity can arise from the ever-increasing division of labor in a non-coercing, rational, and effective manner.[75] This integration perspective thwarts the emergence of unfettered individualism in Spencer's social Darwinism, which replaces solidarities and regulations.

Durkheim sees in social Darwinism a logical consequence of Darwinian principles in terms of the central dogma of competition to survival and natural selection. Darwin's theory is not capable of clarifying moral matters because it removes society's impact on the essential element of moral life. Eventually, Durkheim maintains that the society exerts over the individuals, tempering and neutralizing the brutal effect of the struggle for existence and natural selection.[76]

Durkheim's sociology of social facts helps to see a transcendental, morphological side of the life-world (history, tradition, culture, morality, or language) in its general, collective representations and

---

[74] Cited in Habermas, *The Theory of Communicative Action* II: 49.
[75] Durkheim, *Division of Labor in Society*, XXX.
[76] Ibid., 145.

actions exercising and imposing themselves upon the individual life as an external constraint. "Generality combined with objectivity" is seen, for example, like a communication network "in the case of law, morality, beliefs, customs, and even fashion," has morphological character "without any break in continuity as structural facts influencing human life."[77]

All social constraints in the rational division of labor or education, or well-defined social organization do not necessarily exclude the individual personality, freedom, and moral progress. What remains crucial in Durkheim's structural theory of the life-world can be seen in "the beliefs, tendencies, and practices of the group taken collectively" as a social reality sui generis, which "exists separately from its individual effects."[78]

Social currents of opinions in the public sphere come to terms with the effects of social facts. A morality or a law is no longer individual, but shared, social, and collective functioning as the power of external coercion or a morphological phenomenon which exerts upon individuals.

A social fact *"is general over the whole of a given society whilst having an existence of its own, independent of its individual manifestations."*[79]

For Durkheim, where societies exist, there is altruism found at the very dawn of humanity, in other words, solidarity.[80] Individualism would be tempted to the decay of society without social solidarity. Freely engaged contracts between individuals lay the foundation of social and moral order, rather than replacing it. Contracts presuppose social order which has primacy over individually motivated actions.

---

[77] *Durkheim: The Rules of Sociological Method*, 57.
[78] Ibid., 54-55.
[79] Ibid., 59.
[80] Durkheim, *Division of Labor in Society*, 145.

This perspective takes issue with the individualistic utilitarian approach as an impasse to the problem of social order in modern societies. Individuals form a society and cause association, while the latter reacts upon the consciousness of the individuals, considerably shaping the consciousness. Individuals are more a product of society than they are the author of it.[81] Status group is formed in society through rationalization and with moral significance.

In Axel Honneth's account, Durkheim seeks to establish certain normative conditions underlying market-mediated exchange of labor and its economic system to thwart the problem of a capitalist society under the pressure of competition. The new economic system is injected with the type of moral legitimacy for social integration. Social solidarity should flow from the economic system of division of labor through ration, effective, and cooperative organization.

Given this, there is a parallel between Hegel in *Philosophy of Right* and Durkheim in *Division of Labor in Society*. What is common in Hegel and Durkheim, Honneth argues, all adult members of the society are entitled to contribute to the common good, while receiving an appropriate living wage in return.[82]

However, Durkheim does not share in Hegel's tradition of the State, but with the political democracy of Kant and Rousseau. The moral significance in the capitalist economic system must be championed and furthered by the role of public intellectuals by bridging the interest and need of civil society with the political State. Civil society in its moral significance must be defended from the encroachment of the State in its bureaucratic power and the economic society in its inequality of wealth and privilege.

---

[81] Ibid., 288.
[82] Honneth, *The I in We*, 68-9.

Durkheim finds moral validity not in an autonomous manner, but in agents' collaboration in the social life-world. Defense of civil society with moral integrity cuts through limitations of the self-regulating powers of the market in its unfettered mechanism. Such a sociological project seeks to rationalize institutional conventions and associations in a public moral manner, social networks in a cooperative system, and effective integration of the disadvantaged for safety while featuring meaningful work and moral validity.

Justice and fairness may constitute necessary presupposition within the social democratic framework through the division of labor while generating organic forms of solidarity. Civil society must not entirely be subsumed into the bourgeois dominion of economic society, while the State must work on establishing the balance of the two spheres through collaboration with the association of public intellectuals for common good, equality, and solidarity.

As Durkheim writes, "the division of labor presumes that the worker, far from being hemmed in by his task, does not lose sight of his collaborators, that he acts upon them and reacts to them. He is, then, not a machine who repeats his movements without knowing their meaning, but he knows that they tend, in some way, towards an end that he conceives of more or less distinctly. He feels that he is serving something."[83]

In the analysis of legal code and regulations, Durkheim observes that most civil and commercial law is restitutory in character, while most criminal law is based on penal sanctions.[84] Societies based on mechanical solidarity depend on penal

---

[83] Durkheim, *The Division of Labor in Society*, 372.
[84] In the school of Malinowski, it is argued that pre-modern societies depend considerably on reciprocal obligations based on restitution. Durkheim, *The Division of Labor in Society*, XXIV.

sanctions in contrast to those of organic solidarity prevailing in the modern context.

In his sociology of the division of labor Durkheim is convinced that different economic infrastructures are in interaction with different forms of superstructures, in which society is enlarged and its density would cause new modes of the division of labor. This advanced and qualified division of labor is involved in the underlying legal-judiciary improvement and enhancing moral types of social bonds through the association of professional public intellectuals.

Thus, he cuts through the limitation of historical economic materialism through his structural theory of life-world in explanation of social facts and collective representations, which avoid the consciousness of individual alienation. For Durkheim "religion is the most primitive of all social phenomena... –law, morality, art, science, political forms, etc."[85]

Public Morals and Public Theology

Durkheim is not utopian-romantic for public morals, but of realist-empirical character in facing up to the problem in modern society. In ameliorating the anomic and forced division of labor, he calls attention to the model of institutions, a new corporatism, which is involved in mediating between the State power and the concrete everyday world of the individual.

New types of corporations would be instituted, and their administrative council of these corporations is granted and entitled to regulate labor relations, appointments and promotions, wages, salaries, and condition of work. This model of professional corporations takes a key position in the structure

---

[85] Durkheim, "Marxism and Sociology," in *Durkheim*, 173.

of modern societies which functions as a source of vivifying new social norms and new social bonds regarding the relation between political society and civil society. Durkheim proposes to establish a well-defined, organized group, or a public institution, which assumes the obligation and responsibility regarding the political society, State.[86]

To cut through the pathology of the capitalist system, a model of an institutional council and structure steers between Scylla of state power and Charybdis of economic individualism, seeking the balance between the cult of the individual and social solidarity.

Durkheim's analysis of modern society affirms the moral philosophy of Kant in which we must respect human personality within ourselves and our fellow humans. "In reality, the duties of the individual to himself are duties to society."[87]

What is moral is a source of solidarity. "In short, since the division of labor becomes the predominant source of social solidarity, at the same time it becomes the foundation of the moral order."[88] Durkheim's moral theory is primarily grounded in his social analysis of the division of labor and solidarity, in which justice is filled with charity. Social feelings are in repercussion in the sphere of real rights, and justice "is the necessary accompaniment to every kind of solidarity."[89]

This social scientific approach facilitates public theology in making inroads to the prophetic tradition of religious socialism with a focus toward moral solidarity and public intellectual participation in civil society. Public theology incorporates social scientific analysis of rationalization and social stratification

---

[86] Durkheim, "Preface to the Second Edition," in *The Division of Labor in Society*, XXXVII.
[87] Ibid., 332.
[88] Ibid., 333.
[89] Ibid., 77.

for the common good, moral solidarity, and reform politics in terms of a structural theory of the life-world. It focuses on the regime of civil society, deliberate democracy, and those on the margins of society while featuring the significance of civil society with public intellectuals in connection with State and economic society.

This refers to a new task of public theology to involve diverse social fields (the political, the economic, the cultural, the moral, the family, the education, the religion, etc.) for a better society, which cuts through the pathology of late capitalism, a postcolonial reality of iron cage.

4. Religious Socialism and Social Scientific Inquiry

In the analysis of sociological inquiry into the division of labor, religion, and morality, I return to prophetic reasoning, as expressed in Tillich and Barth. To reconfigure public theology, a social scientific approach relocates a prophetic stance of religious socialism within the legitimacy of late capitalism and its limitations. Religious life is rich, pervasive, and transformative underlying all social phenomena because the economic life does not determine in one way, rather it is influenced and transformed by religious ideas in a prophetic sense.

According to Tillich, it is necessary to extricate Marxism from dogmatic narrowness and restore it following the young Marx in connection with the later Marx of *Das Kapital*.[90]

The capitalist economy is based on the laws of the market as the rational basis of the belief in harmony for the greatest possible advantage for all. However, the experience of the class struggle becomes an empirical reality that is bound to the

---

[90] Tillich, *The Socialist Decision*, 125.

liberal economy. The free enterprise economy results in the irrationality of economic crisis and periods of pauperization. "The actual result of liberal economics was the class rule and imperialistic war, the crisis of the proletarian masses and their utter insecurity."[91]

The socialist demand is characterized by replacing unlimited competition in the creation of crisis through centralized planning, in other words, "central control instead of laissez-faire."[92] Socialism conceives of human nature from the standpoint of reason and posits a shift from the present irrational situation to a future rational situation.

However, Tillich's religious socialist principle repudiates the vulgar Marxist view of human nature in which human being is conceived of as a mechanism. To the degree that the suffering of proletarian mass is increased more and more, its reaction to the pain would result in touching off a revolution.

In Tillich's account, this mechanistic view determines the human person by simple pleasure and pain reactions, in which a person is constructed to become a thing. This repeats an extreme product of bourgeois objectification in concept and actuality, in which a person is supposed to be a commodity, a cog in the machinery of production. Class domination turned persons into things. Socialism is a counter-movement against this process of dehumanization built on in the capitalist system underlying the reality of reification.[93]

In resistance to the pathological reality of reification, I think, it is significant to take into account the sociological analysis of the division of labor and moral solidarity in the public

---

[91] Ibid., 89.
[92] Ibid., 90.
[93] Ibid., 133.

institutions, while upholding a public ethical commitment to those disadvantaged in a social safety net.

Barth: Lordless Powers and Inhumanity

Barth may share in Durkheim's sociological theory, which stands in the political tradition of Kant and Rousseau. In Barth's account of alienation, a human being has enmity against God, murder of fellow humans, and self-destruction of humanity. For Barth, the evil is "enmity against God, fratricide, self-destruction."[94] "Evil is the defiance of Prometheus, the scorn of the *condottieri* and the violent, the self-consuming flame of the super-man, and, best of all, all these combined in one person."[95]

Human refusal can be seen (1) in his/her relationship with God, (2) with his/her fellow persons, (3) with the created order, and (4) with human historical limitation in time.[96] Alienated human beings seek their identity in the desire to become lords. They fall into the social-political consequence of autonomy and play out as the great lords in destroying humanity, society, and nature. Their false autonomy leads to antagonism between human beings while exercising the alienating power of inhumanity in terms of oppression and exploitation of others. This reality of impersonal forces and their false autonomy begin with enmity against God, following theft and murders, which end up with regional and world wars.[97]

For Barth, being "inhuman" means being without one's fellow person. A human being acts as though he/she were an

---

[94] CD IV/1: 400.
[95] CD IV/1: 400.
[96] CD IV/2: 409.
[97] CD IV/2: 436-37.

animal or devil and not a human. "Inhumanity is the denial of our humanity...the aim of hypocrisy is to conceal the inhumanity..."⁹⁸

A notion of co-humanity is a basic form of humanity in Barth who emphasizes moral solidarity in society as a theological criterion; it takes issue with the reality of alienation and reification, which occur in the process of rational organization of the social-economic system. As Barth furthers, "by renouncing our true humanity, we do...achieve a kind of liberation, independence, a superior capacity to act, in the exercise of which we gain a peculiar advantage over others and seem to be the stringer. But...this power is strange and alien in relation to ourselves. It is stronger than we are. Our humanity sets under a rule according to which every man's hand is necessarily against his brother's, and we are all subjects."⁹⁹

In Barth's analysis of the impersonal forces and domination, we observe how the reality of the lordless powers would "become the secret or blatant oppression and exploitation of one's fellow" in terms of active or passive violation of human dignity, honor, and right. Barth characterizes the final upshot by actual transgression: "stealing and robbery; murder in the legal sense; and finally, war, which allows and commands almost everything that God has forbidden."¹⁰⁰

The reality of lordless powers is seen in sociological analysis of the detrimental consequence of the social division of labor and rationalization in imposed and coerced manner. The rationality of prophetic reconciliation runs counter to such a social-political system and reification.

In Barth's critical analysis of Western society, the way of life is rooted in possessive individualism. It is driven by private property

---

[98] CD IV/2: 437.
[99] CD IV/2: 436.
[100] CD IV/2: 436.

and the privatization of values and human relations under institutionalization. It propels the pursuit of markets in other countries, developing foreign policy, the armament industry in Western countries. "It is when interest-bearing capital rather than man is the object whose maintenance and increase are the meaning and goal of the political order that the mechanism is already set going which one day will send men to kill and to be killed."[101]

However, a notion of prophetic rationality of reconciliation, seen in the light of the life-world, aims at establishing a life of co-humanity, parliamentary-participatory democracy, and solidarity with those on the margins in civil society.

If Barth sees the reality of impersonal forces bound to inhumanity, Weber argues that the disenchantment of the world is undertaken through the rationalization of religious charisma and the process of its institutionalization. In the discussion of science as a vocation, the process of disenchantment is undertaken and driven through scientific progress in terms of technical calculations and intellectualization.

Despite scientific pleading and naïve optimism, the various value spheres are in irreconcilable conflict with one another, leading to polytheism, in which the gods of various orders and values are yet disenchanted of their demons. Many old gods assume the form of impersonal forces in their eternal struggle with one another to gain power against "the grandiose moral fervor of Christian ethics."[102]

Science is praised as the way to happiness, yet caught into the reality of impersonal forces. According to Weber, capitalist rationalization has its date in the reality of the iron cage. "For of the last stage of this cultural development, it might well be truly said: "Specialists without spirit, sensualists without heart; this

---

[101] CD III/4: 459.
[102] *From Max Weber*, 149.

nullity imagines that it has attained a level of civilization never before achieved."[103]

However, Barth would not be in agreement with Nietzsche's aristocratic rejection of humanity for the "overman" beyond good and evil. In fact, Nietzsche's will-to-power is without the fellow person.[104] Barth's critique of impersonal forces runs counter to Weber's pessimistic attitude toward this power structure in a polytheistic manner.

But his prophetic rationality of reconciliation does not undermine the significance of rationalization and the social-political system which recognizes human dignity, liberty, and democracy. But it credits a social reality of bureaucracy and inhumanity into the realm of impersonal forces.

Barth: Bureaucracy and Economic Reification

Barth's analysis of bureaucracy is undertaken in his critique of inhumanity and hypocrisy. The inhumanity assumes social-political forms "in the necessary establishment and defense of the institution of law and order."[105] Barth conceptualizes bureaucracy to be a form of reification in the capitalist system.

Its form of inhumanity and hypocrisy may operate "in the functions of the sacrosanct compulsory organization of the totalitarian, or the no less sacrosanct free play of the forces of the democratic state, thus pretending to espouse either the claim of society on the individual or the freedom of the individual in relation to society."[106]

---

[103] Weber, *The Protestant Ethic and the Spirit of Capitalism*, 182.
[104] CD III/2: 240.
[105] CD IV/2: 439.
[106] CD IV/2: 439.

This impersonal form of inhumanity masks itself as ceaseless activity, which "can cloak itself behind pure scholarship or pure art, or behind the promotion of the common interests of a national or economic or intellectual group, or behind officialdom with its concern for the regular functioning of an official apparatus, or simply behind the refinement of a technique with its different applications."[107]

Bureaucracy is a form of inhumanity and hypocrisy, which is based on technological rationality underlying the regular functioning of an official apparatus and different applications. The inhuman element, even in Barth's view of philanthropy, "has such an uncanny power of mastering and using them on the pretext of serving humanity."[108]

In fact, human rationality is in correspondence to the rationality of God's reconciliation in Christ with the world, in which a history of the struggle of Jesus Christ plays a major role in summoning the church to the discipleship against the unreconciled mechanism of impersonal forces.

Alienation and reification of human life lead to comprehensive bureaucratization of human existence and society in which human relation becomes an abstract, anonymous relation.[109] A bureau is a place where human beings are grouped and classified in certain classes, and they are treated, dismissed or doctored in terms of specific plans, principles, and regulations. In the bureaucratic process, a human being is always invisible to a real person and treated "for the sake of simplicity of a general consideration and a general program."[110]

---

[107] CD IV/2: 439.
[108] CD IV/2: 440.
[109] CD IV/2: 680-81.
[110] CD III/2: 252.

Bureaucracy raises its head beyond every bureau, even with the most altruistic of intentions, it causes inhumanity. "It is not the man who works in a bureau, ...but the bureaucrat who is always inhuman."[111] Barth comprehends bureaucracy as "the encounter of the blind with those whom they treat as blind."[112]

In this bureaucratization, human life is misused as a thing under the care of things (food, goods, and life assistance in material, spiritual, technical, civilizing, and cultural arts). These are apparatuses and fittings on which human life and existence are dependent.[113] These things are integrated into human life by taking care of social life, and herein the process of reification becomes compelling and escalates. The order of things must be challenged and changed in light of the Gospel of reconciliation.

Barth's critique of bureaucracy is comprehensive in social-political life by relating it to the reality of impersonal forces. Barth insists on his prophetic reasoning of God's reconciliation against systems of injustice bound to bureaucratic rationalism and domination. In the analysis of the legal form of the free labor contract between the employer and the employee, Barth acknowledges that exploitation takes place in its economic content. Despite the free contract, equality between contract partners does not exist, because the employer has an incomparable advantage over the employee by dictating his/her own interest and advantage.[114]

Because of this double standard, the labor contract becomes a mask for covering inhumanity. "This is social injustice in a form which is less blatant than the simple competition, which is apparently grounded in co-ordination, which may even seem

---

[111] CD III/2: 252.
[112] CD III/2: 252.
[113] CD IV/3. 2: 667.
[114] CD III/4: 542.

to be legitimate in view of its inclusion of free and reciprocal contracts, but which is even more oppressive and provoking in its ostensible show of justice, and can only make industrial peace the more radically impossible of attainment."[115]

Barth encouraged Christian communities to oppose any dictatorship of the totalitarian State as well as the capitalist system of possessive individualism, alienation, and injustice. The church always stands in solidarity with the weak and the poor, fundamentally on the side of the victims of the social-political disorder. As Barth writes, "true Christianity cannot be a private Christianity, i. e., a rapacious Christianity. Inhumanity at once makes it a counterfeit Christianity...It cuts at the very root of the confidence and comfort and joy, of the whole *parresia* [parrhesia], in which we should live as Christians, and of the witness which Christianity owes to the world."[116]

Conclusion: Public Theology and Religious Socialism

In the discussion of Barth and Tillich, I find it significant to review Niebuhr's critique of despotic socialism and its bureaucratic domination. A sociological reading of public theology (according to Durkheim, Weber, and Habermas) can be associated with prophetic reasoning of religious socialism in Barth and Tillich in reference to Niebuhr.

Despite the critique of the problem of Marxist Leninism, Niebuhr does not sidestep the nihilistic dynamics and its danger of capitalism. Thus, he acknowledges that there is a particular truth in Marx's prophecy in increasing frequency and the extent of periodic crises in the capitalist economic system.

---

[115] CD III/4: 542.
[116] CD IV/2: 442.

In a like manner, Barth acknowledges possessive individualism and its autonomy in the fight for private property, possession, and accumulation, which become the self-perpetuating purpose of capitalist society. The struggle for capital is a form of the struggle for existence in a dynamic, yet demonic process. It "consists in the amassing and multiplying of possessions expressed in financial calculations (or miscalculations), i. e. , the "capital" which is in the hands of relatively few, who pull all the strings."[117]

In his critique of capitalist revolution as well as totalitarian state socialism, Barth breaks through Weber's pessimistic diagnosis of pathology of late capitalism and "last man" a la Nietzsche. Barth may be classified into a type of Durkheim's idea of public intellectuals' involvement in their religious construction of social moral reality.

However, Barth's limitation can be seen in his lack of conceptual clarity in dealing with the social problems in social-cultural stratification, in which religious discourse finds elective affinity with diverse social spheres in their material interests. A multicultural, pluralist, democratic society should be enhanced in explicating the life-world among people of different faiths and cultures toward politics of recognition and collaboration.

When public theology analyzes diverse forms of life in social stratification, it acknowledges that religion plays a significant part in shaping civil society, democracy, and interreligious recognition and collaboration. The location of the public sphere as the site of resistance against the reality of impersonal forces (state power and economic domination, simulation of mass media and its political ideology) gives a new impulse to the meaning of civil society.

---

[117] CD III/4: 531-32.

The latter is imbued with a network of associations, voluntary organizations, social democratic movement, citizen initiative, religious community, academic society, cultural solidarity of public intellectuals; these seek to promote the common good, ethical values, participatory democracy, public health, and social, ecological justice. Civil society comes to terms with the life-world as a reservoir of social life and public morals grounded in history, language, culture, communication, and religious texts. Public theology is concerned with the analysis of the religious construction of public spheres and its contribution to public religious ethics in civil society.

In distinction from Habermas,[118] a prophetic reason of reconciliation and *theologia crucis* remains central in public theology and its social scientific approach to diverse spectrum within political, social-cultural, and economic, and educational stratification.

Given this, Tillich's prophetic reasoning of the socialist principle becomes crucial in advancing public theology in this direction. It cuts across economic reductionism while widening the dialectical spectrum of theory and practice in the civil cultural sphere.

An economic aim can be elucidated in four aspects in dealing with the question of needs, the attitude toward technological progress, the attitude toward work; finally, the relation of origin-related economics to international economics.[119]

Technological progress has been systematically advanced by transforming Western civilization while leading the masses out of mute bondage as well as the subjection of nature into technological domination. A capitalist achievement cannot be denied or undermined in terms of technological means of

---

[118] Habermas, *Between Facts and Norms*, 367.
[119] Tillich, *The Socialist Decision*, 154.

production and economic rationalization. But, technological rationalization within the framework of unrestrained free competition and growth is driven by the process of accumulation.

Tillich summons to a return to religious socialist principle as prophetic Protestant principle, which salvages the European society from barbarism. The prophetic principle brings the unlimited possibilities for technological domination under human control to serve humanity and ecological integrity against its self-annihilation.[120]

Tillich's religious socialism points in the same direction to faith and eschatological expectation, which penetrates and purifies limitations of socialist beliefs and Marxist assumption through the concept of the *kairos*. "*Expectation is always bound to the concrete, and at the same time transcends every instance of the concrete...*The vitality and depth of socialist faith lie in the fact that it so distinctly—and so dangerously—embodies this tension."[121] Eschatological expectation is the symbol of prophetic socialism.

The Kingdom of God has broken into our midst through Jesus Christ and continues to break through our midst in terms of *kairos*. This perspective characterizes proleptic discipleship through kairos in its theonomous framework. Theonomous rationality is consistent with the prophetic rationality of reconciliation and *theologia crucis*.

Religious socialist reasoning helps to reinforce public theology in prophetic awareness of *kairos* and *parrhesia*, which are further clarified in the social-scientific framework. For this prophetic direction, Tillich and Barth together with Niebuhr (and Bonhoeffer) remain theological reservoirs for

---

[120] Ibid., 161.
[121] Ibid., 132.

advancing public theology through prophetic realism, *kairos*, and *parrhesia*.

Along with this prophetic principle, a critical theory of social stratification helps to cut across the class-centered model of binary opposition in Marxist theory to further public theology in a democratic, pluralistic society.

Epilogue

In the study of public theology and civil society, I have dealt with the political tradition of modern democracy. In this reading strategy, I undertake a position from the standpoint of the postcolonial, as seen for and from the margins. Public theology is involved in the project of incomplete modernity and the legitimacy of late capitalism while recapturing the prophetic reasoning of religious socialism in a social scientific framework.

Public theology retains a character of constructive theology in correlation with social scientific theory while developing theological appraisal of political, moral philosophy. It is captured in the prophetic reasoning of reconciliation and *theologia crucis* in a proleptic conception of the kingdom of God. It also employs a social scientific approach by reconfiguring the prophetic principle in the context of late capitalism, which besets civil society in its social-cultural stratification.

1. A study of political democracy and liberty weighs in social-democratic orientation through its theoretical retrieval of Rousseau and Kant via John Rawls. This theoretical contribution runs counter to libertarian philosophy, which is embedded in J. S. Mill and social Darwinism beset by laissez-faire capitalism and colonialism.

In differentiating these two traditions from each other, I examine the legacy of Adam Smith whose moral theory of sympathy and his political economy are seen in its anti-colonial orientation. It can be critically renewed and complemented in relation to Marx, Foucault, and Durkheim. In fact, there is a mutation, rupture, or a different paradigm in the theory of justice and civil society in the political tradition of liberal democracy. A Eurocentric type of discourse can be met with a challenge from a prophetic type of resistance within the Western political democratic tradition.

2. A theological interpretation of Kant weighs in the cosmopolitan principle in the framework of anamnesis along with *theologia crucis*, which remains crucial in the prophetic tradition of theology and religious socialism. Christian symbol of the kingdom of God comes to terms with an ethical project in Kant. This reading practice characterizes public theology in terms of philosophical-theological endeavor in undertaking semantic retrieval of the intellectual tradition of political modernity, civil society, and moral theory.

3. Unlike Hobbes's idea of Leviathan and its political absolutism, Locke relocates individual liberty, property, and people's consent within the divine workmanship and the protection of the needy and economically disadvantaged. To sustain human rights and their ethical integrity, the consent of the people becomes the standard and criterion in judging and subjecting them to political power. This political power must not be arbitrary, but separated and specialized into the legislative, executive, and judiciary to cut through political authority and coercion. Ethics of human rights is entitled with resistance or even revolution to the tyranny.

This perspective continues to manifest itself in Rousseau's social contract theory, popular sovereignty, participatory democracy, and civil society. Rousseau's critique of colonialism and slavery is refined philosophically later in Kant's cosmopolitanism. Kant elaborated his duty ethics in the framework of universal history at an evolutionary scale. He incorporates the importance of duty ethics into social contract theory and the republican constitution. Finally, such integration becomes crucial in underlying the ethics of hospitality with a cosmopolitan vision. His distinctive contribution to political ethics is seen in his combination of the concept of law and right with politics.

Political responsibility and reform of the law belong to the type of moral politician committed to remedying the constitution and the idea of reason. This type of political ethics contrasts with political moralists who would fabricate a system of morals. Moralizing politicians, in Kant's view, cannot make progress in a political, legal context.

Rather, the political prudence seeks to affect reforms for its political duty in accordance with the ideals of public law and rights. Reform of moralizing politicians comes to terms with utilizing a revolution in which a legal constitution based on the principle of freedom can be brought about through complete reform.

A theological, philosophical reading of social contract theory features public theology to be grounded in the philosophical tradition of human dignity, ethical socialism, popular sovereignty, and civil society. It differentiates a conception of civil society (Rousseau) sharply from Hegel-Marx tradition, which conflates civil society with bourgeois society under the power of the state. A new model of civil society remains crucial in public theology by distinguishing it from political theology, which was born in political theologians' critical involvement of Hobbes' Leviathan and Carl Schmitt's theory of the totalitarian state. A critical analysis of the state sovereignty, legal-judiciary domination, and its bureaucracy can be a part of public theology, but it does not exhaust major concerns of public theology with diverse public spheres in social stratification.

In so doing, public theology, which I strive for, is defined as a philosophical, constructive discipline, which focuses on civil society stratified in a hierarchical manner. It is concerned with the transformed aspect of civil society in the phase of late capitalism, which is embedded in the postcolonial relation between metropolis and periphery.

4. Kant finds his significance in Albrecht Ritschl in the constructive proposal of Luther's teaching of justification along with Kant's ethical idea of the kingdom of ends. His mode of justification and reconciliation entails social ethical interpretation of Christian theology in the classic sense of public theology. In a critique of his accommodation to the bourgeois culture of the age of Bismarck, I feature a theological model of justification and reconciliation in postcolonial profile through the angle of the theology of the cross (Bonhoeffer) and politics of reconciliation (Barth), which remains crucial in theological interpretation of religious socialism.

Rousseau's political theory finds its significance in Barth who clarifies the relationship between the Christian community and civil community with respect to democracy, social justice, and solidarity in accordance with the direction and orientation toward the kingdom of God.

It is Reinhold Niebuhr that engages in the political tradition of liberal democracy and moral theory, as well as appraising Marxist theory in a critical, constructive manner. His Christian political realism is appreciated as one of the best examples of public theology in reference to political theology and religious socialism (Barth, Tillich, and to some extent Bonhoeffer).

These great thinkers, despite their different orientations and achievements, provide keen insights into advancing public theology and social justice in interrogation with capitalist society as well as Marxist theory.

Appreciating the Christian realism and religious socialist principle, I have attempted to bring sociology of division of labor and moral solidarity (Durkheim) and theory of legitimacy of late capitalism (Habermas) to cut through some limitations of Marx's position. In Weber's critique of Marxist socialism and bureaucracy in the capitalist society and state socialism, I bridge his sociological position with Tillich and Barth in their respective approach to the problem of Marxist theory.

I find that Tillich's creative analysis of Marxist theory has an affinity with Barth's theological interpretation of historical materialism and the reality of lordless powers. It is necessary for public theology to deal with the reality of impersonal forces reified in a society stratified in a hierarchical and unequal manner. I draw attention to Weber's sociological analysis of dictatorship and bureaucracy, and his critical view of socialism in terms of a dictatorship of the bureaucracy finds parallel with Tillich and Barth.

Religious socialist reasoning provides keen insight for public theology to engage effectively in public spheres in civil society, while redefined and elaborated in a social scientific framework. Public theology in this regard is concerned with the legacy of incomplete modernity while elaborating the prophetic reasoning of reconciliation and *theologia crucis* in solidarity with those outcast and maltreated. The hermeneutical standpoint from below finds consonance with Marx's categorical imperative for solidarity and emancipation.

5. Habermas conceptualizes his discourse ethics in the communication rationality in a Kantian sense, such that ideal communication should be universally established for justice, consensus, and recognition of the disadvantaged. Hegel's notion of interaction is wielded to develop ethical reasoning discourse, which can be furthered in taking on the power relations and structure of hegemony among dialogue partners. A language game in different forms of life is socially constructed, and it facilitates ethical inquiry discourse in its commitment to the common good through justice, consensus, and recognition.

Civil society is the foundation for a civil state grounded in general will, and it is not conflated with market bourgeois society like Hegel. The bourgeoisie with its egotistical economic interest should be transformed into citizens, a political subject, who enters into recognition of and solidarity with those on the margins. This perspective takes issue with Hegel's preference for constitutional monarchy.

6. Public theology is primarily concerned with diverse social fields (politics, economics, judiciary legitimacy, networks of information, immigration problems, neo-racism, culture, and

religion) in a society reified and stratified in a hierarchical and inequitable manner. Problems of public theology cannot be adequately comprehended without considering the neocolonial condition, which is saturated with diverse fields in society. It does not leave the incomplete project of modernity (liberty, equality, and justice) behind by jumping up to the postmodern theory of deconstruction and its global sovereignty under the Empire. Immanent critique, which is based on the principle of negation, is at the heart of the dialectical theory. It calls for a project in measuring the great ideals of modernity (justice, equality, freedom, and solidarity) in a constructive fashion against the social background, which they emerge.

If public theology provides a broader conceptual framework in dealing with social, political, economic, and cultural issues within social stratification, it engages in analyzing social discourse, power relations, and struggle for symbolic goods and capitals in reifying the public spheres. The cultural form of leadership or a cultural hegemony is indispensable in understanding cultural life and its sustainability for grassroots movement (anti-racism, the immigration problem, politics of recognition) for sustaining civil society under the life-world.

7. Thomas McCarthy synthesizes the critical theory of genealogy with Habermas' communicative rationality by advancing a critique of enlightenment metanarrative of a universal principle in an attempt to require a critical history of the present. Our self-understanding has to be altered by suspending and scrutinizing the actual genealogies of accepted ideas and principles of practical reason.

Despite his critique of racial ideology inherent in Kant and Rawls, McCarthy remains in a reconstructive spectrum by correcting ideological elements in modern colonialism and racism against neoliberal globalizers and neoconservative ideology of intervention.

McCarthy is convinced of an intersubjective notion of communicative reason in dialogue with non-Western cultures, such that its rationality is embodied and embedded in society, culture, and history. A critical history with a practical intent recasts Kant's moral theory in the sense of discourse ethics, in other words, reworking Kantian categorical imperative upon the discourse-ethical principle of equal participation and democratic consensus toward alternative modernities.

I incorporate McCarthy's critical theory of racism and progress into strengthening public theology, which is concerned with theological, ethical deliberation of the kingdom of God, justice, and solidarity in public spheres and social institutions. Accordingly, theological foci, such as grace, sin, redemption, and eschatology, are communicated and reinterpreted to the secular mind in society and the world through strenuous endeavors for enhancing the public use of reason. It is performed in an interdisciplinary framework, especially assessing the western tradition of modern democracy and its political, moral theory for people and civil society with deliberate democracy in the late modernity. The latter is characterized by the cosmopolitan condition in the aftermath of colonialism in search of legacy and a project of incomplete modernity.

8. Public theology is featured in its engagement with the public sphere of civil society in the sense of *res publica* made up

of non-governmental organizations, social institutions, and faith communities. Public theology stands in the prophetic tradition of Christian political realism and religious socialism along with the theology of the cross. It seeks to guide the sphere of civil associations and institutions against the domination of political society (the state) and the privileged strata of economic society (bourgeois dominion) along with bureaucratic systems.

In a nutshell, a project of public theology and civil society travels with Kant by examining other philosophical schools of modern democracy and justice through theological appraisal. Christian political realism shows one of the best examples, which involves a modern theory of political democracy and its incomplete project in view of Marxist theory. Christian political realism is associated with the theological interpretation of religious socialism. Finally, a prophetic reasoning of reconciliation and Biblical symbol of the kingdom of God provide public theology with a comparative study of religion, which remains crucial in recognition of and collaboration with other religious communities in democratic, pluralistic society toward interreligious common good and solidarity.

Bibliography

Aristotle, *Nicomachean Ethics*, trans. H. Rackham. Cambridge and London: Harvard University Press, 1994.

_____. *The Politics*, ed. and trans. Ernest Barker. New York: Oxford University Press, 1946.

_____. *A New Aristotle Reader*, ed. J. L. Ackrill. Princeton, New Jersey: Princeton University Press, 1987.

Arrighi, Giovani *The Long Twentieth Century: Money, Power, and the Origins of Our Times*. London: Verso, 1994.

Augustine, *City of God*, trans. Gerald G. Walsh, et al. Garden City, N. Y.: Doubleday, 1958.

Barth. K. *Church Dogmatics*, 4 vols. trans. and eds. Geoffrey W. Bromiley and G. T. Thomson. Edinburgh: T. & T. Clark. 2004.

_____. *Protestant Theology in the Nineteenth Century*, New Edition. Grand Rapid, MI: Wm. B. Eerdmans, 2002.

_____. *Karl Barth: Theologian of Freedom*, ed. Clifford Green. Minneapolis: Fortress, 1991.

_____. "The Christian Community and the Civil Community (1946)," in *Karl Barth: Theologian of Freedom*, ed. Clifford Green. Minneapolis: Fortress, 1991. Pp. 265-96.

_____. *Christian Life. Church Dogmatics IV, Part 4, Lecture Fragments*, trans. Geoffrey W. Bromiley. Grand Rapids: Eerdmans, 1981.

Beaud, Michael. *A History of Capitalism 1500-1980*, trans. Tom Dickman and Anny Lefevre. New York: Monthly Review, 1983.

Benjamin, Walter. *Illuminations*, trans. Harry Zohn. New York:

Schocken Books, 2007.

Bonhoeffer, Dietrich. *Sanctorum Communio: A Theological Study of the Sociology of the Church* vol. 1. Ed. Clifford J. Green and trans. Reinhard Krauss and Nancy Lukens. Minneapolis: Fortress,1998.

_____. *Creation and Fall: A Theological Exposition of Genesis 1-3*, ed. John W. De Gruchy and trans. Douglas S. Bax. Minneapolis: Fortress, 1997.

_____. *Letters & Papers from Prison*, ed. Eberhard Bethge. New York: The Macmillan Press, 1967.

_____. *Who Is Christ for Us?* eds. and trans. Craig L. Nessan and Renate Wind. Minneapolis: Fortress, 2002.

Boss, Judith A. Ed. *Ethics for Life: A Text with Readings*, 3rd ed. New York: The McGraw-Hill, 2004.

Bourdieu, Pierre and Loic J. D. Wacquant. *An Invitation to Reflexive Sociology*. Chicago: The University of Chicago Press, 1992.

Brueggemann, Walter. *The Prophetic Imagination*. Minneapolis: Fortress, 2002.

Campbell, Timothy and Adam Sitze, eds. *Biopolitics; A Reader*. Durham and London: Duke University Press, 2013.

Chakrabarty, Dipesh. *Provincializing Europe: Postcolonial Thought and Historical Difference*. Princeton University Press, 2000.

Cohen, H. "Kant," *Marxismus und Ethik*, ed. Hans. J. Sandkűhler et al. Frankfurt am Main: Suhrkamp, 1974. 745-86.

Colletti, Lucio. *From Rousseau to Lenin: Studies in Ideology and Society*, trans. John Merrington and Judith White. New York and London: Monthly Review Press, 1972.

Cone, James H. *The Cross and the Lynching Tree*. Maryknoll, New York: Orbis, 2011.

Danto, Arthur C. *Nietzsche as Philosopher*. New York: Columbia University Press, 1980.

Dobb, Maurice. *Studies in the Development of Capitalism.* Rev. ed. New York: International, 1963.

Duchrow, Ulrich and Franz J. Hinkelammert. *Transcending Greedy Money: Interreligious Solidarity for Just Relations.* New York: Palgrave, 2012.

Durkheim, Emile. *Montesquieu and Rousseau.* Ann Arbor: University of Michigan Press, 1960.

_____. *Durkheim: The Rules of Sociological Method and Selected Texts on Sociology and its Method*, ed. Steven Lukes and trans. W. D. Halls. New York: The Free Press, 1982.

Fetscher, Iring. *Rousseaus politische Philosophie: Zur Geschichte des demokratischen Freiheitsbegriffs.* Frankfurt am Main: Suhrkamp, 1968.

Foucault, Michel. *The History of Sexuality: An Introduction* I, trans. Robert Hurley. New York: Vintage, 1990.

Franck, Andre G. *Dependent Accumulation and Underdevelopment.* New York: Monthly Review, 1979.

Franklin, Julian H. Trans. and ed. , *Constitutionalism and Resistance in the Sixteenth Century: Three Treatises by Hotman, Beza, and Mornay*, New York: Pegasus, 1969.

Gollwitzer, Helmut. *Krummes Holz-aufrechter Gang: Zur Frage nach dem Sinn des Lebens.* Munich: Chr. Kaiser. 1985.

_____. *An Introduction to Protestant Theology*, trans. David Cairns. Philadelphia: The Westminster Press, 1982.

Gonzalez, Justo L. *The History of Christianity II: The Reformation to the Present Day*, rev. and updated. New York: Harper One, 2010.

Gramsci, Antonio. *Selections from the Prison Notebook.* New York: International Publishers, 1971.

Grotius, Hugo. *On the Law of War and Peace: Student Edition*, ed. Stephen C. Neff. Cambridge: Cambridge University

Press, 2012.

Gustafson, James. *Ethics from a Theocentric Perspective II: Ethics and Theology.* Chicago, IL: University of Chicago Press, 1992.

Habermas, J. *The Structural Transformation of the Public Sphere: An Inquiry into a Category of Bourgeois Society*, trans. Thomas Burger. Cambridge: MIT, 1993.

_____. *Between Naturalism and Religion: Philosophical Essays,* trans. Ciaran Cronin. Malden, MA: Polity Press, 2008.

_____. *Justification and Application: Remarks on Discourse Ethics,* trans. Ciaran Cronin. Cambridge, Mass.: The MIT Press, 1987.

_____. *Between Facts and Norms: Contributions to a Discourse Theory of Law and Democracy.* Cambridge: Polity Press, 1996.

_____. *The Theory of Communicative Action II: Lifeworld and System: A Critique of Functionalist Reason*, trans. Thomas McCarthy. Boston: Beacon Press, 1987.

_____. *Legitimation Crisis*, trans. Thomas McCarthy. Boston: Beacon, 1973.

_____. *Theory and Practice*, trans. John Viertel. Boston: Beacon, 1973.

Hardt, Michael and Antonio Negri, *Empire*. Cambridge, Mass.: Harvard University Press, 2000.

Hegel, G. W. F. *The Phenomenology of Mind*, trans. J. B. Baillie. Mineola, New York: Dover, 2003.

_____. *Hegel's Philosophy of Right*, trans. T. M. Knox. Clarendon Press, 1952.

_____. *Philosophy of Right*, trans. S. W. Dyde. Kitchener, Ontario: Batoche Books, 2001.

_____. *Lectures on the Philosophy of Religion*, ed. and trans. Peter C. Hodgson et al. Berkeley and Los Angeles, 1984-87.

_____. *Hegel: Theologian of the Spirit*, ed. Peter C. Hodgson. Minneapolis: Fortress, 1997.

Horkheimer, Max. *Eclipse of Reason*. New York: Bloomsbury, 1974.

Hume, David. *An Enquiry Concerning the Principles of Morals* (1751). London: A. Millar, 2014.

Husserl, Edmund. *The Essential Husserl: Basic Writings in Transcendental Phenomenology*, ed. Donn Welton. Bloomington and Indianapolis: Indiana University Press, 1999.

Kant, I. *Basic Writings of Kant*, ed. Allen W. Wood. New York: The Modern Library, 2001.

_____. *The Moral Law: Groundwork of the Metaphysic of Morals*, trans. H. J. Paton. London: Routledge and Kegan Paul, 1785/1991.

_____. *The Conflict of the Faculties*, trans. Mary J. Gregor and Robert Anchor, in *Kant, Religion and Rational Theology*, ed. Allen W. Wood and George di Giovanni. Cambridge: Cambridge University Press, 1996. Pp. 233-327.

_____. *Critique of the Power of Judgment*, trans. Paul Geyer and Eric Matthews. Cambridge: Cambridge University Press, 2000.

_____. *The Metaphysics of Morals* [1797], trans. and ed. M. Gregor. Cambridge University Press, 1996.

_____. "Of the Different Races of Human Beings," trans. J. M, Mikkelsen, in R. Bernasconi and T. Lott (eds.), *The Idea of Race*. Indianapolis: Hackett, 2000. Pp. 8-22.

_____. *Groundwork of the Metaphysic of Morals* (1785), trans. H. J. Paton, New York: Barnes and Nobles, 1967.

_____. *Lectures on Ethics*. Indianapolis: Hackett, 1775-1780/1963.

Kelsen, Hans. *The Law of the United Nations*. New York: Praeger, 1950.

Kleingeld, Pauline. *Kant and Cosmopolitanism: The Philosophical Ideal of World Citizenship*. Cambridge: Cambridge University Press, 2012.

Kolakowski, Leszek. *Main Currents of Marxism: 2. The Golden Age*, trans. P. S. Falla. Oxford and New York: Oxford University Press, 1978.

Kwame Anthony, Appiah. *Cosmopolitanism: Ethics in a Word of Strangers*. New York: WW Norton, 2006.

Lehmann, Paul L. *Ethics in a Christian Context*. New York and Evanston: Harper & Row, 1963.

Leith, John H. Ed. *Creeds of the Churches: A Reader in Christian Doctrine from the Bible to the Present*, 3rd ed. Louisville: John Knox Press, 1982.

Lenin, V. I. *The State and Revolution: The Marxist Teaching on the State and the Tasks of the Proletariat in the Revolution*. Foreign Language Press: Peking, 1976.

Locke, John. *Two Treatises of Government*, ed. Mark Goldie. London: J. M. Dent; Vermont: Charles E. Tuttle, 1993.

Lukacs, Georg. *History and Class Consciousness: Studies in Marxist Dialectics*, trans. Rodney Livingstone. Cambridge, Mass.: The MIT Press, 1971.

Luxemburg, Rosa. *Socialism or Barbarism: Selected Writings Rosa Luxemburg*. Ed. Paul Le Blanc and Helen C. Scott. New York: Pluto Press, 2010.

Macpherson, C. B. *The Political Theory of Possessive Individualism: Hobbes to Locke*. Oxford: Oxford University Press, 1962.

_____. *The Life and Times of Liberal Democracy*. Oxford, UK: Oxford University Press, 1979.

Marcuse, Herbert. *Reason and Revolution: Hegel and the Rise of Social Theory*. Boston: Beacon Press, 1960.

Marquardt, F. W. *Theological Audacities: Selected Essays Friedrich-Wilhelm Marquardt*, eds. Andreas Pangritz and Paul S. Chung. Eugene, OR: Pickwick, 2010.

Marx, Karl. *Critique of Hegel's Philosophy of Right*, trans. Joseph

O'Malley. Oxford: Oxford University Press, 1970.

_____. *Capital: A Critique of Political Economy* I, trans. Ben Fowkes. London and New York: Penguin, 1990.

_____. *Karl Marx Selected Writings*, ed. David McLellan. Oxford: Oxford University Press, 1988.

McCann, Dennis. *Christian Realism and Liberation Theology: Practical Theologies in Creative Conflict.* Eugene, OR: 1981.

McCarthy, Thomas. *Race, Empire, and the Idea of Human Development.* Cambridge: Cambridge University Press, 2010.

McGrath, Alister E. *Iustitia Dei: A History of the Christian Doctrine of Justification*, 2nd ed. Cambridge: Cambridge University Press, 1998.

McNeil, John T. *The History and Character of Calvinism.* London and Oxford: Oxford University Press, 1954.

Mill, J. S. *On Liberty*, ed. E. Rapaport. Indianapolis: Hackett Publishing, 1978.

_____. *Considerations on Representative Government* (1861). South Bend, IN: Gateway, 1962.

Milton and Rose Friedman. *Free to Choose.* New Work: Houghton Mifflin Harcourt, 1980.

Moltmann, J. *God for a Secular Society: The Public Relevance of Theology*, trans. Margaret Kohl. Minneapolis: Fortress, 1999.

_____. *The Crucified God: The Cross of Christ as the Foundation and Criticism of Christian Theology.* Minneapolis: Fortress Press, 1993.

Morgan, Michael L. Ed. *Classics of Moral and Political Theory*, 4th ed. Indianapolis and Cambridge: Hackett Publishing Company, 2005.

Niebuhr, H. R. *Christ and Culture.* New York: Harper and Row, 1951.

Niebuhr, Reinhold. *An Interpretation of Christian Ethic.* New York: N. Y.: Harper and Row, 1963.

_____. *The Nature and Destiny of Man* 1. II. New York: Charles

Scribner's, 1941. 1943.

_____. *The Essential Reinhold Niebuhr*, ed. Robert M. Brown. New Haven and London: Yale University Press, 1986.

_____. *Reflections on the End of an Era*. New York: Charles Scribner's, 1934.

_____. *Reinhold Niebuhr: His Religious, Social, and Political Thought*. Ed. Charles W. Kegley and Robert W. Bretall. New York: The Macmillan Company, 1986.

_____. *The Self and the Dramas of History*. New York: Charles Scribner's, 1955.

_____. *Moral Man and Immoral Society: A Study in Ethics and Politics*. New York, London: Charles Scribner's, 1934.

Nozick, Robert. *Anarchy, State, and Utopia*. New York: Basic Books, 1974.

Pannenberg, Wolfhart. *Systematic Theology* 2, trans. Geoffrey W. Bromiley. Edinburgh: T & T; Grand Rapids: Eerdmans, 1994.

Polanyi, Karl. *The Great Transformation: The Political and Economic Origins of Our Time*. Boston: Beacon, 1957.

Rachels, James and Stuart Rachels, *The Elements of Moral Philosophy*, 6th ed. New York, NY: McGraw-Hill, 2010.

Rawls, John. *A Theory of Justice*. Rev. ed. Cambridge, Mass.: The Belknap Press of Harvard University Press, 1999.

_____. *The Law of Peoples*. Cambridge, MA: Harvard University Press, 1999.

Ritschl, Albrecht. *The Christian Doctrine of Justification and Reconciliation: The Positive Development of the Doctrine,* trans. H. R Mackintosh and A. B. Macaulay. Clifton, N. J.: Reference Book, 1966.

Rousseau, Jean-Jacques. *The First and Second Discourses*, ed. Roger D. Masters and trans. Roger D. and Judith R. Masters. New York: St

Martin's Press, 1964.

———. *On the Social Contract with Geneva Manuscript and Political Economy*, trans. Judith R. Masters and ed. Roger D. Masters. New York, N. Y: St. Martin's Press, 1978.

Said, Edward. *The Edward Said Reader*, eds. Moustafa Bayoumi and Andrew Rubin. New York: Vintage, 2000.

Sandel. Michael J. *Justice. What's the Right Thing to Do?* New York: Farrar, Straus and Giroux, 2009.

Smith, Adam. *Theory of Moral Sentiments*. Ed. A. L. Macfie and D. D. Raphael. Indianapolis: Liberty Press, 1982.

———. *The Wealth of Nations*. New York: Bantam, 2003.

Schmitt, Carl. *The Concept of the Political*, trans. George Schwab. Chicago: The University of Chicago Press, 1996.

———. *The Leviathan in the State Theory of Thomas Hobbes: Meaning and Failure of a Political Symbol*, trans. George Schwab and Ema Hilfstein. Westport, CT: Greenwood Press, 1996.

Spencer, Herbert. *Social Statics: The Conditions Essential to Human Happiness Specified, and the First of Them Developed.* New York: S. Appleton, 1864.

Stackhouse, Max. *Public Theology and Political Economy: Christian Stewardship in Modern Society*. Grand Rapids: Eerdmans, 1987.

Taylor, Charles. *Hegel.* Cambridge: Cambridge University Press, 1975.

Tillich, Paul. *Systematic Theology* I. III. Chicago: The University of Chicago Press, 1951. 1963.

———. *The Socialist Decision*, trans. Franklin Sherman. New York and San Francisco: Harper & Row, 1977.

———. *Political Expectation*, ed. James L. Adams. New York: Harper & Row, 1971.

Tracy, David. *The Analogical Imagination*. New York: Crossroad, 1981.

Wagoner, Bryan L. *Prophetic Interruptions: Critical Theory, Emancipation, and Religion in Paul Tillich, Theodor Adorno, and Max Horkheimer (1929-1944)*. Macon, GA: Mercer University Press, 2017.

Weber, Max. *The Protestant Ethic and the Spirit of Capitalism*, trans. Talcott Parsons. Mineola, New York: Dover, 2003.

_____. *From Max Weber: Essays in Sociology*, eds. H. H. Gerth and C. Wright Mills. New York: Oxford University Press, 1958.

Williams, Reggie L. *Bonhoeffer's Black Jesus: Harlem Renaissance Theology and an Ethic of Resistance*, rev. ed. Waco, TX: Baylor University Press, 2021.

Online Link

https://www. britannica. com/topic/Declaration-of-Independence/Text-of-the-Declaration-of-Independence

Index

A

American Declaration of Independence 124
Analogia relationis 265
Anamnesis 242
Aristotle 11, 39, 57, 58, 108, 109, 111, 116, 146, 147, 148, 153, 154, 157, 158, 181, 189, 191, 192, 194, 204, 210, 251, 350
Aufhebung 60
Augustine 29, 36, 37, 201, 202, 235, 249, 250, 251, 252, 253, 254, 257, 259, 260, 261, 262, 263, 265, 267, 268, 284, 287, 288, 350
Augustinian political realism 23

B

Barmen Declaration 128, 129, 305
Barth 14, 22, 26, 27, 28, 29, 32, 34, 37, 44, 52, 54, 59, 60, 64, 65, 128, 158, 162, 170, 195, 196, 246, 247, 256, 263, 264, 265, 266, 288, 291, 292, 294, 295, 303, 304, 305, 306, 307, 308, 309, 310, 311, 312, 328, 330, 331, 332, 333, 334, 335, 336, 337, 339, 344, 345, 350
bellum omnium contra omnes 115, 174
Biopolitics 98, 101, 104, 111, 126, 351
Bolshevism 313
Bureaucracy 333, 334, 335

C

Calvinism 121, 123, 126, 356
Calvinist theory of resistance 108, 118, 121
Chiliasm 235

Code Noir 189
Colonial racism 88
Critique of Ideology 300
Cuius regio, eius religio 130

D

Deontology 31
Difference Principle 151
Durkheim 26, 27, 30, 162, 181, 292, 320, 321, 322, 323, 324, 325, 326, 327, 330, 336, 337, 342, 345, 352

E

Eigensetzlichkeit 237
Encyclopedia 157
English Reform Bill 178, 179
Enlightenment 13, 20, 31, 32, 60, 64, 91, 157, 158, 159, 182, 209, 219, 229, 249, 279, 280, 312, 318
Eurocentric Position 19

F

Fiat justitia 309
French Revolution 32, 87, 174, 176, 219, 225, 235, 313

G

Gollwitzer 129, 303, 352
Gospel ethic 25

H

Habermas, J. 353
Historical Materialism 300
homo sacer 104, 116
Horkheimer 26, 296, 297, 353, 358

I

Immanent critique 347

J

Jim Crow laws 140
justitia originalis 263, 266

L

Leviathan 13, 108, 109, 110, 112, 113, 114, 115, 118, 119, 120, 121, 124, 125, 126, 127, 128, 130, 131, 132, 133, 135, 140, 196, 214, 299, 342, 344, 358
Life-world 217, 218

M

Marquardt, F. W. 355
Marx's Orientalism 20
Massacre of St. Bartholomew 121
massa perditionis 310, 311
Mill, J. 356
Mill, J. S. 356
Moltmann, J. 356

N

National Socialism 108, 128, 132, 264, 282, 287, 305, 312, 313
Nazism 102, 127, 282
Niebuhr, H. R. 356

O

Oriental despotism 20, 21, 182
Orientalism 20, 22

P

Panopticon 79, 80, 81
primus inter pares 264, 265
privatio boni 59, 256
Protestant principle 296, 307, 339

Q

Quaternity 58

R

Realpolitik 286, 287
Reformation 13, 110, 179, 222, 249, 262, 280, 282, 288, 303, 307, 352
Renaissance 249, 279, 280, 282, 317, 359

S

Schopenhauer 268
Scots Confession 123
Sittlichkeit 46, 178
Slavery 142, 189, 223
Social Darwinism 215
Social Stratification 17
Stalinism 102
Stoic Principle 204
Survival of the fittest 90

T

Theodicy 235
Theologia crucis 257
Theonomous Ethics 205

W

Weber 15, 17, 27, 30, 237, 299, 300, 320, 332, 333, 336, 337, 345, 359
Workmanship 133
World Spirit 59

www.ingramcontent.com/pod-product-compliance
Lightning Source LLC
Chambersburg PA
CBHW020350080526
44584CB00014B/966